Using Mental Image in Counselling and Psychotherapy

A guide to more inclusive theory and practice

Valerie Thomas

Routledge
Taylor & Francis Group
LONDON AND NEW YORK

First published 2016
by Routledge
2 Park Square, Milton Park, Abingdon, Oxon, OX14 4RN

and by Routledge
711 Third Avenue, New York, NY 10017

Routledge is an imprint of the Taylor & Francis Group, an informa business

© 2016 Valerie Thomas

The right of Valerie Thomas to be identified as author of this work has been asserted by her in accordance with sections 77 and 78 of the Copyright, Designs and Patents Act 1988.

All rights reserved. No part of this book may be reprinted or reproduced or utilised in any form or by any electronic, mechanical, or other means, now known or hereafter invented, including photocopying and recording, or in any information storage or retrieval system, without permission in writing from the publishers.

Trademark notice: Product or corporate names may be trademarks or registered trademarks, and are used only for identification and explanation without intent to infringe.

British Library Cataloguing-in-Publication Data
A catalogue record for this book is available from the British Library

Library of Congress Cataloging-in-Publication Data
Thomas, Valerie, 1952– author.
  Using mental imagery in counselling and psychotherapy : a guide to more inclusive theory and practice / Valerie Thomas.
    pages cm
  Includes bibliographical references and index.
  1. Imagery (Psychology) 2. Counseling psychology. 3. Psychotherapy. I. Title.
  BF367.T495 2016
  153.3'2—dc23
  2015024836

ISBN: 978-0-415-72885-0 (hbk)
ISBN: 978-0-415-72886-7 (pbk)
ISBN: 978-1-315-67323-3 (ebk)

Typeset in Times
by Apex CoVantage, LLC
Printed and bound in Great Britain by
Ashford Colour Press Ltd, Gosport, Hampshire

Using Mental Imagery in Counselling and Psychotherapy

The therapeutic potential of working with clients' mental images is widely acknowledged, yet there is still little in the counselling and psychotherapy literature on more inclusive approaches to the clinical applications of mental imagery. *Using Mental Imagery in Counselling and Psychotherapy* is a unique, accessible guide for counsellors and psychotherapists who wish to develop their expertise in this important therapeutic practice.

Contemporary practitioners have at their disposal a large repertoire of imagery methods and procedures comprising the contributions from different therapeutic schools and clinical innovators. Valerie Thomas identifies some of the common features in these approaches and offers a transtheoretical framework that supports integrative practitioners in understanding and using mental imagery to enhance therapeutic processes. The book:

- Examines the development of the theory and practice of mental imagery within a wider context of the history of imagination as a healing modality;
- Describes the different ways that mental imagery has been incorporated into therapeutic practice and evaluates recent developments;
- Reviews explanations of the therapeutic efficacy of mental imagery and considers how recent theoretical concepts provide a means of understanding the role that mental images play in processing experience;
- Includes reflections on ways to develop more inclusive theory and proposes a model that can inform integrative practice.

Using a wide range of clinical vignettes to illustrate theory and cutting-edge research, Valerie Thomas proposes a new integrated model of practice. Providing clear and detailed guidance on applying the model to clinical practice, the book will be essential reading for psychotherapists and counsellors, both in practice and training, who wish to harness the therapeutic efficacy of mental imagery.

Valerie Thomas is a counsellor, psychotherapist and supervisor in private practice. Formerly, she was a Senior Lecturer at Anglia Ruskin University and Course Leader for Counselling training.

"This book is an exciting contribution to the use of mental imagery in counselling and psychotherapy. Grounded in the real-world, practical experience of the author, and developed from her in-depth Doctoral studies, it offers an original, inclusive model, well rooted in the diverse history of mental imagery in therapeutic work. It is presented in terms as vivid, imaginative and, above all, useful as the way of working it describes. It should be an inspiration for practitioners from across the psychological therapies, regardless of their theoretical orientation, and deserves a place on the bookshelf of everyone who seeks to work with the immense fund of creative opportunities the imagery of human minds can offer us."
—Dr Stephen Goss, Principal Lecturer, Metanoia Institute, and
Co-Editor, *British Journal of Guidance and Counselling*

"This book is a highly practical and persuasive guide to developing a more inclusive practice with mental imagery. I wholeheartedly recommend it to all psychotherapists and counselors who recognize the importance of imagination in the therapeutic process."
—Anees A. Sheikh, Ph.D., Professor Emeritus of Psychology,
Marquette University, Editor, Baywood's Imagery and
Human Development Series

"A welcome and comprehensive approach to imagery as part of the warp and woof of therapeutic and counselling work. Its wide-ranging approach to theory, and very specific guidelines to practice, makes the vital and much neglected usefulness of imagery accessible to any practitioner. Highly recommended."
—Dr. Dina Glouberman, Skyros Holistic Holidays founder,
Imagework pioneer, author of *Life Choices, Life Changes,
The Joy of Burnout, and You are what you imagine*

Contents

Acknowledgements vii
Preface ix

1 Introduction   1

PART I
Towards more inclusive theory   11

2 An historical perspective on the therapeutic use of imagination   13
3 The story of using mental imagery in counselling and psychotherapy   23
4 Explanations for the therapeutic efficacy of mental imagery   42
5 Identifying common features in the use of mental imagery in talking therapies   53
6 Developing a more inclusive model of mental imagery in therapeutic practice   66

PART II
Towards more inclusive practice   73

7 An introduction to the model in practice   75
8 The building image   85
9 The path image   111

10 The plant image	133
11 Integrating a more inclusive approach to mental imagery into ongoing therapeutic work	159
12 Practice issues	176
13 Conclusion	185
Index	187

Acknowledgements

Many people have helped me in the process of producing this book. However, the single most important group consists of the clients who placed their trust in me as I developed my understanding of how to integrate imagery more deeply into talking therapies. It is to these people that I owe a special debt of gratitude – they taught me this practice.

Along the way, my friends and family have been a source of constant support. One person, in particular, deserves a name check: my dear friend and colleague, Mark Neary. Without his endless enthusiasm and encouragement, I doubt that I would have completed this task.

I would also like to acknowledge permission to reprint the explanation of conceptual metaphor theory in Chapter 4 originally published in the *British Journal of Counselling & Guidance* (see www.tandfonline.com/doi/full/10.1080/03069885.2013.811216).

Reference

Thomas, V. (2014). 'Drawing on Creative Reflective Practices in Counselling research: An example of using mental imagery to enhance researcher reflexivity', *British Journal of Counselling & Guidance*, 42, 1: 43–51.

Preface

An enduring fascination with the therapeutic power of mental images and symbols has shaped my vocation and professional life. Early experiments in creative reflective exercises and therapeutic practice led me into teaching the therapeutic applications of mental imagery to counselling and psychotherapy students, and more lately, to conducting research into its practice. This book is another stage on a journey that began in my early 20s when I came across Carl Jung's (1968) work in *Man and His Symbols* and then read *Seeing with the Mind's Eye*, the seminal book written by Mike and Nancy Samuels (1975) that helped to introduce the practice of visualisation into popular culture during the 1970s.

Twenty-five years ago I embarked on my profession as a therapist working in the drugs field. In those early years I started to draw on my experience with mental imagery to help clients alleviate some of their physiological drug withdrawal symptoms and also, more significantly, manage and contain some of the difficult accompanying emotional states. Over time, three main themes crystalised in this work: the building image representing psychological structure; the plant image representing personality traits and psychological development; and the path image, which is used to represent living a purposeful life. I was impressed by the way these concrete representations helped substance-misusing clients (from a very diverse range of backgrounds) make sense of and work with their difficulties. Later on I developed this work further with cancer patients and integrated the use of these imagery themes in counselling and psychotherapy with a more general clinical population.

Perhaps I would have remained a practitioner but for a significant change that occurred in the mid-1990s when London experienced an epidemic of crack cocaine misuse. I started to notice a pattern emerging whereby crack cocaine users consistently reported that the roofs of their representational building images were damaged. When I turned to the literature to find an explanation I was not able to find any examples of similar patterns identified by other clinical practitioners. Instead of answers, my search of the relevant literature generated another question – why, despite the large amount of literature within different therapeutic schools, was there so little general treatment of mental imagery? I decided, then, to use the opportunity presented by undertaking a doctorate in psychotherapy to design a research study to identify some commonalities in therapeutic practice with mental imagery. The findings that ensued from a grounded theory study identified the different ways in which mental images operate as communications between the conscious and nonconscious parts of the self. I recall the Eureka moment when I realised that these findings offered a basis for a more inclusive model for general therapeutic practice with imagery.

The therapeutic potential of clients' mental imagery has been recognised since the inception of psychotherapy. Many of the great clinical innovators of the 20th century have contributed to our understanding of the different ways mental images can facilitate therapeutic processes. At different times its practice has been advanced by particular schools, such as the humanistic therapies in the 1970s and the current explosion of interest within contemporary cognitive behavioural approaches. And yet, there appears to be little obvious interest in developing more inclusive frameworks that would allow integrative therapists a way of drawing on the wide range of methods and procedures developed by different schools and clinical innovators. This book is a modest attempt to address that gap. It presents a coherent framework for inclusive practice with mental imagery and provides a guide for a deeper integration of its practice within talking therapies – an integration where working with the client's mental images is regarded as an intrinsic part of the therapeutic process. This is the guidebook I was looking for at the beginning of my therapeutic practice.

References

Jung, C., von Franz, M-L., *et al.* (1968). *Man and His Symbols*, New York: Dell Publishing.
Samuels, M. and Samuels, N. (1975). *Seeing with the Mind's Eye: The history, techniques, and uses of visualization*, New York: Random House.

Chapter 1

Introduction

The original pioneering geniuses of psychotherapy, Freud and Jung, helped to re-establish the faculty of imagining, expressed in the form of mental images, as a source of valid knowledge about the self and its operations. Since that time, mental imagery has gone through cycles of neglect and rediscovery; these rediscoveries have been made either by individual clinical pioneers who went on to develop idiosyncratic systems or by particular therapeutic schools where mental imagery comprises a set of techniques harnessed to a particular paradigm.

Shorr underscores the fundamental role that imagination plays in talking therapies when he poses the rhetorical question:

> Is there a psychotherapeutic procedure that does not depend on the patient's ability to recall and recreate situations and persons, real or imagined, which are a central part of a person's inner world regardless of whether they are verbalised in a therapy session?
>
> (1983: 464)

And yet, surprisingly, there is little general treatment of this subject in the field, apart from some notable exceptions such as Singer (2006; Singer and Pope, 1978) and Sheikh (2002). Why, despite its ubiquity, has the theory and practice of mental imagery in counselling and psychotherapy not followed the more usual recent trajectory of theoretical convergence? How can integrative counsellors and psychotherapists find a way of developing a coherent approach that can draw on radically different practices? It is important to note here that this integration needs to include approaches that would appear to be completely incompatible in practice – such as depth psychology's commitment to following the image without attempting to interpret or change it and cognitive behavioural therapy methods where mental images are reshaped to rational curative ends. How can more inclusive frameworks be developed for this practice? This book is an attempt to answer these questions.

The premise of this book

The patchwork development of the theory and practice of mental imagery within counselling and psychotherapy makes more sense when viewed in the light of wider historical and cultural contexts. In premodern Western Europe, imagination was a healing modality – viewed both as a cause of physical maladies and also as a potential cure. This role rapidly came to an end with the advent of Cartesian dualism in the 17th century. From this point on, if the faculty of imagining was understood to be purely a mental function then it could not be implicated in physiological processes. Furthermore, as a mental function it was compared unfavorably with rational thought and viewed as an inferior or 'primitive' type of thinking. This narrow view of imagination, one that conflates it with illusory thinking, has had a profound impact on Western culture and mental imagery as a subject has suffered as a consequence – academic psychology did not begin to consider mental images as worthy of investigation until the 1950s.

This historical and cultural context shaped the development of mental imagery as a therapeutic application in talking therapies through the 20th century. Although clinical experience consistently demonstrated the therapeutic potential of working with clients' mental images, developments in theory and practice were piecemeal and mainly informed by the paradigms espoused by particular therapeutic schools or clinical innovators. In the first decades of the 21st century it is evident that our thinking about mental imagery in counselling and psychotherapy has not followed the trajectory of theoretical convergence that is now commonly seen in the field. Instead the development of more inclusive theory has been stalled and two factors appear to be significant. First, Western thinking is still fundamentally shaped by Cartesian dualism and this means that, in popular culture, imagination as a valid healing modality continues to be automatically deprivileged. Second, the relational turn in counselling and psychotherapy has led to less interest in therapeutic methods that focus on the client's subjective processes. It is no coincidence that the main site for developing new therapeutic procedures with mental imagery is contemporary cognitive behavioural therapy (CBT) – the school least committed to intersubjectivity.

However, this post-Cartesian landscape is changing: a combination of a body of empirical neuroscientific research findings and theoretical developments across a range of disciplines are laying the grounds for a re-integration of body and mind. These developments are relevant to the therapeutic application of mental imagery because the faculty of imagining is now being understood as an embodied process; in particular, Lakoff and Johnson's (2003) theory of conceptual metaphor points to mental imagery having a mediating role between physiological and cognitive processes. Lakoff emphasises the importance of these developments, when he states with reference to the discovery that the same neurons fire for the action of grasping as when the concept grasp is expressed:

> It is hard to underestimate how far the idea that concepts are physically embodied, using the sensory motor system of the brain, is from disembodied Enlightenment reason – from the usual view of concepts as disembodied abstractions, entirely separate from the sensory motor system.
> (Lakoff, 2009: 252)

These wider developments indicate that it is time for the field of counselling and psychotherapy to embrace more inclusive approaches to the theory and practice of mental imagery. This book argues that one way of approaching this task is to identify commonalities in its practice across the different therapeutic schools. The general acceptance that mental images operate as a means of communicating between conscious and nonconscious parts of the self offers a potential locus of integration. This book goes on to propose a model that takes the basic distinctions noted in clinical practice between directive and receptive imagery and further differentiates these out into a range of communication functions operating within a therapeutic context. This model provides a potential transtheoretical framework that offers the possibility of integrating the practices and perspectives and techniques with respect to mental imagery across a wide range of modalities. Furthermore, it will also show how using mental images to represent fundamental dimensions of the self, theorised as conceptual metaphors, can be integrated into ongoing therapeutic work. This more inclusive practice recognises the significant role that mental images play in communicating between parts of the self and seeks a fuller and deeper integration of mental imagery within talking therapies to enhance therapeutic processes.

Who is it for and what are its aims?

This book is written primarily for counselling and psychotherapy practitioners with an integrative or pluralistic approach who want to develop their thinking about and practice with mental imagery. It will also appeal to all practitioners who have a particular interest in developing their work with creative imagination-based methods and who view imagery and symbols as an important means of facilitating therapeutic processes. It has been written on the assumption that the reader has a thorough grounding in counselling and psychotherapy theory and practice that would also include some familiarity with the way mainstream approaches make therapeutic use of clients' mental images.

It has also been written with researchers, counselling educators and academics in mind, in the hope that it will prompt more interest in developing more inclusive theory and practice with mental imagery.

The aims of the book are summarised below. It is intended to:

- shed light on the current state of the theory and practice of mental imagery by setting it within a much wider historical and cultural context;
- consider how more inclusive theory can be developed through identifying commonalities in its practice;
- introduce a potential framework for inclusive practice, i.e. the interactive communicative model of mental imagery;
- provide a detailed guide to using this model in clinical practice working with a set of mental images deemed to represent conceptual metaphors;
- encourage a deeper ongoing integration of mental imagery within talking therapies.

The rational and imaginal perspectives

As Hackmann *et al.* note, there has been ' . . . a long tradition of psychology models which suggest a contrast between nonverbal/imaginal and verbal modes of processing' (2011: 36). This distinction has been labeled in different ways, for example, Bruner (1986) refers to the former as 'narrative' and the latter as 'logical-scientific' or 'paradigmatic'. Any work that focuses on the therapeutic use of mental imagery will need to explore the relationship and interaction between these two different types of cognitive processing. However, selecting acceptable generic terms for the two different modes suitable for a more inclusive approach has been a challenge. In the counselling and psychotherapy literature these modes have been described and explained in various ways according to the theoretical positions held by the different schools and a range of terms have been used to refer to this difference. Inevitably, each pair of commonly used terms comes with a set of assumptions. Referring to the non-verbal/imaginal mode as the 'unconscious', for example, immediately links it to a psychodynamic model of the self. Using older more symbolic terms such as the 'underworld' assumes a location that is extra-psychic. I considered borrowing the term 'cognitive unconscious' from cognitive linguistics but this would award it a particular ontological status. Basic generic distinctions such as 'right/left brain' found in popular culture are unsuitable for similar reasons as well as being too simplistic to warrant serious consideration.

In the end I have decided that the best solution is to follow Hillman's (1975, 1979) example of referring to these two modes as two different perspectives: the 'rational perspective' (a shorthand label for everything associated with this mode i.e. literal, empirical, analytical, conceptual, verbal, linear, etc.) and the 'imaginal perspective' (a shorthand for everything associated with this mode, i.e. symbolic, non-linear, emotional, intuitive, etc.) In general I will be using these terms through the text. These terms allow the most freedom from an identified position. However, there are limitations to this shorthand nomenclature and on occasion I have needed to use other terms.

The scope of this book

There is a very wide range of applications of mental imagery across therapeutic and other cognate disciplines. Because the scope of this field is so vast it has been necessary to impose some limitations. The explicit focus of this book is the therapeutic use of mental imagery in counselling and psychotherapy. Therefore, although reference is made in the text on occasion to the following, they are not the subject of significant attention:

- Other modalities that make significant use of mental imagery such as hypnotherapy and art therapy. These are particular ways of working with mental images, each having a set of specific procedures.
- Dreams. This book focuses on mental images that are produced in a conscious relaxed state rather than imagery recalled from unconscious states

such as sleeping. This is a somewhat artificial boundary, of course, and in therapeutic practice clients' dream imagery may well become the starting point for further active work as one would with an image produced in a guided visualisation.
- Transpersonal imagery. Transpersonal therapeutic work makes significant use of imagery and symbols. However, an in-depth consideration of this subject sits outside the remit of this book. The work presented in this book focuses mainly on the use of imagery to represent aspects of the self. However, this does not mean that it is an explicitly secular work as imagery can appear in these settings that incorporates or depicts transpersonal dimensions.
- Self-help and self-development literature. Although this genre includes some excellent guides to using imagery procedures, these techniques are designed for individual creative practices rather than being delivered within a therapeutic setting.

Overview of the contents

The book is divided into two parts: the first part (Chapters 2–6) sets the context and deals with the theory; and the second part (Chapters 7–12) provides a guide to more inclusive practice. Although the second half can be read as a stand-alone guide, it is supported by the preceding theoretical section.

It is important to note this is not designed to be a scholarly text although it does address theoretical matters. Some of the debates concerning mental imagery raise complex epistemological and ontological questions. In order to make the material presented in this book accessible for the general reader I have taken shortcuts wherever it is possible and when it will not undermine the argument.

NB: Part One presents the background to the use of mental imagery in counselling and psychotherapy. In order to do this I have drawn on a wide range of scholarly work by experts in these fields. Any mistakes in the ensuing synthesis are purely my own.

Part one: towards more inclusive theory

Chapter 2 presents an overview of the history of imagination as a healing modality. It starts with a description of the premodern view of imagination as an integral part of healing practices. It then goes on to discuss the impact of Cartesian dualism on Western culture's approach to illness and health and, in particular, the end of imagination as a healing modality. It discusses the way that mental imagery was also deprivileged within the emerging discipline of psychology until the mid-20th century.

Chapter 3 returns to the late 19th century to trace the way that, beginning with Freud, the psychotherapeutic use of mental images developed as different sets of techniques within the main therapeutic approaches. As it assumes the reader will be familiar with the range of mental imagery methods developed within mainstream schools over the 20th century, these sections will be presented in summary. It then goes on to consider the contributions of clinical pioneers, working outside the mainstream, who developed influential image-based therapies, particularly those from the European waking dream tradition such as Desoille's (1966) directed daydream method and Leuner's (1984) *Guided Affective Imagery*. It ends by discussing the current developments within contemporary cognitive approaches including an account of some of the new imagery approaches for trauma such as rescripting.

Chapter 4 considers how the field has dealt with explaining the therapeutic efficacy of mental imagery. These explanations can be grouped into two types – i.e. empirical models and phenomenological descriptions. It then goes on to consider an attempt from within the field to generate a more transtheoretical explanation, i.e. Ahsen's (1984) image/somatic/meaning model (ISM). It then describes a particularly important and relevant theory from another discipline, i.e. conceptual metaphor developed by cognitive linguists, Lakoff and Johnson (2003). It discusses how this theory can explain the operations of mental imagery as a bridge between nonconceptual cognitive processing and later emerging higher-order conceptualisation processes. It concludes that conceptual metaphors can provide potential ground for the integration of both the empirical and phenomenological perspectives on mental imagery.

Chapter 5 discusses another way of moving beyond the empirical/phenomenological divide that has characterised the study of mental imagery in counselling and psychotherapy by returning to the field and identifying basic commonalities in its practice. It considers some of the simple distinctions and basic operational differences that are generally accepted in clinical practice across the different schools, including the particularly important distinction that is made between receptive and directive imagery in therapeutic practice. It then goes on to consider, in detail, a typology of communication functions that emerged from a recent research study.

Chapter 6 goes on to discuss how the typology of communication functions identified in the previous chapter can provide the basis for an inclusive theoretical framework of mental imagery in therapeutic practice. It explains how the six different identified functions model the way that mental images operate as an interactive communication process between the rational and imaginal perspectives. The chapter concludes by offering some thoughts on the advantages of the model and also acknowledges its limitations.

Part two: towards more inclusive practice

Chapter 7 provides an introduction to the interactive communicative model of mental imagery in practice. It explains how this model can operate as a more inclusive framework for therapeutic work. It identifies the main principle that informs the model in practice – i.e. maintaining a dynamic balance between the rational and imaginal perspectives. Other important aspects of therapeutic work with mental imagery are considered, such as: induced relaxation; how both the therapist's and client's attitudes towards imagery influence the work; and the issue of interpreting imagery. The second part of the chapter goes on to introduce and provide a context for the next three chapters, each of which present guidance on using particular framing images that represent a fundamental dimension of human experience. It explains how these framing images are theorised as conceptual metaphors.

Chapters 8, 9 and 10 demonstrate the application of the interactive communicative model illustrated through using three particular framing images. This set of images comprise: the building image to represent psychological structure, the path image to represent leading a purposeful life and the plant image to represent personality traits and psychological. The three chapters have a similar format: each one is designed to be a manual and reference text for working with a particular framing image. Different stages of the work are considered from the initial diagnostic procedure through to ongoing longer term work. In addition, specific communication functions of imagery are emphasised as especially pertinent to particular stages of the work. These chapters are extensively illustrated with case vignettes.

Chapter 11 considers how these framing images can be integrated into ongoing work in counselling and psychotherapy. Viewed in the light of the interactive communicative model, it discusses the way that different communicative functions of mental imagery come to the fore dependent on therapeutic need and illustrates how a deeper integration of mental imagery into talking therapies can facilitate long-term therapeutic shifts. It begins with some general observations about the therapist's approach and then examines some of the different aspects of incorporating imagery, with specific reference to the three framing images, into ongoing clinical work.

Chapter 12 considers some of the more significant issues that are relevant to developing a more inclusive practice with mental imagery. This discussion includes matters relating to safe practice such as: contra-indications to its use; working with induced relaxation states; and managing clients' problematic reactions to imagery. Other aspects of practice include strategies for increasing clients' capacity to make productive use of mental imagery. It includes some consideration of the way that the subjective processes facilitated by mental imagery operate within the intersubjective context of the therapeutic relationship.

A note on the clinical work presented in this book

It is important to emphasise that this book is not intended to offer another system based on the formulation of one clinician's body of work (this is not intended to disparage the important and valuable contributions made by clinicians who have generated their own systems of therapeutic imagery). The imagery work presented here is used purely to illustrate more inclusive theory applied to practice. Admittedly, in order to provide some guidance this imagery work has been formulated along particular lines and this can give it a somewhat prescriptive flavour, whereas, in practice, my experience has shown me that that this work is endlessly fluid and creative. Notwithstanding the detailed guidance on procedures, the main aim of this book is to encourage a deeper more creative ongoing engagement with mental images. I would hope that therapists will be able to draw on its guidance in whatever way that suits their own individual approach.

However, it is important to acknowledge the limitations imposed by using illustrations drawn exclusively from my own casebook as this work is inevitably shaped by my clinical experience and personal history, as well as wider cultural influences. As described in the preface, my formative clinical work was undertaken in London with substance misusers in crisis, many of whom had life histories characterised by trauma. Traces of this clinical experience can be detected in the way that the guidance in this book emphasises structural issues, security, stabilisation and temporary containment.

Another influential experience that has shaped my attitude to imagery would be my early training as an archaeologist specialising in prehistory. I can see how I have been drawn to using mental images to reveal causes and early conditions, as well as an interest in noting continuities and discontinuities over time.

On another note, it is also important to acknowledge that I have drawn on the work with many clients to illustrate the guidance to more inclusive practice in Part Two. The identities of the clients have been anonymised and I have sought permission for publishing these short examples wherever possible. It is important to emphasise that these vignettes are not offered as rounded case studies – the imagery is highlighted and other important aspects of the therapeutic process are left out. Having said that, I believe that, taken as a whole, these snapshots of clinical work deliver a good sense of the ways that mental images operate in therapeutic processes. Hopefully, these examples will stimulate practitioners to develop their skills with more inclusive practice that is presented in this book.

A note on terms and conventions

The terms 'mental images', 'mental imagery' and 'visualisation' will be used interchangeably throughout the text. These terms refer to mental depictions, whether these be recreations of previously experienced events or depictions that have no external referent.

The terms 'counselling', 'psychotherapy', 'talking therapies' and 'therapy' will be used interchangeably in the text.

I will be making significant reference throughout this book to the theory of conceptual metaphor. When I do, I will be using the accepted convention of small capital letters for representing conceptual metaphors throughout the text, e.g. PEOPLE ARE PLANTS.

References

Ahsen A. (1984). 'ISM: The Triple Code Model for Imagery and Psychophysiology', *Journal of Mental Imagery*, 8, 4: 15–42.
Bruner, J. (1986). *Actual Minds, Possible Worlds*, Cambridge, MA: Harvard University Press.

Desoille, R. (1966). *The Directed Daydream*, New York: Psychosynthesis Research Foundation.
Hackmann, A., Bennett-Levy, J. and Holmes, E. A. (2011). *Oxford Guide to Imagery in Cognitive Therapy*, Oxford: Oxford University Press.
Hillman, J. (1975). *Re-visioning Psychology*, New York: Harper & Row.
——. (1979). *The Dream and the Underworld*, New York: Harper Perennial.
Lakoff, G. (2009). *The Political Mind*, New York: Penguin.
——. and Johnson, M. (2003). *Metaphors We Live By*, 2nd edn, Chicago: University of Chicago Press.
Leuner, H. (1984). *Guided Affective Imagery: Mental imagery in short-term psychotherapy*, New York: Thieme-Stratton Corp.
Sheikh, A. A. (ed) (2002). *Therapeutic Imagery Techniques*, Amityville, NY: Baywood Pub.
Shorr, J. E. (1983). *Psychotherapy through Imagery*, 2nd edn, New York: Thieme-Stratton Inc.
Singer, J. L. (2006). *Imagery in Psychotherapy*, Washington, DC: American Psychological Association.
——. and Pope, K. S. (eds) (1978). *The Power of Human Imagination: New methods in psychotherapy*, New York: Plenum Press.

Part I

Towards more inclusive theory

Part I

Towards more inclusive theory

Chapter 2

An historical perspective on the therapeutic use of imagination

Over the last three decades, one of the main directions in counselling and psychotherapy has been towards increasing theoretical convergence. However, there is little evidence for more inclusive theorising regarding the therapeutic use of mental imagery. Since the faculty of imagining appears to be implicated in all creative processes, why has the study and development of mental imagery procedures remained confined within the parameters of particular schools and approaches? The first two chapters of this book attempt to shed some light on this puzzle by situating this practice in a much wider historical and cultural context. In particular, the discussion will focus on how this therapeutic application has been, and, even more importantly, still is, impacted by the advent of Cartesian dualism and the establishment of a scientific worldview. In order to capture a large and complex landscape, I have taken a broad-brush approach that identifies the main themes pertinent to this question, drawing on scholarly work by experts on the history of imagination as a healing modality, particularly McMahon (1976; McMahon and Hastrup, 1980) and Achterberg (2002).

This chapter begins by explaining how the faculty of imagining lost its role in the treatment of physical illnesses; a radical change neatly captured in the statement by McMahon and Hastrup, 'In the predualistic era the expression "It's all in your imagination" signified a key medical principle. In the modern era it came to signify justification for dismissing the patient as untreatable' (1980: 206). The following chapter then goes on to consider how the use of mental imagery was reprised as a therapeutic procedure for treating psychological problems and how this developed over the course of the 20th century.

The premodern use of imagination as a healing tool

Anthropological studies, archaeological evidence and historical records have given us a picture of medical practices in premodern cultures that display some remarkably consistent features. One of these features is the shaman: the person who has the power to use altered states of consciousness to access symbolic landscapes in order to diagnose and treat illnesses. As Achterberg notes, 'The shamans' work is conducted in the realm of the imagination, and their expertise in using that terrain for the benefit of the community has been recognised throughout recorded history' (2002: 11). It seems clear that in shamanic cultures the distinction between technological medicine such as setting a broken bone and imaginative medicine for curing sickness of the soul has generally been recognised. In these cultures the shaman occupies the top of the hierarchy with technological specialists such as bone setters at the bottom. The shaman is applied to as a last resort after physical interventions have failed.

There were local variants of shamanic practices across the world and some of these survived in remote regions shielded from Western influence until relatively recently such as the Sami peoples of Siberia. The following section begins with the shamanically informed healing practices in early Greek civilisation and goes on to trace how the role of imagination fared in the development of Western medicine.

In ancient Greece, people held the same fundamental understanding of the human condition as the shamanic tradition; mind and body were viewed as one integrated system. Consequently, all illnesses were considered to be psychosomatic and the faculty of imagining had a legitimate role as an important healing tool. There is evidence of its use in this capacity from reports of the healing practices employed in the Asclepian temples (Asclepius is the Greek god of healing). One particular practice appears to have used a form of incubation therapy where patients were helped into hypnagogic states. The temple priests then interacted with the patients' hypnagogic images based on the principle that these dramatic enactments could heal the patients' illnesses.

Aristotle (384–322 BC) and Galen (AD 130–200), two of the earliest Greek writers on healing and medicine, were trained in the Asclepian tradition and both of them wrote explicitly about their understanding of the ability of imagination to operate directly on the physical system. Aristotle identified mental images as the necessary pre-existing condition that arouses emotion, which in turn produces physical effects in the body. An important consequence of this view was the emphasis placed on controlling emotion. Aristotle's conceptualisation of the effect of images and imagination became a central tenet of later medical understanding, i.e. the importance of engaging the patient's imagination to bring about healing. Later on in the second century AD, Galen recorded his belief in the diagnostic properties of patients' dreams. He subscribed to Hippocrates' theory that the physiological system comprised four humours, i.e. black bile, yellow bile, phlegm and blood. It was believed that all four humours needed to be in balance to ensure good health; an excess or deficit of a humour would result in disease and disability. Particular dream images would indicate imbalances in this system: 'Images of loss, disgrace or grief, for example, signified excessive melancholy; those of terror, fighting, wounds and the like, indicated predominance of choler' (McMahon, 1976: 180).

After this high point in the early development of Western medicine, little further progress was made until the Renaissance. Throughout this long period there were hardly any advances made in understanding how the body actually worked and little was known with any accuracy of the body's anatomy. The explanatory models used were still rooted in the early Greek thinking and these age-old medical practices were not challenged until the early 16th century when Paracelsus (1493–1541) revolutionised medical practice. However, even though he pioneered new treatments such as the use of chemicals and minerals, these practices remained wedded to the unquestioned belief that the mind and the body form one inseparable entity. This conviction allowed him to restate the important role of imagination in health: the faculty of imagining is so powerful that it can both cause and cure diseases. During the Renaissance, the wide range of healing practitioners operating in Western Europe, including wise women, priests and monks, would have shared this understanding of the power of imagination. McMahon acknowledges the difficulty that we have in understanding this from a 21st-century perspective, stating that, 'The key to an understanding of such pre-Cartesian theory lies in recognizing that imagery was understood to be as much a physiological reality as it is today regarded as a psychological reality' (1976: 181).

However, a radical transformation of the theory and practice of medicine was waiting in the wings heralded by the founding of the Royal College of Physicians in England in 1518. Its charter outlawed the practice of medicine by women and certain male craftsmen and laid the foundations for an elite medical profession. And then, a century later, came an intellectual revolution, Cartesian dualism, that would create the grounds for a new view of imagination; one that would result in its removal from medical practices and reduce it to 'a wispy and evanescent process that lacks flesh and blood substance' (Price-Williams, (1992: 246). From thence on an increasingly powerful medical establishment, wedded to a new rationalist materialist worldview, would defend itself against any re-emergence of imagination as a legitimate healing modality.

Cartesian dualism and its impact on imagination as a healing modality

It is important to remind ourselves of the enormity and speed of the paradigm shift that began in 17th-century Europe. Through Descartes's (1596–1650) publications, a new perspective came into being that asserted itself as completely separate from the world captured eloquently in Harpur's description:

> The new consciousness was centred around a subject, an *ego* as we now call it, which was so narrow, so focused, so bright, that it threw the rest of the psyche into dark shadow. All the twilight intercourse between consciousness and the unconscious ceased.
>
> (2003: 47)

Descartes's (1641) philosophical writings brought about a fundamental change in the way that people conceptualised the relationship between mind and body.

In essence, Descartes's quest to prove the immortality of the soul meant that the soul had to be separated off from the body. Mind and body could, no longer, be viewed as one entity: man was redefined as an immortal soul residing in a purely mechanical body. Although many of his contemporaries disputed his conclusions – some even deriding him as mad – it would appear that the zeitgeist was ripe for this idea. In other words, it was time for a differentiation between the different domains of human existence to happen. From that point on, the body was given over to anatomy and physiology and the mind to philosophy or psychology. Within a very short period of fifty years an intellectual revolution had taken place laying the ground for great progress in the 19th and 20th century in science-based medicine.

With particular relevance to the subject of mental imagery, Cartesian dualism paved the way for the removal of imagination as a credible and viable healing modality. By separating mind and body, mental imagery lost its biological base: mental images were henceforth understood to be purely contents of the mind. If there were any apparent mutual influences between the two then these were the product of divine influence. Imagination could not possibly cause, cure or influence physiological conditions such as illness.

However, there was another important consequence of this dualistic view that exacerbated the diminishment of imagination as a valid means of knowledge. Once imagination could no longer be partly physiological and partly mental, it lost its function as a mediator between the mind and body. Reduced to the status of purely mental operations, imaginary processes, such as mental imagery, were compared unfavourably with analytic and rational thinking; the latter better suited to the purposes of materialism with its quest for objective truth and universal laws. Imagination became increasingly under attack, Hobbes (1588–1679), for example, asserted in his influential philosophical treatise, *Leviathon* (1996), that imagination was the property of children, lunatics and the uneducated (see Chapter 4 for further discussion of these critiques). The characteristic features of the new worldview, i.e. fact-based and literal, were antithetical to imaginative knowing.

And so it was that imagination, conflated with illusory thinking and fantasy, was condemned, along with traditional healing practices and practitioners, to the margins of a new world. It was accepted as long as it stayed within the boundaries of its proper sphere of influence, i.e. literature and art. However, it no longer had any place within medicine or healing. Mental images languished in exile, not deemed to be a proper object of study until reprised by psychology in the second half of the 19th century.

After Descartes

Despite plenty of opposition from Enlightenment scholars who criticised this mechanistic view, Cartesian dualism held sway and, over the next two centuries, links between mind and body were either ignored or suppressed. Some conditions, however, could not be so easily dismissed, for example, any attempt to explain the etiology of 'nervous complaints' would inevitably require a means of connecting mental states to physiological conditions. Enlightenment thinkers wrestled with this conundrum trying to find an explanation that adhered to the basic principles of dualism. One solution that gained a favourable reception in the 18th century was the theory of parallelism originally proposed by Leibniz (1646–1714) and more fully developed by Hartley (1705–1757) that explained correspondences between mind and body as fortuitous, arising from identical responses to the same stimuli.

Despite the prevailing view and hostile climate of opinion, there were some attempts to re-establish healing practices that acknowledged the link between body and mind. One of the most notable of these, as well as being particularly salient to the therapeutic practice of mental imagery, is the work of Mesmer (1734–1815). His story is also an illustration of how the established medical profession dealt with challenges to its materialistic dualistic worldview. Mesmer developed a practice that used a combination of suggestion, altered states of consciousness and the use of magnets that were reported to result in remarkable cures. These procedures were aimed at a range of illnesses that would nowadays be viewed as psychosomatic such as temporary paralysis, depression and asthma. Mesmer's theory was that there was a fluid he called 'animal magnetism' that moved through the body and was implicated in physiological conditions. Treatment with physical magnets could rebalance this energy and when this happened the physical malady would disappear. People flocked to his practice and its success attracted attention from the authorities. A Royal Commission of Inquiry was set up and came to the conclusion that there was no basis for the theory of animal magnetism and that the cures had been brought about by imagination only. As, from a dualistic position, imagination is purely the content of the mind, the Commission reached the only conclusion that would be coherent with this worldview: the medical conditions purportedly healed through mesmerism were illusory in the first place. This decision marked the end of Mesmer's battle to get the medical establishment to accept his healing procedure.

There were further attempts by other notable physicians to advocate the role of imagination in health. The English physician, Falconer (1744–1824), for example, highlighted the operation of cures brought about by ineffective remedies and proposed that patients' confidence in these cures was the reason. Later on in the 19th century, Tuke (1827–1895) came across a report of a dramatic railway accident where one uninjured passenger emerged completely cured of severe rheumatism. He became an advocate of placebo therapy and published texts on the power of imagination to effect cures of medical conditions. However, all of these attempts came to nothing as the medical establishment rose up to defend dualism labeling all opposition as the work of 'quacks' – a label that would automatically have the practitioner ostracised by society and bereft of patients.

A more recent example from the 20th century can be found in the work of the Simontons (1978), a pioneering husband and wife medical team, who studied the impact of using visualisation techniques with their cancer patients. Their clinical observations led them to believe that patients could use their imagination to help actively strengthen self-healing mechanisms. In order to do this, patients were taught to visualise their immune system overpowering the cancer. This method was informed by a new theory (although now this has lost some of its credibility) that the immune system holds the key to the progression of the disease. Very early on, the Simontons noticed that the imagery their patients produced was indicative of their beliefs about the progression of the illness (this echoes Galen's belief, mentioned earlier, that dream images are diagnostic). Patients who produce weak imagery symbolising the immune system – for example, visualising this as rain falling onto rocks that represent the tumours – are revealing their hopelessness regarding the capacity of their physical system to fight the disease. In these cases, the Simontons realised the importance of helping patients create changes in the imagery that would convey a stronger message to the subconscious mind of faith in the power of the immune system. The patients would then be encouraged to practise this twice a day and to monitor any changes in the imagery of the illness as they went along. This practice became an established part of the repertoire of complementary treatments and remains popular to this day (see Thomas [2009] for a description of visualisation procedures current in complementary healthcare practice with cancer patients). Yet, despite the increased acknowledgement of the importance of psychosocial factors in the progression of cancer and the emergence of psycho-oncology as a new discipline, the Simontons' work has not been received favourably by the medical establishment. Developing the Simontons' work and building on their insights has been mainly undertaken by medical practitioners and specialists working outside the mainstream e.g. Cunningham (2010) and Dossey (1997). Imagination as a healing modality remains generally restricted to nonconventional complementary and alternative medicine and the accusation of 'quackery' is still current. Although some inroads have been made by psychologists who have developed imagery interventions designed to be adjuncts to orthodox medical treatment (Brigham, 1996; Graham, 1995).

In the following section I go on to discuss how imagination fared in the role of treating psychopathology.

19th-century psychology and mental imagery

Cartesian dualism created the grounds for different disciplines to arise that dealt with the body and the mind separately. During the 19th century, psychology emerged as a separate discipline rather than just a branch of philosophy and with this came an opportunity for establishing mental imagery as a serious focus of intellectual investigation. Many studies were carried out during this time that used introspective methods to identify, among other things, different types of images. It also led to a reconsideration of the role of imagery in arousal – for example, the American psychologist William James's (1842–1910) influential theory of ideo-motor action that appears to reprise an earlier Aristotelian theory of the role of mental images in influencing physiological states.

But, despite these promising beginnings, psychology was a fledgling discipline at the beginning of the 20th century and its main proponents were concerned to establish it as a scientific discipline. Dualism soon reasserted its power as the dominant paradigm and any novel element or theory that challenged its fundamental principles was suppressed. This orthodox position was personified in the form of the influential American behaviourist, Watson (1878–1958), who issued a notorious rebuttal of mental imagery (Watson, 1913). The behaviourists rejected mentalist concepts such as imagery because, they claimed, there was no evidence for the contents of the mind, substituting drives, instead, as the agents of arousal. This hostility to introspective methods and mentalist concepts resulted in imagery being ignored as a serious subject of research in psychology until the 1960s.

Meanwhile, in continental Europe, the study of mental imagery was less constrained by experimental psychology, and there was more focus on how psychological factors were implicated in psychopathology. This focus, of course, did not pose any challenges to the dominant orthodoxy of dualism as psychology and mental illness both pertained to the mind. During the latter half of the 19th century there was an increasing interest in descriptions of disassociated states and altered states of consciousness, and systematic methodical research was carried out into the nature of dreams and visions. One important influential example is Charcot (1825–1893), a prominent French neurologist (among whose students were Janet and Freud) who became interested in studying hysteria in his patients and came to the conclusion that this state could have arisen from an emotional reaction to a traumatic accident. Meanwhile, other psychologists and psychiatrists were experimenting and developing Mesmer's therapeutic methods, rebranding his procedures as hypnotherapy. And, similarly to Mesmer's patients over a century previously, their patients were reporting successful cures. Furthermore, these experimental procedures often contained an imagery component, and it is striking how much these 19th-century accounts seem to hark back to premodern practices in Ancient Greece, discussed earlier, such as the incubation methods in the Asclepian healing temples.

Importantly, and especially pertinent to the history of the therapeutic use of mental imagery, practitioners were beginning to identify that during hypnotic states their patients would produce mental images that seemed to be the products of a helpful unconscious source. James and Myers (1843–1901), who at this time were studying psychic methods such as automatic writing, were coming to a similar conclusion, i.e. that these methods appeared to be a means of accessing subconscious material and, furthermore, bringing this material to light could be therapeutically beneficial. These conclusions arising out of a combination of clinical observations and introspective investigations marked the beginning of the reprisal of the faculty of imagining as a valid therapeutic method. Mental images were not just expressions of a degraded type of thinking but instead were potentially helpful and useful communications from another part of the mind.

European psychiatrists and psychologists in the last quarter of the 19th century started to explore the therapeutic potential of mental imagery in earnest. This interest focused, in particular, on the phenomenon of the 'unconscious' (the term that emerged as the generally accepted designation for the region of the mind where repressed experience was believed to be stored) and its imaginative nature was identified as one of its main characteristics. Myers coined the useful descriptive term 'mythopoetic' (Ellenberger, 1970), which captures the imaginative processes evident in the tendency of the unconscious to weave fantasies.

However, it is important to note that, although some of these new methods appear to share similar features to earlier premodern healing approaches, the modern understanding of the unconscious was different to the premodern view. Probably the most significant difference is where the source of the images is located: in the premodern era this mythic reality was externalised as a noncorporeal environment but in the modern era it is clearly located within the individual and specifically within the person's mind. Hillman's elegant aphorism captures this paradox of similarity and radical difference: 'Mythology is a psychology of antiquity. Psychology is a mythology of modernity' (1979: 23).

Attempts were made to develop therapeutic applications based on these discoveries and this new kind of work was termed 'psychotherapeutics' in 1872 and 'psychotherapy' in 1891. One of the great pioneers in this regard was Janet (1889–1947), the French psychologist, who developed a theory that split-off parts of the self expressed themselves symbolically. He helped his patients gain access to these parts of the self hidden from their conscious awareness through a technique that stimulated the production of imagery. He believed that once these images were brought into consciousness they then needed to be changed or eradicated for the patient to improve. Janet's influence on Freud's ideas is well-documented but it is also worth noting how similar this technique sounds to the rescripting techniques developed more recently within cognitive behavioural therapy (CBT), i.e. substituting a different image for a problematic intrusive memory.

It was in this fertile milieu that Freud refined his psychoanalytic method (Jones, 1951). And, at a pivotal moment at the beginning of the 20th century, as psychology closed its doors to anything that smacked of unorthodox theory and practice, psychotherapy emerged as the sole container for the study and development of the therapeutic application of mental imagery. The following chapter will examine how this development unfolded over the 20th century right up to the present day. However, before I turn to a more detailed discussion of the history of the use of mental imagery in counselling and psychotherapy, there is one important final part of the story of psychology and mental imagery that happens in the latter half of the 20th century.

Psychology finally reclaims mental imagery

As mentioned earlier, Watson's rebuttal of mental imagery had a powerful lasting impact; almost no research was conducted by psychologists into mental images in the following four decades. However, by the late 1950s, this entrenched position began to be undermined by the increasing body of evidence from hard science that everyone dreams and that normal people in abnormal situations, e.g. prison, produced imagery. Faced with this evidence, behaviourists started to revise their hard-line position and began to study how imagery was implicated in behavioural change. In a very short space of time there was an explosion of interest in mental imagery. After a dearth of interest and publications, almost overnight, mental imagery was reclaimed with enthusiasm across several disciplines including psychology. One particularly important factor implicated in this rediscovery was the gathering pace of the human potential movement in America and the UK. New humanistic therapies were being developed that focused on exploring and facilitating creative self-development. Pioneers such as Fritz Perls (1893–1970) were developing a range of innovative mental imagery methods to help people experience their emotions and explore their creative potential (his important contributions will be discussed in detail in the following chapter). A cultural shift was happening and a new generation was attracted to exploring altered states of consciousness, the imagination and nonrational domains of human experience. Seminal books were published at this time, such as *Seeing with the Mind's Eye* (Samuels and Samuels, 1975), that introduced the general public to the potential of mental images as a means of self-development. These early texts received an enthusiastic reception and unleashed a flood of popular self-help literature containing visualisation techniques for positive personality and behavioural change.

Academic psychology, too, was freeing itself from the shackles of behaviourism and positivism. Biochemical and neuropsychological investigations prompted interest in mental processes such as visualisation and how the use of mental imagery could influence behaviour. Research studies provided evidence for the positive impact that imagery rehearsal could have on sports performance. Since then imagery as a behavioural intervention has become a sophisticated specialist application used in a wide range of contexts such as sports performance training. Mental images as an instrumental means of shaping the personality along desired lines have become well-established in the repertoire of popular psychology and self-help literature.

Meanwhile, running parallel to the story of how psychology reclaimed mental images, another complex narrative was unfolding – i.e. the therapeutic application of mental imagery in counselling and psychotherapy. The following chapter presents its history, considering the contributions of important innovators and tracking the shifting perspectives on this practice across the different therapeutic schools.

References

Achterberg, J. (2002). *Imagery in Healing: Shamanism and modern medicine*, 2nd edn, Boston: Shambhala.

Brigham, D. (1996). *Imagery for Getting Well: Clinical applications of behavioral medicine*, New York: Norton.

Cunningham, A. (2010). *The Healing Journey: Overcoming the crisis of cancer*, 3rd revised edn, London: Healing Journey Books.

Descartes, R. (1641). *Meditations on First Philosophy*, in *The Philosophical Writings of René Descartes*, trans. J. Cottingham, R. Stoothoff and D. Murdoch, 1984, vol. 2, 1–62, Cambridge: Cambridge University Press.

Dossey, L. (1997). *Meaning and Medicine: Lessons from a doctor's tales of breakthrough and healing*, reprint edn, New York: Bantam Doubleday Dell Publishing Group.

Ellenberger, H.F. (1970). *The Discovery of the Unconscious*, New York: Basic Books.

Graham, H. (1995). *Mental Imagery in Healthcare: An introduction to therapeutic practice*, London: Chapman & Hall.

Harpur, P. (2003). *The Philosophers' Secret Fire: A history of the imagination*, Chicago: Ivan R. Dee Pub.

Hillman, J. (1979). *The Dream and the Underworld*, New York: Harper Perennial.

Hobbes, T. (1996). *Leviathon*, ed. R. Tuck, Revised student edn, Cambridge: Cambridge University Press.

Jones, E. (1951). *The Life and Work of Sigmund Freud*, vol 1, New York: Basic Books.

McMahon, C. E. (1976). 'The Role of Imagination in the Disease Process: Pre-Cartesian history', *Psychological Medicine*, 6: 179–184.

—— and Hastrup, J. L. (1980). 'The Role of Imagination in the Disease Process: Post-Cartesian history', *Journal of Behavioral Medicine*, 3, 2: 205–217.

Price-Williams, D. (1992). 'The Waking Dream in Ethnographic Perspective', in B. Tedlock (ed) *Dreaming: Anthropological and psychological interpretations*, 246–262, Santa Fe, NM: School of American Research Press.

Samuels, M. and Samuels, N. (1975). *Seeing with the Mind's Eye: The history, techniques, and uses of visualization*, New York: Random House.

Simonton, O.C. and Mathews-Simonton, S. (1978). *Getting Well Again: A step-by-step self-help guide to overcoming cancer for patients and their families*, New York: J.P. Tarcher Inc.

Thomas, V. (2009). 'Using Visualisation Techniques with Cancer Patients (Abstract only)', Online Cancer Education Forum, *European Journal of Cancer Care*, 18, 2.

Watson, J.B. (1913). 'Psychology as the Behaviorist Sees It', *Psychological Review*, 20, 2: 158–177.

Chapter 3

The story of using mental imagery in counselling and psychotherapy

This chapter picks up the story of imagination as a healing modality at a pivotal moment in the late 19th century when the therapeutic potential of mental images was being rediscovered. A creative modern reworking of the premodern practices seen in the Asclepian temple tradition was starting to be crystalised in early psychotherapeutic methods. Although, as previously noted, there were significant differences; psychotherapeutic practice focused on healing psychological problems and the potentially helpful source of imagery had been relocated from a mythic reality to an unconscious part of the mind.

The story of using mental imagery in counselling and psychotherapy from those early beginnings up to the present day is a complex one. However, two main themes can be picked out in this narrative: the first theme consists of the way in which different schools have theorised and applied the therapeutic function of mental images; and the second one comprises the influential individual pioneers working outside the mainstream schools who have developed and formulated image-based work. Of course, in reality, these two groups are not so clearly distinct – each one has influenced the other – and their interweavings form the fabric of this story. However, for the sake of clarity, this chapter addresses these two themes separately. It begins with an account of the way that the use of mental imagery was developed within the main therapeutic approaches of the 20th century – I am grouping these into three very general orientating categories i.e. psychodynamic, humanistic and cognitive behavioral therapy (CBT). These approaches will be presented chronologically starting with Freud's initial experiments with mental images then moving on to Jung's pioneering work and the flowering of mental imagery in the humanistic approaches of the 1970s, and ending with the imagery methods currently being developed within contemporary CBT approaches. It will also include a consideration of some of the influential image-based psychotherapies that were being developed in parallel through the course of the 20th century. Some of this narrative will be familiar to the reader, in particular its development within the mainstream approaches and, consequently, these sections will be delivered in summary (for a more detailed treatment of this subject, readers are referred to Singer's [2006] scholarly account). Other presumably less well-known parts of this story will be dealt with in more detail, particularly the European waking dream tradition and recent developments within contemporary CBT. The chapter ends with some reflection on the current state of theoretical development and practice in mental imagery in the early 21st century.

The early days of therapeutic practice with mental imagery: the psychodynamic school

Freud and psychoanalysis

As discussed in the previous chapter, Freud (Jones, 1951) was developing his theories during the last decades of the 19th century when there was widespread enthusiastic experimentation with a range of methods that appeared to allow access to nonconscious parts of the mind. Charcot (1825–1893) and Janet's (1842–1910) pioneering work influenced Freud's early experiments where he sought to use hypnosis to help his patients relive traumatic events. In 1892, Freud (Breuer and Freud, 1955) dispensed with hypnosis and used a technique of pressing his hand on the patient's forehead to stimulate imagery and then interpreting the arising images and fantasies. Later on, he ceased to encourage this active generation of imagery and instead began to rely on other methods such as free association that he believed offered a better means for allowing a free flow of unconscious contents to arise in the patient. From then on, his work with mental imagery became restricted to interpreting his patients' dreams and spontaneous fantasies (Freud, 1900).

This shift away from the initial active use of mental imagery can be explained by Freud's developing formulation of psychoanalytic practices and his view of the defensive nature of the unconscious. In terms of the former, Freud believed that methods for actively generating mental images would conceal the patient's transference and defences. Verbal methods for accessing uncensored unconscious material were viewed as less problematic in this regard. In terms of the latter, Freud believed that the unconscious is a receptacle for all the material and experiences that the conscious mind, particularly during childhood development, could not assimilate and this material is generally negative or culturally unacceptable. Consequently, the unconscious both discloses information through dream images and fantasies but also uses these images to ward off the re-experiencing of repressed material. In other words, images should not be taken at face value. The manifest image is viewed as the product of processes of symbolization, condensation and displacement. Interpretative strategies are required to explore its multiple latent meanings. Images were increasingly viewed by Freud as a manifestation of the patient's resistance.

In summary, once the fundamental principles of the practice of psychoanalysis had been firmly established this included a particular therapeutic use of mental images limited mainly to dream imagery and fantasy. This classic approach is characterised by understanding the patient's imagery as screen memories, i.e. what a screen conceals. The emphasis is on latent content and what the mental image conceals rather than the manifest content and what it might reveal. No one can doubt the greatness of Freud's legacy with regard to mental imagery: his revolutionary psychoanalytical method effectively re-established mental images as important therapeutic tools. However, his interpretative framework is stamped with 'the hermeneutics of suspicion' (Ricoeur, 1970) – a byproduct of which is an enduring perception in popular culture that dream images are invariably disguised communications about sex.

During the 1970s, a more active engagement with patients' mental images did resurface within this school and this was prompted by a combination of factors. Psychoanalytic approaches are not immune to cultural shifts and, as discussed in the previous chapter, during that decade there was a widespread resurgence of interest in the study of mental imagery. But, perhaps more significantly, revisions of the psychoanalytic school had taken place during the previous decades, in particular, object relations and self-structure approaches, that were less concerned with drive theory. These developments paved the way for exploring more active use of mental images. A good example of these new approaches is Silverman's (1987) 'imploding psychodynamic themes' technique where the patient is actively encouraged by the analyst to conjure up affect-laden imagery. Silverman makes the case that this active technique is more likely to facilitate the patient's process of working through inner conflict than the traditional approach of interpreting spontaneous fantasies.

Yet, despite openness to a more active role of the analyst, it is fair to say that in general, mental images do not appear to represent a significant focus of interest in current psychoanalytic theorising and contemporary psychoanalytically informed relational practice.

Jung and analytical psychology

Jung (1875–1961) remains one of the most influential figures in terms of therapeutic practice with mental images and symbols. Similarly to Freud, he believed that mental imagery operates as a means of communication from the unconscious to the conscious mind. However, he departed radically from Freud in the way that he viewed the structure and nature of the unconscious and this resulted in a different approach to the use of mental images in therapeutic practice. Although Jung's theory of the unconscious will be familiar to many readers, it is worth highlighting the main points relevant to mental imagery. His radical views were formulated out of his own investigations into himself. From 1912 to 1917, Jung (1961) opened himself up to direct experiences of exploring the arising contents of his unconscious mind. He discovered through this process that the unconscious is not solely repressive as Freud believed it to be; noting instead that it appeared to be performing a range of tasks such as compensating for undeveloped parts of his conscious personality and anticipating the future. These investigations informed his view of the unconscious as creative and purposive, with both a transcendent and balancing function; summed up by Price-Williams (1992) as, '. . . . the process whereby imaginative productions are used as revelations of unknown parts of the self, which need to be confronted or worked through in the normal waking life' (1992: 248).

Not only was Jung's understanding of the nature of the unconscious different from Freud's, he also developed a new structural model that comprises two strata, i.e. an individual personal unconscious that emerges out of a deeper collective unconscious structured by archetypal patterns. Jung believed the collective unconscious constitutes a common psychic substrate of a suprapersonal nature that is present in everyone. He defined the archetype as essentially an '. . . unconscious content that is altered by becoming conscious and by being perceived, and it takes its colour from the individual consciousness in which it happens to appear' (Jung, 1991: 5). Furthermore, he asserted that these innate *a priori* psychic structures have the capacity to direct psychological life. It is not surprising, therefore, given this fundamentally different perspective of the unconscious, that Jung's analytical psychology would take a very different approach to therapeutic work with mental images.

Similarly to Freud, Jung had discovered that the unconscious appeared to operate independently to the person we consider ourselves to be and psychological integration required becoming conscious of these hidden dimensions of the self. He also believed that the unknown parts of the self communicated with the conscious personality through nonverbal means, in particular, imagery, symbols, dreams and creative impulses. However, in practice, Jung's different model of the unconscious meant that he was interested in the manifest content of dreams and imagery produced by the patient. Although he, like Freud, sought meaning in imagery he believed the correct interpretation lay in the direction of amplification, i.e. creating the right conditions for the image to unfold its meaning for the patient. Although he believed that the patient is the best person to understand the meaning of the image, he thought that it was important for the therapist to hold onto an interpretative framework grounded in universal symbols. It would not be necessary to share this interpretation with the patient but it would helpfully inform the therapist's thinking.

In practice Jung asked the patient to make meaning of their fantasies and dreams by gently asking them nonleading questions. Over time he became unsatisfied by relying on dreams, believing that they did not provide a direct enough dialogue between the conscious and unconscious. This dissatisfaction prompted the development of his influential method of active imagination which he described as follows:

> In cases of this sort, the patient is simply given the task of contemplating any one fragment of fantasy that seems significant to him – a chance idea, perhaps, or something he has become conscious of in a dream – until its context becomes visible, that is to say, the relevant associative material in which it is embedded.
>
> (Jung, 1991: 49)

It is interesting to note that, although active imagination is commonly cited as one of the most important original therapeutic methods using mental imagery, Jung never intended it to be employed in this way. Although he originally developed it in a therapeutic setting, he came to view it as an introspective method that patients could use on their own for the purposes of individuation work. Furthermore, Hollis warns us that we have also lost sight of its original aim:

> This technique so common to Jungian parlance is still often misunderstood. Jung did not mean free association, meditation or guided imagery. Active imagination needs to be understood literally as the *activation of the image*, a technique which invites *Auseinandersetzung* or a dialogue with the unconscious. Active imagination affords the unconscious its own freedom, its own integrity. It seeks an expanded consciousness that arises out of an encounter with the intrapsychic other. (italics in original)
>
> (2000: 67)

Theorists and clinical innovators have continued to build on Jung's insights into the way that mental images can be used to facilitate therapeutic and individuation processes. Hillman (1926–2011) is particularly relevant due to his radical views concerning the nature of the unconscious (which he termed 'the imaginal'). In Hillman's (1975) archetypal psychology, similar to Jung's method of active imagination, the perspective of the imaginal is privileged over the rational perspective in therapeutic work. However, he goes much further than Jung in this regard because he considers that any attempt to impose a curative agenda on the imaginal perspective, in other words to subject mental images to interpretation or procedures, is fundamentally misguided. The imaginal perspective needs to be accepted on its own terms and these terms do not include any goals for personality integration. In this regard, Hillman aligns himself with the premodern Asclepian healing tradition, particularly in the way that he rejects the idea that mental images are purely mental properties. And in terms of the range of therapeutic practices with mental imagery in counselling and psychotherapy, his archetypal psychology represents the extreme end of a continuum, the other end being CBT procedures that use directive imagery for reparative purposes.

In the following sections I will consider how Jung's insights and methods went on to influence both the humanistic school and the individual clinical innovators in their approaches to working with mental imagery.

New therapeutic mental imagery methods in the 1960s and '70s: the humanistic school

Humanistic therapies draw upon a wide repertoire of imagery procedures and techniques, many of which were originally developed during the 1960s and '70s. In general, this approach to imagery highlights the creative potential of the client's images and the use of imagery as a means of bypassing the censorship of the conscious personality. Of course, this is a very broad church and includes a wide range of approaches that have all contributed particular methods to the repertoire. One example of this range would be the influential humanistic-transpersonal model of psychosynthesis founded by Assagioli (1888–1974). He (Assagioli, 1965) noted that imagery is particularly beneficial because of its capacity to tap into many aspects of the total personality and integrate different levels of sensation, emotion, cognition and intuition. A particularly influential member of this school with regard to mental imagery is Ferrucci (2009) whose seminal text, *What We May Be*, helped to propagate the use of visualisation in the wider humanistic field. Even humanistic schools such as the person-centred approach with its inherent distrust of techniques have generated contributions to this repertoire; one example being Gendlin's (1981) 'focusing' method where the therapist helps the client use mental images to first concretise and then gain more insight into vague undifferentiated bodily sensations.

Despite the range of theory and practice across the humanistic schools, it is possible to make some general observations as to its use of mental imagery. Similarly to the Jungian school, the focus in humanistic approaches is on the manifest content of the mental image not its theorised latent content. Alongside this is also a belief that it is the client, and not the therapist, who is best placed to interpret the imagery.

However, there are some subtle differences. In general, humanistic therapies (with the exception of psychosynthesis) are less concerned with structural models of self and the unconscious and are more interested in finding ways to unfold human potential. Imagery is viewed as one of a range of creative modes for achieving that goal. Thus, there is more focus on developing methods and a more interactive approach to the use of mental images. Although Jung's understanding of the therapeutic application of mental imagery developed in a very different way to Freud, they shared one thing in common: their interest lay solely in clients' mental images as meaningful communications from the unconscious. In other words, their interest was restricted to receptive imagery. Although humanistic therapies draw heavily on Jung's work, a more active approach is taken to the therapeutic use of imagery and this has resulted in a large body of techniques and procedures. Helping clients make sense of their mental images represents just one aspect of this work. Methods have been developed for helping clients actively interact with their imagery productions. Instead of waiting for communications to arise spontaneously in the form of dreams and fantasy, guided imagery techniques have been developed that are designed for a more directive investigation of the unconscious mind.

Of all the humanistic approaches, it is probably gestalt therapy that has contributed the most to this more dynamic and interactive use. Its founder, Perls (1893–1970), was particularly opposed to, what he considered to be, the over-intellectualisation evident in psychoanalysis, and consequently one of the main aims of his therapeutic approach is to bypass the client's conscious thinking processes. In gestalt therapy, clients are encouraged to express the image creatively using all the senses in order to allow its meaning to be grasped. Although Perls made creative use of client images that arose spontaneously during the session, he had a particular interest in working with dream imagery. He developed an identification technique whereby clients are instructed to experience themselves as elements of their dream. He believed that re-experiencing the dream in this way is a much more effective therapeutic process than relying on intellectual interpretations; explaining his method as follows in his characteristically direct way:

> You see how you can use *everything* in a dream. If you are pursued by an ogre in a dream, and you *become* the ogre, the nightmare disappears. You re-own the energy that is invested in the demon. Then the power of the ogre is no longer outside, alienated, but inside where you can use it. (italics in original)
> (Perls, 1992: 189)

Probably his most well-known mental imagery technique is his two-chair procedure. This is a dynamic technique whereby clients are facilitated in dialoguing with imaginal representations in an empty chair; these could include aspects of themselves, dream elements and representations of real people. The therapist encourages the client to conduct a dialogue both from the client's own position and also from the position of the represented figure or element. Perls believed, as the previous quote makes clear, that the process of thoroughly identifying with these projected elements or aspects would lead to insight and integration. Although, it is fair to say that Perls's reputation has suffered in recent years – his clinical approach has been criticised as overly directive – there can be no disputing his positive legacy with regard to a body of innovative and creative mental imagery methods. His empty chair technique is just one example of his original methods that remain standard in the humanistic repertoire (interested readers can read verbatim extracts from his work [Perls, 1992] using this technique in a series of seminars delivered in the Esalen Institute from 1966–1968).

By the end of the 1980s, the enthusiasm with which the humanistic schools had embraced mental imagery was starting to fade. The relational turn in counselling and psychotherapy was gathering momentum and interest was moving away from the subjective world of the client to the intersubjectively constructed nature of therapy. However, this is not the end of the story of the development of mental imagery within the main therapeutic schools in therapy, by any means. Another school with a radically different approach was beginning to investigate mental images as a means of working with a range of challenging clinical presentations. And I shall pick up this narrative later on at the end of the chapter when I consider contemporary developments in theory and practice.

The relational turn and the decline of interest in mental imagery

In the last couple of decades of the 20th century there were two interrelated factors that contributed to a general wane of interest in the therapeutic use of mental imagery: both of these factors were connected to the relational turn in counselling and psychotherapy.

The first factor relates to the impact of changing intellectual fashions in Western culture. Nearly all of the main therapeutic approaches that were developed before the last couple of decades of the 20th century share a modern psychological conception of the self as autonomous and bounded. Within this general model of the self, change is posited as an intra-psychic process, and mental imagery would be viewed as being generated from and within the subjective interior of the individual mind. However, a postmodern perspective on the nature of the self is very different: it is not understood to be a fixed psychological construct. Instead, the self is a fluid and socially constructed identity, or a 'multiplicity of self-accounts' (Gergen and Kaye, 1992) – selves are only realised as products of relatedness. In other words, our self-identity is fictive with no ontological basis.

By the beginning of the 21st century the impact of this new understanding of the nature of the self on the field of counselling and psychotherapy was evident in the increasing emphasis on the co-constructed nature of therapy. New therapeutic approaches were emerging, such as narrative therapy (White and Epston, 1990; McLeod, 1997), that do not depend on psychological models of the self: difficulties that the clients bring would be theorised as arising within the intersubjective field of action rather than the individual subjective interior. This postmodern perspective on the nature of the self has significant implications for a therapeutic practice with mental imagery as the source of the client's presenting issues are no longer situated subjectively. Furthermore, a postmodern-informed perspective asserts the primacy of language in therapeutic practice as language is the means by which social narratives about reality are constructed.

The second factor relates to developments within the field whereby research in counselling and psychotherapy had established the fundamental importance of the therapeutic relationship. Research findings from the 1970s that indicated there was no real difference between particular therapeutic approaches generated interest in identifying the common factors implicated in successful therapy. In their influential reviews of the research literature, Asay and Lambert (2000) estimated that the therapeutic relationship has twice the impact that the use of therapeutic techniques have on therapeutic progress. These findings cemented the shift of focus in psychotherapeutic theory and practice away from subjectivity and onto intersubjectivity.

It is not surprising then that the relational turn in counselling and psychotherapy with its emphasis on the linguistically constituted nature of human experience combined with research evidence for the importance of the relationship has resulted in a general lessening of interest in mental imagery as a therapeutic technique. It is also not surprising that the one place where mental imagery is being developed is in the therapeutic approach least influenced by postmodern perspectives on the self, i.e. CBT and its contemporary variants. However, before I discuss these recent developments, it is important to consider other influential clinical approaches to imagery produced by the clinical innovators working outside the mainstream.

The contributions of individual clinical innovators

Another important contribution to the field comprises the work of individual clinician-theorists who have produced their own particular versions of image-based psychotherapies. Although, it is important to emphasise that these imagery approaches have not developed in isolation. They draw extensively on the theory and practices originating from within the main schools and they also, in their turn, developed imagery methods that were imported particularly into humanistic approaches. In general it would appear that the independent rediscovery of the therapeutic efficacy of imagery and the development of standard imagery scripts or procedures based on the therapist's knowledge and experience is a common theme in the history of therapeutic imagery. Although there are some very significant differences in these individual, and often, idiosyncratic approaches, they all have one thing in common, i.e. mental imagery is regarded as the primary means for therapeutic work. In this section I will consider the approaches developed by some of the more notable and influential clinician-theorists. Throughout this discussion it is important to bear in mind the point made by Watkins (1984) in her classic scholarly account of the European imagery tradition that, although these clinical innovators invite imagination into the consultancy room, their attitudes and beliefs determine how mental imagery is used and it is usually put to the service of their particular interests. This section will begin with a brief overview of early 20th-century pioneers before focusing on some of the particularly influential later clinician-theorists.

As previously mentioned, Freud's early interest in inducing mental images in his patients had been stimulated by the work of influential pioneers, in particular, Janet. Although Freud soon substituted verbal free association as a means of accessing the patient's unconscious, there were other psychotherapeutic innovators who continued to experiment with imagery. One example was Happich (1932) who continued the use of mental images in free association, believing that this direct experience of imagery rather than verbal conceptualisation is necessary for personality change. Happich stimulated the arising of a stream of images in the client by suggesting various imaginal landscapes – e.g. mountains, etc. Another of these early pioneers was Clark (cited in Watkins, 1984) who used induced reverie in his patients to explore the contents of the unconscious. In Clark's method, patients are asked to imagine their childhood. Clark would then help his patients work out what was memory and what was fact, and in so doing be able to identify where the fixations and problems lay.

The imaginal content of this introspective route was not the only focus of inquiry – Frank (1910) had discovered the importance of deep relaxation for the production of hypnagogic imagery. He believed that whilst patients are in this state they are able to discharge repressed emotional energy. Later on, Schultz and Luthe (1969) explored the potential for training in deep bodily relaxation states to help patients develop skills in eliciting and working with images – a method that they later termed 'autogenic training'. They were interested in facilitating a cathartic discharge in their patients that released tension and dissolved emotional complexes without any need to analyse the contents.

Over the following decades, there was a general trend, particularly within continental Europe, towards developing more systemised approaches that are based on formulations of the individual innovators' clinical work and informed by their espoused theoretical approach. The following section focuses on two influential image-based therapies developed during this period: Desoille's (1966) directed daydream; and Leuner's (1984) guided affective imagery (GAI).

Desoille (1890–1966), a French psychotherapist who originally trained as an engineer, developed an approach in the 1930s that he termed the 'directed daydream'. This method represents probably the first version of the type of guided imagery journeys that have become an established part of the humanistic repertoire of creative therapeutic procedures. His approach is informed by the Jungian theory of the collective unconscious. He was also influenced by his teacher, Caslant (1865–1940), who had been particularly interested in directional movement within inner space. Caslant (1921) noted that ascension and descension, in particular, were associated with different experiences for his patients – ascending tended to lead to more expanded and positive emotional states whereas the reverse was associated with descent. Desoille used these ideas as a way of mapping inner landscapes. He believed that if clients are helped to ascend then they would be contacting more spiritual or expanded parts of the self where they could engage with their current difficulties from a higher perspective. If they descended then they would be going into their own personal unconscious where they would directly encounter repressed material.

The aim of Desoille's method is for clients to encounter the collective unconscious and understand the larger context of their personal problems. However, he believed that in order for difficulties to be resolved, the person has to actively engage with the archetypes as a means of generating new inner dynamics. In order to do this, Desoille's method has the patient enter one out of six possible imaginary landscapes; each one deemed to represent a particular psychological theme, for example, a descent into the depths of the ocean is used for the patient to confront suppressed parts of themselves. The patient is then directed through a process of exploring and interacting with imagery that, according to Desoille, arises out of both the personal and collective unconscious. An important aim of this procedure is to help the patient discharge stored-up negative emotions such as anxiety and fear. Desoille devised a particular set of interventions for these therapeutic purposes that he had synthesised from myths and fairytales.

From the perspective of later developments of using guided imagery in therapeutic practice, Desoille's system appears highly directive, forcing the patient's experience into a rigid mould. Although his method helps people to gain experience of working with their imagery, ' . . . it is compromised by a detailed schedule of places to get to and things to be accomplished that the therapist thought were important' (Watkins, 1984: 80). Yet, despite these limitations, it is important to appreciate that Desoille's directed daydream method paved the way for further systemisation of the therapeutic use of imagery and the importation of imagery methods into counselling and psychotherapy.

Another notable innovator in this field is Leuner (1918–1996). His GAI system employs a similar basic method to Desoille's of conducting the patient on imagery journeys – his system comprises a set of ten particular journeys each one representing a specific psychological theme. One example involves the exploration of a house deemed to represent the patient's personality (this is particularly pertinent to the clinical work presented in the second part of this book where readers will have an opportunity to compare and contrast two different clinical approaches to the same theme).

These journeys are used in two ways. First, the landscapes of each journey are designed to be general and allow the patient to project his/her fantasies into them – Leuner believes this gives plenty of scope for diagnosis. His method draws upon a combination of self-evident and psychoanalytical interpretation; an example of this would be guiding a patient to explore the course of a river deemed to represent the course of their life. A self-evident interpretation would be that the origin of the river represents the beginnings of the person's life. However, Leuner then goes on to view this through a psychoanalytically informed interpretative frame by explicitly linking problems at the river's source to oral stage difficulties with mother. The second way the journeys are used is similar to Desoille's. Leuner believes that the patient can be assisted through deep psychotherapeutic processes by engaging with repressed material symbolised in the imagined landscape; rather than working these through in the form of becoming conscious of their enactments within the context of the therapy dyad.

Leuner's approach is less directive than Desoille, as can be seen in the following piece of guidance for therapists, 'Our basic rule reads instead: *Every patient develops mental imagery according to his individual style, and it is the therapist's duty to accept this individual style and to adjust to it*' (italics in original) (1984: 133). The patient is encouraged to allow the imagery to unfold spontaneously and the resulting images and experiences are discussed with the therapist with a view to integration. However, he does have a set of techniques he employs where necessary, such as confronting threatening figures or animals in order to strengthen the ego. These techniques structure the patient's experience along certain lines leading Watkins to detect a 'hero' myth operating in Leuner's approach – everything that remains in the unconscious can become threatening, therefore its contents need to be brought up into the world of the ego.

Despite some of the criticisms that can be leveled at the methods developed by Desoille and Leuner, their systemised image-based therapies have played a very important role in establishing the use of mental imagery as a primary means of working with therapeutic processes. Contributions have also been made to this European waking dream tradition by other clinical innovators, including the influential work of the Italian psychotherapists Frétigny and Virel (1968). In their method, termed 'oneirotherapy' (derived from *oneiro*, the Ancient Greek word for dream), their patients are encouraged to create spontaneous imagery and to fully participate in the unfolding inner drama until a catharsis or resolution is achieved.

Outside Europe, image-based therapies often drew on a range of approaches. One important example would be Shorr's (1983) 'psycho-imagination' method that integrates Rorschach projective tests with imaginary situations. Psycho-imagination therapy comprises a repertoire of procedures that can be used in psychotherapy such as asking the client to imagine two different objects in order to represent and work with an inner conflict. Another example of an unusual hybrid is Ahsen's (1968) eidetic psychotherapy that draws on humanistic and cognitive behavioural approaches: it is a highly systemised approach to working with mental imagery where diagnostic and therapeutic procedures are intertwined. His clinical methods are rarely referred to within the counselling and psychotherapy literature; therefore I am not describing this work in any detail here. However, his important theoretical contributions have been taken up in the wider field of the therapeutic application of mental images and these will be discussed in detail in Chapter 5.

Finally, it is worth mentioning an interesting and unusual example of an image-based therapy developed elsewhere than Europe and North America, i.e. Tajima and Naruse's (1987) 'Tsubo' mental imagery method. In general, working with mental imagery is contra-indicated for clients with serious mental health issues because of the danger of the client becoming overwhelmed by unmanageable unconscious material (see the discussion of contra-indications in Chapter 12). However, in this particular case, Tajima and Naruse have developed a method of using imagery that is designed to create a safe boundary between clients and their material. This imagery method gives the client a means of exploring difficult feelings and material in a controlled way. In this procedure, the client is helped to visualise a tsubo (a tsubo is a large earthenware container) in which they can place difficult feelings or objects. They are then helped to enter the tsubo and passively feel the feelings within and then leave and seal up the tsubo. This process is repeated over time until the client has been able to integrate their repressed material into their conscious awareness. It has been used effectively with clients experiencing delusional ideation.

In conclusion, there has been a steady stream of clinical innovators working outside the mainstream schools who, despite their differences, all share a common commitment to mental imagery being the primary means of working with or facilitating the client's therapeutic process. A general criticism that could be made of their work is that these individual clinicians incline towards presenting a formulation of their own practice as a complete and fully formed therapeutic approach. In other words they tend not to acknowledge the partial nature of their clinical formulations. Furthermore, it is unusual in their work to come across significant explicit consideration of other factors, apart from imagery, that are implicated in therapeutic processes. However, having said that, their foregrounding of mental imagery allowed them to generate new insights into its therapeutic application and produce a range of techniques and methods that have been adopted and further developed in the wider counselling and psychotherapy field. Although their ideas are sometimes idiosyncratic and their methods often harnessed to unreflected attitudes to the imaginal, no one can dispute the creativity and vigour of their therapeutic enterprise and the contributions they have made to sustaining and developing interest in and practice with mental images in psychotherapy.

Recent developments: contemporary cognitive behavioural approaches

Meanwhile, as interest in the psychotherapeutic use of mental imagery increasingly waned towards the end of the 20th century, there was one approach where the opposite trajectory happened: currently, it is the CBT school, particularly the more recent variants, that is proving to be at the forefront of developments in the field. Although structured imagery interventions have been part of the CBT repertoire of therapeutic procedures right from its inception, it is only recently that mental imagery has become the focus of sustained investigation. This interest has been driven by advances in theory and knowledge; specifically, the increased understanding of how images create and maintain psychopathology. In this section I will identify the main characteristics of this school's use of imagery in practice, before then going on to give a brief overview of its development (readers who are interested in a more in-depth history are referred to Edwards [1989, 2007, 2011] scholarly accounts). It ends with a discussion of some of the current innovations in practice concluding with a clinical illustration of imagery rescripting, a method that is rapidly becoming established as a treatment for trauma.

As would be expected, CBT approaches have employed mental imagery differently to the psychodynamic school and the humanistic schools. Historically (although this is changing in contemporary applications), the focus has been on the directive use of mental imagery. Informed, by the materialist, scientific worldview, there has been little interest per se in the imaginal perspective as a valid way of knowing. Mental images have not been valued as they are in psychodynamic and humanistic approaches as a means of understanding and unfolding aspects of the self hitherto hidden from awareness. Instead, mental images have been used primarily as instruments to modify and restructure dysfunctional schemas. Other important distinctive features are this school's focus on autobiographical imagery rather than symbolic images. This focus is apparent in the way that CBT methods make extensive use of memories and behavioural rehearsal in imagination.

And yet, in the early days of CBT, some of these defining characteristics were not so pronounced. Right at the beginning, Beck (1970) was advocating a very different kind of practice with mental imagery to the directive type that would become standard later on. He believed that it was therapeutically beneficial to explore clients' dream images and gain more understanding of the meanings they attributed to them (Beck's original psychoanalytical training is evident here). However, this early interest in the therapeutic potential of receptive imagery soon faded away, not to resurface until the beginning of the 21st century, as the focus turned to developing procedures that involved the manipulation of mental images to impact on behaviour and emotions – procedures more coherent with the classic CBT treatment model.

Quite early on, the clinical utility of mental images for treating anxiety and panic attacks was noted and a range of techniques were developed. Some of these are diagnostic in nature and focus on identifying components in the self-schema that contribute to maladaptive thinking, e.g. recalling the events that precipitated a panic attack. However, most of the procedures that employed imagery developed during this time were focused on changing dysfunctional behaviour. One example would be the classic desensitisation technique for treating phobias. The premise of this behaviourist treatment is that through a managed exposure to the phobic target the person will be able to learn how to manage anxiety. In this procedure, clients are asked to visualise progressively more anxiety – producing encounters with the phobic object and at the same time they are taught to practise relaxation techniques in a managed way.

Other imagery techniques were also developed that exploit the human tendency to rehearse events and behaviours in imagination; these procedures are informed by classical conditioning theory that changes in the internally rehearsed event will promote changes in actual behaviour. Two types of covert modelling have been developed as standard therapeutic interventions. The first type is the coping model deemed suitable for anxiety as it involves imagining stages of developing skills. The mastery model, on the other hand, requires the client to visualise competence right from the start. These methods have been increasingly taken up in other non-therapeutic contexts such as sports training and are popular techniques in self-help literature.

Over time, cognitive behavioural therapists expanded beyond using mental imagery solely as a component of behaviourist interventions and started to recognise the usefulness of working with imagery more generally within a cognitive framework. These strategies, as might be expected, are mainly directive and emphasise cognitive restructuring. The final decades of the 20th century saw the development of a wide range of applications, two examples from the literature being: reducing traumatic grief reactions by visualising less aversive images (Fidaleo et al., 1999); and changing negative behaviour through visualising the inner critic (White, 1988).

However, by the end of the 20th century, a significant shift had begun: mental imagery itself had become, not just the method, but also an increasing focus of clinical work. This change was brought about by radical revisions within this school concerning the role of emotion and the limitations of language. Rachman's (1980) seminal paper challenged the idea that emotion is just a product of cognition, arguing instead that it is a type of information processing. As clinical experience strongly suggests that imagery has a special relationship with emotion, this has led to interest in the way that mental imagery is implicated in the development and maintenance of psychopathologies. An increasing body of empirical support for the direct link between mental images and emotions has resulted in imagery interventions designed to process and transform negative affect (Holmes and Mathews, 2010).

Another factor implicated in the new interest in clients' mental imagery is the growing recognition of the limitations of linguistic-based retrieval for both early memories and also later traumatic ones. Research evidence (Holmes and Mathews, 2010) increasingly supports the generally accepted clinical understanding that mental imagery is a means of accessing nonconscious processes, particularly clients' early implicit or procedural memory. These research findings provide the evidence-based rationale for developing imagery procedures designed to expose the primary patterns or schemata laid down during the preverbal formative cognitive stage. In other words image-based methods are starting to be seen as having more potential to help clients identify underlying assumptions than the more traditional linguistic-based ones. Moreover, it is not only early life experience that is laid down in schemata, it is now generally accepted, based on clinical experience, that later traumatic events can be imprinted in the adult mind in a similar way. This combination of research findings and clinical observation opened the door to new image-based methods for treating trauma (see Chapter 4 for further relevant discussion of how CBT theorises the therapeutic efficacy of mental imagery).

This new appreciation of the importance of clients' mental images has led to reprising earlier methods from other approaches particularly the humanistic school; one rather surprising example is the recent interest in Jung's method of active imagination. Cognitive therapy theorists have noted the way that mental images can unfold and deliver new material. Considered from the perspective of cognitive therapy, working with the client's spontaneous imagery, ' . . . can trigger an autonomous cognitive shift through which clients may become aware of their cognitive distortions, or of possible solutions' (Hackmann *et al.*, 2011: 15). Central to some of the current thinking is the notion that imagery operates as an emotional bridge that can disclose the source of the person's difficulties. In one study of images in agoraphobia (Day *et al.*, 2004), all the participants reported current intrusive imagery and the majority made a link between the images and earlier traumatic experience. The research study noted that making this link had been therapeutically beneficial to some of the participants (self-reported avoidant scores had reduced significantly over one week later).

As a consequence of research and theoretical developments, a range of new imagery methods and techniques are now being incorporated into contemporary CBT practice. The established techniques can generally be grouped into ones that increase positive imagery and ones that reduce the impact of negative imagery. An example of the former would be 'compassionate mind training' (CMT) (Gilbert, 2010), which aims at creating new imagery to support the self. One of its methods is to use mental images to access the neurophysiological systems that underpin the affect of self-soothing. An example of the latter would be imagery rescripting, which is rapidly becoming an established method for treating post-traumatic stress disorder (PTSD). The premise of rescripting is that deliberate changes made to the negative mental images associated with the condition will result in equivalent changes to the emotional response. Furthermore, as much of the consequent post-trauma disturbance is associated with memory, modifying the traumatic memory is a powerful means of treatment. Rescripting draws on previously developed methods of imaginal exposure and covert modelling discussed earlier. First, the client is directed to recreate the memories of the original trauma. Then they are guided through a process of replacing these memories with either mastery or coping imagery (it is striking how similar this sounds to Janet's original therapeutic experiments in the late 19th century of substituting a different image for the patient's problematic intrusive imagery). A standard technique for achieving this replacement is through visualising a 'survivor' self coming to the aid of the 'victim' self. The following case vignette is an illustration of imagery rescripting in action taken from the work of Smucker, who along with Dancu (Smucker and Dancu, 1999) helped to establish this method within the clinical repertoire. The following text is my highly abridged version of the original (Smucker et al., 2002: 90–96).

> Bob, a restaurant manager in his mid-twenties, experienced a robbery at his work premises. He and his co-workers were closing the establishment when three armed robbers arrived demanding money. Bob was forced at gunpoint to open the safe and cash registers. Afterwards he reported PTSD symptoms including: sleeplessness; obsessively checking his house security; poor concentration; and repetitive intrusions of traumatic memories. He was assessed for psychological treatment and he was assigned to imaginal exposure therapy. After eight sessions Bob was still not desensitised to the memory of the actual robbery and it was decided to employ imagery rescripting. In this session he was encouraged to visualise the actual robbery and to imagine his 'survivor' self entering the scene. Bob reported that he could visualise his survivor self attempting to attract the attention of the armed robber and alert him to the terrible mistake he was making. Bob reported that this started to give him a feeling of empowerment as he realised that he had managed to stay calm throughout the ordeal and had been able to pacify the robber when the safe opened to reveal little cash. By the end of the imagery rescripting Bob started to recognise that even though the robber was holding a gun to his head, it would be himself rather than the robber who would win in the end. At the end of the rescripting session his Subjective Units of Distress (SUDs) rating, originally at 10 has reduced dramatically to 0. In regular follow up meetings over one year he reported that intrusive memories of the trauma and other PTSD symptoms were no longer present.

Before concluding this section on the CBT approaches to mental imagery, it is worth emphasising how wide-ranging the current interest is. Although, the more established CBT image-based methods display the school's characteristic directive and instrumental approach, contemporary literature provides evidence for increasing creative exploration and experimentation. One example is the attention being paid to client metaphors and symbolic imagery. This is particularly significant as historically this school has mainly confined its interest in mental images to autobiographical imagery. New techniques have been developed that are designed to elicit clients' metaphorical imagery in relation to their presenting difficulty. The ensuing metaphoric images can then be explored or actively manipulated. Clinicians in this school have noted, ' . . . the way in which a metaphorical image can crystallize the meaning of a difficult emotional experience . . . ' (Hackmann et al., 2011: 204) and how a change to the image is linked to new perspectives on the experience. Indeed, some of the published case studies show remarkable similarities to humanistic approaches such as Gendlin's (1981) 'focusing' method.

It seems appropriate to end this section with Hackman *et al.*'s summary statement that captures the excitement generated by this surge of interest in mental imagery within CBT:

> 50 years ago, in the heyday of behaviourism, imagery was not considered worthy or appropriate for experimental investigation, though interestingly it was incorporated into behavioural treatments such as systematic desensitization. Now the empirical study of imagery links clinical research, cognitive psychology, neuroscience and clinical treatments, creating a body of knowledge that strongly suggests the rich potential of imagery-based interventions in therapeutic practice.
>
> (2011: 204)

For readers who want to know more about developments within this school I would recommend the comprehensive overviews presented in the text cited above by Hackman *et al.* and Stopa's (2009) edited work that draws together current practice, research and theory on images of the self in cognitive therapy.

Reflections on current theory and practice

Different schools and approaches over the course of the 20th century and into the 21st century have made and continue to make their own contributions to our understanding of the therapeutic application of mental imagery. At particular points in the history of talking therapies, different therapeutic approaches have been at the forefront in terms of generating theory and innovations. And operating in parallel to the mainstream have been influential clinician-theorists who have also contributed to the theory and practice. Each school and each pioneering clinician has developed characteristic ways of using mental images to promote therapeutic processes. All of these contributions inform the rich repository of therapeutic imagery techniques and methods that are currently at our disposal.

However, it is also important to consider the significant limitations of this patchwork development. The way that mental imagery has developed as a therapeutic application has been informed by the different theoretical models espoused by the schools and clinicians. These theoretical positions have shaped clinical practice, e.g. the emphasis on imagery communications from the imaginal perspective evident in psychodynamic approaches and the emphasis on communications from the rational perspective in CBT approaches. The limitations of the clinical innovators operating outside the main schools are also demonstrated in their tendencies to present the formulations of their own clinical practice as complete approaches rather than explicitly acknowledging their partial and provisional nature. What is striking, in terms of a wide historical overview, is the way that our theorising about mental imagery has not moved beyond this patchwork stage and continues to be driven by advances within particular therapeutic schools rather than being informed by theoretical convergence.

And yet, despite all the radical divergences in theorising and application, there has been one consistent agreement across all schools and individual clinicians right from the beginning of psychotherapy: clinical practice with mental imagery is therapeutically efficacious. In the following chapter I consider how the different approaches account for its efficacy and, in particular, if there are any explanations or theoretical models that could provide some common ground for more inclusive theory.

References

Ahsen A. (1968). *Basic Concepts in Eidetic Psychotherapy*, New York: Brandon House.
Asay, T. and Lambert, M. (2000). 'The Empirical Case for the Common Factors in the Therapy: Quantitative findings', in M. Hubble, B. Duncan and S. Miller (eds), *The Heart and Soul of Change: What works in therapy*, 33–56, Washington, DC: American Psychological Association.
Assagioli, R. (1965). *Psychosynthesis*, New York: Hobbs, Dorman & Co.
Beck, A. (1970). 'The Role of Fantasies in Psychotherapy and Psychopathology', *Journal of Nervous and Mental Disease*, 150, 1: 3–17.
Breuer, J. and Freud, S. (1955). 'Studies on Hysteria' in J. Strachey (ed) *The Standard Edition*, vols 4 & 5, London: Hogarth.
Caslant, E. (1921). *Méthode de Dévelopment des Facultés Supranormales*, Paris: Edition Rhea.
Day, S. J., Holmes, E. A. and Hackmann, A. (2004). 'Occurence of Imagery and Its Link with Early Memories in Agoraphobia', *Memory*, 12: 416–427.
Desoille, R. (1966). *The Directed Daydream*, New York: Psychosynthesis Research Foundation.
Edwards, D.J.A. (1989). 'Cognitive Restructuring through Guided Imagery: Lessons from Gestalt therapy', in A. Freeman, K. M. Simon, L. E. Beutler and H. Arkowitz (eds), *Comprehensive Handbook of Cognitive Therapy*, 283–297, New York: Plenum.
———. (2007). 'Restructuring Implicational Meaning through Memory-Based Imagery: Some historical notes', *Journal of Behavior Therapy and Experimental Psychiatry*, 38: 306–316.
———. (2011). 'From Ancient Shamanic Healing to Twenty-First Century Psychotherapy: The central role of imagery methods in effecting psychological change', in A. Hackmann, J. Bennett-Levy and E. A. Holmes, *Oxford Guide to Imagery in Cognitive Therapy*, xxxiii-xliii, Oxford: Oxford University Press.
Ferrucci, P. (2009). *What We May Be: Techniques for psychological and spiritual growth through psychosynthesis*, foreword by Laura Huxley, New York: J.P. Tarcher/Penguin.
Fidaleo, R., Proano, T. and Friedberg R. (1999). 'Using Imagery Techniques to Treat PTSD Symptoms in Bereaved Individuals', *Journal of Contemporary Psychotherapy*, 29, 2: 115–126.
Frank, L. (1910). *Die Psychoanalyse*, Munich: Reinhart.
Frétigny, R. and Virel, A. (1968). *L'Imagerie Mentale*, Geneva: Mont Blanc.
Freud, S. (1900). 'The interpretation of dreams', in J. Strachey (ed) (1962) *The Standard Edition*, vols 4 & 5, London: Hogarth.
Gendlin, E. T. (1981). *Focusing*, 2nd edn, New York: Bantam.
Gergen, K. and Kaye, J. (1992). 'Beyond Narrative in the Negotiation of Therapeutic Meaning', in K. Gergen and S. McNamee (eds), *Therapy as Social Construction*, 166–185, London: Sage.

Gilbert, P. (2010). *Compassion-Focused Therapy: Distinctive features*, Hove: Routledge.
Hackmann, A., Bennett-Levy, J. and Holmes, E. A. (2011). *Oxford Guide to Imagery in Cognitive Therapy*, Oxford: Oxford University Press.
Happich, C. (1932). 'Das Bildbewusstsein als Ansatzstelle Psychischer Behandlung', *Zentreblatt Psychotherapie*, 5: 663–667.
Hillman, J. (1975). *Re-visioning Psychology*, New York: Harper & Row.
Hollis, J. (2000). *The Archetypal Imagination*, College Station, Texas: Texas A & M University Press.
Holmes, E. A. and Mathews, A. (2010). 'Mental Imagery in Emotion and Emotional Disorders', *Clinical Psychology Review*, 30: 349–362.
Jones, E. (1951). *The Life and Work of Sigmund Freud*, vol 1, New York: Basic Books.
Jung, C. G. (1961). *Memories, Dreams and Reflections*, Aniela Jaffe (ed), New York: Random House.
——. (1991). 'The Archetypes and the Collective Unconscious', in *The Collected Works of C. G. Jung, v*ol 9, part 1, 2nd edn, trans. R.F.C. Hull, London: Routledge.
Leuner, H. (1984). *Guided Affective Imagery in Short-term Psychotherapy: The basic course*, New York: Thieme-Stratton Corp.
McLeod, J. (1997). *Narrative and Psychotherapy*, London: Sage.
Perls, F. S. (1992). *Gestalt Therapy Verbatim*, reprint (1969), Gouldsboro, ME: The Gestalt Journal Press Inc.
Price-Williams, D. (1992). 'The Waking Dream in Ethnographic Perspective', in B. Tedlock (ed), *Dreaming: Anthropological and psychological interpretations*, 246–262, Sante Fe, New Mexico: School of American Research Press.
Rachman, S. (1980). 'Emotional Processing', *Behaviour Research and Therapy*, 18: 51–60.
Ricoeur, P. (1970). *Freud and Philosophy: An essay on interpretation*, trans. Denis Savage, New Haven, CT: Yale University Press.
Schultz, J. H. and Luthe, W. (1969). *Autogenic Methods*, New York: Grune & Stratton.
Shorr, J. E. (1983). *Psychotherapy through Imagery*, 2nd edn, New York: Thieme-Stratton Inc.
Silverman, L. H. (1987). 'Imagery as an Aid in Working through Unconscious Conflicts', *Psychoanalytic Psychology*, 4: 45–64.
Singer, J. L. (2006). *Imagery in Psychotherapy*, Washington, DC: American Psychological Association.
Smucker, M. R. and Dancu, C. (1999). *Cognitive-behavioral Treatment for Adult Survivors of Childhood Trauma: Imagery rescripting and reprocessing*, Northvale, NJ: Jason Aronson.
——, Weis, J. and Grunert, B. (2002). 'Imagery Rescripting for Trauma Survivors with PTSD', in A. A. Sheikh (ed), *Therapeutic Imagery Techniques*, 85–94, Amityville, NY: Baywood Pub.
Stopa, L. (ed) (2009). *Imagery and the Threatened Self: Perspectives on mental imagery and the self in cognitive therapy*, London: Routledge.
Tajima, S. and Naruse, G. (1987). 'Tsubo Imagery Therapy', *Journal of Mental Imagery*, 11, 1: 105–118.
Watkins, M. (1984). *Waking Dreams*, 3rd revised edn, Dallas, Texas: Spring Publications Inc.
White, D. J. (1988). 'Taming the Critic: Use of imagery with those who procrastinate', *Journal of Mental Imagery*, 12, 1: 125–134.
White, M. and Epston, D. (1990). *Narrative Means to Therapeutic Ends*, New York: Norton.

Chapter 4
Explanations for the therapeutic efficacy of mental imagery

Counselling and psychotherapy schools provide a range of accounts of the therapeutic efficacy of mental imagery that are informed by different theoretical perspectives. However, despite the differences, all these explanations have one thing in common; an acknowledgement that mental images appear to operate consistently and reliably as a communicative bridge between the conscious and non-conscious parts of the mind (generally referred to throughout this book as the rational and imaginal perspectives). This chapter considers how efficacy has been understood, both within the counselling and psychotherapy field and beyond, and discusses how these explanations contribute to more inclusive theory making.

I begin by briefly reviewing the history of Western understanding post-Descartes of the nature of mental imagery that has resulted in two different accounts, i.e. empirical models and phenomenological descriptions; both types are then considered in more detail. I will then go on to consider theoretical approaches that can bridge the divide between the two. This discussion will focus in detail on Ahsen's (1984) image/somatic/meaning model (ISM) and the theory of conceptual metaphor developed by the cognitive linguists, Lakoff and Johnson (2003).

What is the nature of mental imagery?

From the Enlightenment onward, the Western understanding of the nature of mental imagery has been characterised by two different views of the imagination, i.e. the empirical and the phenomenological. This situation broadly reflects the two distinct Western philosophical traditions, i.e. the North American and British analytic schools and the continental European phenomenological tradition. This distinction is apparent in the field of counselling and psychotherapy. How each school understands the way that mental imagery operates is dependent on which view is taken of the imagination. This is a complex philosophical debate so what follows is a simplified historical account.

As previously mentioned (see Chapter 2), in the immediate aftermath of the publication of Descartes's philosophical treatise, imagination was subjected to a fierce critique. Hobbes's (1588–1679) argument that imagination was a poor relation of rational thought was buttressed by other philosophers such as Locke

(1632–1704) who defined imagination as a 'decaying sense'; in other words, the power to summon up an image depends on the fading sensate inscriptions of past experience. These ideas were further elaborated by Hume (1711–1776), who asserted that imagination simply reproduces the sensory experiences impressed upon the mind so that we can think about them when they are absent – it is the faculty of imagining that also gives us the sense of a continuous world. In other words, imagination is a mechanical function related to sense impressions. This view of imagination has continued right up to the present day and it was particularly evident during the surge of research into mental imagery during the 1970s. At that time computational cognitive theorists argued for a hypothetical language-like representational system apparently built into the brain. Although those models are less in favour now, the quest continues for a convincing explanatory model for the way that mental images operate as quasi-perceptual experiences.

On the other side of this historical divide stands a group of philosophers and artists who rejected this narrowly empirical view of imagination. Kant (1724–1804) was among the first to clearly articulate a broader understanding of the nature of imagination. Although he accepted Hume's view of the mechanical operations of imagination, he proposed that this was only one type: there is another kind of imagination that is productive and transcendent, mediating between intellect and the senses. In this regard his ideas foreshadow Jung's (1991) theory of archetypes. Kant's view of imagination as constitutive – part of the nature of the experience that expresses it – was further developed by Schelling (1775–1854) and Hegel (1770–1831). Imagination has a transcendent function in Hegel's system where the universe is understood to be an intelligent entity with human beings as participatory agents of the unfolding process of consciousness. The Romantic poets, artists and writers of the early 19th century including Goethe (1749–1832), Coleridge (1772–1834), Wordsworth (1770–1850), Keats (1795–1821) and Shelley (1792–1822), also completely rejected the mechanical view of imagination – viewing it instead as the door to divinity. This view was perhaps most fully articulated in Blake's (1757–1827) poetic works where he clearly equates imagination with reality. As with the empirical view, this Romantic tradition has continued to be an influential perspective on imagination up into the present day.

In the following sections I go on to consider how these two distinct views have informed the different ways that counselling and psychotherapy schools account for the efficacy of mental imagery.

The empirical view

As would be expected, cognitive behavioural therapy (CBT) is the main approach that is informed by the empirical view of mental imagery. This perspective has resulted historically in a focus on autobiographical memory and simulation or covert modelling that draws on reality-based imagery. It has also led to recent attempts to develop explanatory models of the therapeutic efficacy of mental imagery that are grounded in the operations of the brain and evidenced through research. As mental images have only recently become the focus of sustained interest, these are early days in terms of developing fully worked out explanatory models of the therapeutic efficacy of mental imagery. However, there are some already-established models that CBT theorists are drawing on in the drive to deliver empirical explanations.

A particularly important model, in this regard, is Teasdale and Barnard's (1993) theory of interacting cognitive subsystems (ICS). Their model represents a robust attempt to operationalise the functional relationship between conscious and nonconscious cognitive processes (or, to use the terms employed throughout this book, between the rational and the imaginal perspectives). It is an information processing model and is based on experimental evidence that information is coded in different ways by the brain. In this model, nine interacting subsystems are postulated, two of which code memory and meaning. The first of these two subsystems is expressed straightforwardly in propositional code – in other words, these are memories/cognitions/concepts that the self has conscious access to. In the other subsystem the recording memory is implicational and is expressed in more inchoate bodily sensations and metaphoric communications. Because of the different ways that information and memory are coded, there is no direct connection between the information processing in these two subsystems. An example of this would be when someone prepares to give a public presentation. They may have conscious access to the contents of the proposed and rehearsed speech but may also experience anxiety or threat issuing from earlier negative experiences coded in implicational memory. In general, what is stored in implicit memory such as earlier threatening experiences have a much more direct unconscious route into awareness. These two subsystems map onto the general distinction made in psychological models between verbal and emotional processing. Teasdale and Barnard argue that this model explains why not only early memories are laid down in implicational memory but also later traumatic experience as an adult. This would explain why traumatic memories can hijack the person's awareness and be resistant to cognitive treatment interventions. Teasdale and Barnard's ICS model explains the therapeutic efficacy of mental imagery because mental images are one way in which information is coded in implicational memory. This model is frequently cited in the literature (Hackman *et al.*, 2011; Stopa, 2009) as providing a rationale for using imagery as a means of accessing and transforming memories that underpin maladaptive cognitions and behaviours.

Another empirically based model that has been used to account for the therapeutic potential of mental imagery is Kosslyn *et al.*'s (2001) theory of functional equivalence. As with the ICS model, this theory is based on empirical research. In this particular case, the findings that the same neural structures are activated both in imagining an action and also in performing the same action has led to the idea that mental imagery resembles real perception. If this is the case then it would explain why just imagining something could have a direct impact on the body and the emotions.

Due to the increasing interest in the clinical use of mental imagery in CBT it would be expected that there will be a rapid development in explanatory theoretical modelling in the near future.

The phenomenological view

The phenomenological (or descriptive) position generates a different approach to understanding the efficacy of mental imagery. As would be predicted, there is the lack of interest in developing general explanatory models in relation to the operation of imagery. Where explanations are offered, they are either framed by the therapeutic model itself or they rely on consistent clinical observations such as the generally acknowledged facility of mental imagery to bypass the usual censorship of the person's conscious mind.

Instead of explanations, the focus is on gaining a detailed description and understanding of the phenomenon itself. Watkins encapsulates this phenomenological approach as follows:

> Each image discloses its own character – the particular way it shapes and expresses the nature of the imaginal – by being itself. It tells what it is doing by doing it, by acting itself out. Whether it means to tell – that is, whether we can impute an intentionality to it – must be decided according to each phenomenon.
> (1984: 99)

In other words, mental imagery is not viewed primarily as an epiphenomenon of the brain but rather as something that needs to be understood on its own terms. Hillman argues robustly against the empirical position, stating that: 'Psychic images are not necessarily pictures and may not be like sense images at all. Rather they are *images as metaphors*' (italics in original) (1979: 54). He goes on to say that psychology makes a fundamental mistake of trying to employ sense perception for interior domains of the self (this identification of mental imagery with metaphoric thinking will be considered in more depth in the final section on conceptual metaphor). Both Hillman and Watkins refer back to the earlier ideas of Myers who, as previously noted, first coined the term 'mythopoetic' (Ellenberger, 1970), which he used to describe the tendency of the unconscious mind to weave fantasies. Jung's active imagination and some types of guided imagery are examples of the mythopoetic function in action.

Bridging the divide

In general, there has been few robust attempts to provide an account for the efficacy of mental imagery that bridges the divide between the empirical and phenomenological perspectives. This is not surprising given the radical epistemological differences between these two views. However, there is one important exception, Ahsen's (1984) tripartite image/somatic/meaning model (ISM).

Ahsen followed a now familiar trajectory for pioneering clinician-theorists working with mental imagery. He began by rediscovering its therapeutic potential in his clinical practice, which he then went on to formulate into a body of techniques and procedures he has termed 'eidetic' psychotherapy (Ahsen, 1968). This approach consists of a highly systemised intertwining of diagnostic and therapeutic procedures. What is unusual in his work is the way in which he draws on both humanistic and cognitive behavioural approaches. His empirical leanings are obvious both in his commitment to developing an evidence base for work with mental imagery and also in the similarities between eidetic psychotherapy and CBT practices: eidetic psychotherapy procedures are directive and follow set structures and formulas with an emphasis on diagnosis and identifying the source of maladaptive cognitions and behaviours.

However, despite Ahsen's empirical leanings, he perceived limitations in the cognitive-behavioural perspective (although it is important to note that his view was informed by an earlier and more narrow CBT understanding of mental imagery) stating:

> There is an unfortunate emphasis on the limited notion of image as representation, which reduces the mental image to the status of being a mere inert picture or copy rather than a process. Such definitions, in fact, minimise the important role of the concreteness of the image, a dynamic which leads to interaction and not just representation.
>
> (1993: 27)

Ahsen's (1968) emphasis on process led him to a more integrative perspective on both the theory and practice of working with imagery. This can be seen in the way that some aspects of eidetic psychotherapy resemble humanistic approaches where therapeutic processes are facilitated through the client focusing on and experiencing their own arising imagery. Ahsen went on to propose a model that could explain why working with clients' mental images could lead to a re-experiencing of the precipitating events. The basic premise of his ISM model is that every important experience is impressed in memory in the form of a semi-permanent representation which he termed an 'eidetic'. Furthermore the mental image operates as a container for all the elements involved in this eidetic. When the mental image surfaces, the memory contained within it is available for instantaneous playback. This totality is captured in his three-dimensional model of imagery; the core component is the visual representation and the other two elements comprise the somatic aspect and the associated meaning. Not all three are necessarily present at the same time. Ahsen views the self as a vast multiplicity of ISM states rather than a unified structure. Presenting issues are related to particular ISM states that require surfacing and re-experiencing in order to transform dysfunctional ways of being.

Although Ahsen's transtheoretical model of imagery is rarely referenced in the counselling and psychotherapy literature, elsewhere it has been widely accepted as an important model by writers on imagination as a healing modality including Achterberg (2002) and Sheikh (2002). It is worth noting that one of Ahsen's clinical specialisms is substance misuse and this is likely to have driven his theory-making towards an attempt to explain the interlinking between psychological and physiological conditions.

Singer, another influential American psychologist, has also placed a great deal of importance on integrating the empirical and phenomenological positions in relation to mental imagery practice. Singer's seminal work in this field needs very little introduction: during the 1970s, his co-edited book *The Power of Human Imagination* (Singer and Pope, 1978) helped to establish the academic respectability of mental imagery. His commitment to the centrality of imagination-based processes in talking therapies is evident in his following statement:

> Although many features of psychotherapy call for verbalization, clarity of communication, questioning of assumptions, or identification of misguided attributions, almost all treatment approaches do rely on patients' awareness of the reality and potential of their imagery capacities.
>
> (Singer, 2006: 86)

This commitment informs his interest in developing transtheoretical perspectives in the practice of mental imagery. Although his work does not focus specifically on explaining the efficacy of mental imagery, his thoughts regarding the commonalities and distinctions in mental imagery practice between psychodynamic/humanistic practice on one hand and cognitive behavioural on the other are instructive. He notes how the ways different therapeutic schools use imagery is informed by their theoretical positions; historically, the empirically informed CBT school has tended towards using imagery as reparative interventions whereas other phenomenologically informed schools place more emphasis on clients' imagery narratives. He draws our attention to a central task in psychotherapy: how to help clients effectively integrate the two radically different modes of processing and encoding experience, i.e. the rational and imaginal perspectives (Singer refers to these using Bruner's [1986] terms 'logical/paradigmatic' and 'narrative'). Due to this centrality, he observes that in practice therapists, despite their school affiliations, are increasingly integrating methods that draw on both modes of thought. He then proposes ways in which a wider range of techniques can be incorporated into both schools that begin to close the gap.

In the following and final section I consider how disciplines outside the field of counselling and psychotherapy can contribute to our understanding of how mental imagery works. It will focus in particular on how the theory of conceptual metaphor has the potential to integrate different views on the nature of imagery.

Conceptual metaphor: a potential means of integrating empirical and phenomenological perspectives

There is a very close link between linguistic metaphors and mental imagery (this similarity is explicitly recognised in the distinction noted in the CBT literature between 'autobiographical' and 'metaphoric' imagery). Put simply, metaphors are linguistic expressions of thinking in pictures. And, just as with mental imagery, there is a general acceptance within counselling and psychotherapy that working with both client and therapist generated metaphor can be therapeutically beneficial. Indeed, there have been some well-known therapists such as Kopp (1971) whose therapeutic proficiency is directly linked to their acknowledged mastery of the use of metaphor in clinical work. Probably the most well-known would be Erickson (1901–1980), the founder of hypnotherapy (Erickson and Rossi, 1979), who was particularly skilled at creating apt metaphors for clients' presenting problems. The aptness of these metaphors is predicated on a structural similarity to the client's difficulty that does not include explicit reference to the problematic issue. A well-chosen metaphor can then allow a nonthreatening means for the client to explore and potentially transform their perception of their difficulties. And yet, despite the universal recognition of the usefulness of metaphor in therapy, it has been viewed until recently as merely a helpful linguistic tool that the therapist could employ to promote therapeutic insight. However, over the last couple of decades, there is evidence for a new understanding of the therapeutic potential of metaphor, and this has been informed by a revolution in the way in which we understand the role of metaphor in cognition. The recognition that metaphor is integral to the way we think has, by association, very significant implications for the study of mental imagery in counselling and psychotherapy. Lakoff and Johnson's (2003) theory of conceptual metaphor has become increasingly well-known and influential across a wide range of disciplines: it is assumed, therefore, that most readers will be familiar with its basic premise but perhaps not fully conversant with some of its implications for therapeutic practice. Because of the importance accorded to this theory in this book – not only do I highlight its potential to integrate empirical and phenomenological perspectives, it also explicitly informs the imagery practice presented in Part Two – I am restating its basic principles in some detail below before discussing its relevance for the therapeutic practice of mental imagery.

In cognitive linguistics theory, language is understood to arise out of our embodied experience of the world and to be primarily metaphoric in expression. Furthermore, these metaphors function in a fundamental way to structure our thinking and perception. It is the most familiar unconscious metaphors that are the most basic in terms of this structuring process. Lakoff and Johnson assert that we are continuously employing concrete phenomena (which they term the 'source domain') to articulate abstract concepts (which they term the 'target'). These source domains are generated out of our embodied experience situated within a particular cultural and historical context. A clear illustration of this is provided in Kövecses's (2002) discussion of the universality of metaphoric conceptualisations of anger: across a range of unrelated languages, e.g. English, Zulu, Japanese and Hungarian, there is a remarkably similar conceptualisation of anger as energy held in a pressurised container. Lakoff and Johnson (2003, 1999) argue that this universality arises from the embodied experience of physiological symptoms of this state. However, there are variations in linguistic metaphorical expressions that are influenced by cultural factors. For example, in Japanese the pressurised container is in the 'hara', i.e. belly and intestines, whereas in English it is situated in the head.

The key concept in Lakoff and Johnson's theory is conceptual metaphor. These metaphors are understood to be underlying schema or 'experiential gestalts' that can generate a whole range of linguistic metaphorical expressions. These schema are often so fundamental that we do not recognise their metaphorical nature – for example, when we use spatial metaphors for our experience of time, such as 'there are good times ahead'. Here the source domain is our experience of being physically located in space and this is mapped onto the more abstract phenomenon of time.

However, whatever metaphor is used, it structures our experience and perception of the target phenomenon; it will highlight particular aspects of the target phenomenon and hide others. Lakoff and Johnson (2003) use the example of the conceptual metaphor ARGUMENT IS WAR (small capital letters are the accepted convention for conceptual metaphors) to illustrate this process. If this conceptual metaphor is operating, then the participants engaged in this activity become opponents who are out to win through scoring points; these would be viewed as the entailments of the metaphor. Argument activities that do not cohere with the conceptual metaphor would disappear as possibilities; for example, there would be no room for collaborative experiences of argument.

Linguistic metaphors represent only the surface level expressions of underlying cognitive structures. Gibbs *et al.* emphasise the nonverbal nature of conceptual metaphors, stating that these ' . . . image schemas are imaginative and nonpropositional in nature and operate as organizing structures of experience at the level of bodily perception and movement' (2004: 1192). A research study conducted by Gibbs and O'Brien (1990) provides some tangible support for the use of mental imagery to represent conceptual metaphor. In a series of experiments, participants were asked to form mental images of metaphoric idioms. Gibbs and O'Brien argue that the remarkable consistency of these images supports the theory that these images were generated by conceptual metaphor. In addition, Lakoff (2001) argues that conceptual metaphor theory could be a particularly effective means of interpreting dreams.

Furthermore, in more recent work, Gallese and Lakoff (2005) have proposed an extension of the ontological base for conceptual metaphor to encompass all abstract thinking. The groundbreaking discovery of mirror neurons (Rizzolatti *et al.*,1996), i.e. the same neurons fire not only when we perform an action but also when we watch someone else perform the same action, is the basis of their claim that imagining and understanding originate from the same neural substrate (readers who are interested in recent developments within conceptual metaphor theory are referred to Gibbs's [2011] evaluation of current research and thinking).

The theory of conceptual metaphor is impacting on a wide range of disciplines from archaeology to comparative philosophy, and has started to make its presence felt in the field of counselling and psychotherapy. Lawley and Tompkins (2000) have developed a new counselling and coaching approach, which they term 'symbolic modelling', that focuses on the surfacing of clients' embodied metaphors, thereby bringing about meaningful change. Furthermore, other writers, such as Wickman *et al.* (1999), have identified the contribution that conceptual metaphor could make to theoretical integration; stating that it ' . . . provides a potentially powerful counselling framework generalizable across theoretical orientations' (1999: 389).

In conclusion, it would appear that cognitive linguistics is providing both the theoretical grounds and, more recently, the empirical evidence for the argument that mental imagery arises out of embodied experience (Gibbs and Berg, 2002). This embodied meaningfulness offers a potential solution to the long-debated symbol grounding problem, i.e. the attempt to connect symbols to objective referents in the external world – meaningfulness is embedded in human perception and action.

The implications of this new understanding of metaphor for therapeutic work with mental images is clear – i.e. using mental imagery (or image schemas) provides direct access to the individual's fundamental patterns of thought, behaviour and meaning making. And more than this, conceptual metaphor offers a potential explanation for the therapeutic efficacy of mental imagery that can integrate empirical and phenomenological perspectives.

Some final comments

Although all the main counselling and psychotherapy schools agree that working with mental imagery is therapeutically efficacious, attempts to use explanations for its efficacy as a locus of integration is problematic: this is due to the divide between two different views of the nature of mental imagery. This barrier has been so great that even Ahsen's (1984) descriptive transtheoretical ISM model that captures the links between body, image and meaning-making has gained little purchase on the field of counselling and psychotherapy; this is despite it being accepted in other disciplines that use imagination as a healing modality. Casting around for other theoretical means to bridge the empirical and phenomenological perspectives on mental imagery has led writers and theorists to consider developments in other new disciplines of embodied cognition and cognitive linguistics. In this regard, it would appear that Lakoff and Johnson's theory of conceptual metaphor that attributes a primary role to metaphor in the structuring of cognition holds the most promise. By association, conceptual metaphor does two things for the practice of mental imagery in talking therapies. First, it offers a robust explanation for its therapeutic efficacy: mental images operate as bridges between nonconceptual cognitive processing and later emerging higher-order conceptualisation. Second, it presents a means for integrating two different perspectives on the nature of imagery and the two different types of imagery, i.e. autobiographic, reality-based imagery and symbolic or metaphoric imagery. Conceptual metaphor theory supports the empirical position by offering an explanation of the physiological grounding of mental representations that bears resemblances to Kossyln *et al.*'s theory of functional equivalence. At the same time, due to its focus on the metaphoric nature of cognition, it also accords with the emphasis placed on narrative and experience by the phenomenological position. And finally, by implication, this theory strongly suggests that the usual role generally assigned to mental imagery in therapy, i.e. as merely a useful technique or procedure, needs to be reassessed – mental imagery is a primary means of interacting with the fundamental cognitive processes that are shaping the person's perception and behaviour.

References

Achterberg, J. (2002). *Imagery in Healing: Shamanism and modern medicine*, 2nd edn, Boston: Shambhala.
Ahsen A. (1968). *Basic Concepts in Eidetic Psychotherapy*, New York: Brandon House.
——. (1984). 'ISM: The Triple Code model for imagery and psychophysiology', *Journal of Mental Imagery* 8, 4: 15–42.
——. (1993). *Imagery Paradigm: Imaginative consciousness in the experimental and clinical setting*, New York: Brandon House.
Bruner, J. (1986). *Actual Minds, Possible Worlds*, Cambridge, MA: Harvard University Press.
Ellenberger, H. F. (1970). *The Discovery of the Unconscious*, New York: Basic Books.
Erickson, M. and Rossi, E. (1979). *Hypnotherapy: An exploratory casebook*, New York: Irvington.
Gallese, V. and Lakoff, G. (2005). 'The Brain's Concepts: The role of the sensory-motor system in conceptual knowledge', *Journal of Cognitive Neuropsychology*, 22, 3/4: 455–479.
Gibbs, R. W. (2011). 'Evaluating Conceptual Metaphor Theory', *Discourse Processes*, 48, 8: 529–562.
—— and Berg, E. A. (2002). 'Mental Imagery and Embodied Activity', *Journal of Mental Imagery* 26, 1–2: 1–30.
—— Costa Lima, P. L. and Francozo, E. (2004). 'Metaphor Is Grounded in Embodied Experience', *Journal of Pragmatics*, 36: 1189–1210.
—— and O'Brien, J (1990). 'Idioms and Mental Imagery: The metaphorical motivation for idiomatic meaning', *Cognition*, 36: 35–68.
Hackmann, A., Bennett-Levy, J. and Holmes, E. A. (2011). *Oxford Guide to Imagery in Cognitive Therapy*, Oxford: Oxford University Press.
Hillman, J. (1979). *The Dream and the Underworld*, New York: Harper Perennial.
Jung, C. G. (1991). 'The Archetypes and the Collective Unconscious', in *The Collected Works of C. G. Jung*, vol 9, part 1, 2nd edn, trans. R.F.C. Hull, London: Routledge.
Kopp, S. B. (1971). *Guru: Metaphors from a psychotherapist*, Palo Alto, CA: Science & Behavior Books.
Kosslyn, S. M., Ganis, G. and Thompson, W. L. (2001). 'Neural Foundations of Imagery', *Nature Reviews Neuroscience*, 2, 9: 635–642.
Kövecses, Z. (2002). *Metaphor: A practical introduction*, Oxford: Oxford University Press.
Lakoff, G. (2001). 'How Metaphor Structures Dreams: The theory of conceptual metaphor applied to dream analysis', in K. Bulkeley (ed) *Dreams: A reader on religious, cultural and psychological dimensions of dreaming*, 265–284, New York: Palgrave.

—— and Johnson, M. (1999). *Philosophy in the Flesh*, New York: Basic Books.
—— and Johnson, M. (2003). *Metaphors We Live by*, 2nd edn, Chicago: University of Chicago Press.
Lawley, J. and Tompkins, P. (2000). *Metaphors in Mind: Transformation through Symbolic Modelling*, London: Developing Company Press.
Rizzolatti, G., Fadiga, L., Gallese, V. and Fogassi, L. (1996). 'Premotor Cortex and the Recognition of Motor Actions', *Cognitive Brain Research*, 3, 2: 131–141.
Sheikh, A. A. (2002). 'Eidetic Psychotherapy Techniques' in A. Sheikh (ed) *Therapeutic Imagery Techniques*, 145–154, Amityville, NY: Baywood Pub.
Singer, J.L. (2006). *Imagery in Psychotherapy*, Washington, DC: American Psychological Association.
—— and Pope, K.S. (eds) (1978). *The Power of Human Imagination: New methods in psychotherapy*, New York: Plenum Press.
Stopa, L. (ed) (2009). *Imagery and the Threatened Self: Perspectives on mental imagery and the self in cognitive therapy*, London: Routledge.
Teasdale, J. and Barnard, P. (1993). *Affect, Cognition and Change: Remodelling depressive thought*, Hillsdale, NJ: Earlbaum.
Watkins, M. (1984). *Waking Dreams*, 3rd revised edn, Dallas, Texas: Spring Publications Inc.
Wickman, S., Daniels, M., White, L. and Fessmire, S. (1999). 'A "Primer" in Conceptual Metaphor for Counselors', *Journal of Guidance and Counseling*, 77, 44: 389–394.

Chapter 5

Identifying common features in the use of mental imagery in talking therapies

The move towards psychotherapy integration that began in the 1970s stimulated some, admittedly short-lived, interest in more general theorising with regard to the therapeutic use of mental imagery. However, apart from the aforementioned exceptions of Ahsen's (1984) and Singer's (2006) work, these attempts have tended, on the whole, to reflect the empirical/phenomenological divide discussed in the previous chapter; and, consequently do not provide a satisfactory means of integrating radically different therapeutic approaches.

Is there another way to move beyond this split that has done so much to halt the movement towards theoretical convergence in the theory and practice of mental imagery? In the previous chapter I discussed the potential for explanations of the therapeutic efficacy of mental imagery to deliver some grounds for integration: in this chapter I consider whether observations from clinical practice can identify common features across the different schools. This chapter identifies some of the simple types of imagery and basic operational differences that are generally accepted in therapeutic practice including the particularly important distinction that is made between receptive and directive imagery. I will then go on to consider a set of six common therapeutic functions that have been identified in a recent research study. As this typology of functions forms the basis of the transtheoretical model that I will be presenting in the following chapter, each function will be described and discussed in considerable detail.

Commonalities observed in clinical practice

In general, the commonalities accepted across the different schools with regard to therapeutic practice with mental imagery are simple descriptive categories that rest on basic distinctions. These categories have arisen out of observations from clinical practice. Two examples of these simple distinctions would be between latent and manifest imagery and between autobiographical and metaphoric imagery. In the first pairing, the client's mental images are either viewed as concealing meaning, i.e. latent, or as revealing meaning, i.e. manifest. Psychoanalytically informed therapy regards mental images as having hidden meanings and these images need to be deciphered to extract the real communication: other schools, particularly the humanistic ones, regard imagery as self-evident, in other words the surface image is regarded as the communication and the therapeutic method would involve further amplification of the image itself. The distinction in the second pairing rests on the difference between reality-based imagery such as memories or simulations (rehearsing behaviours in imagination) and nonliteral imagery such as symbols. More recently, the increased interest in mental imagery within contemporary cognitive behavioural therapy (CBT) has led to the naming of other distinctions. One example would be the difference regarded as important for therapeutic work with post-traumatic stress disorder (PTSD) between veridical and nonveridical imagery. The former relates to accurate truthful autobiographical memories of the trauma, whereas the latter refers to memories that are not factually correct.

However, there is another important simple distinction that rests on the production of the image rather than the nature of the mental image itself. This is the generally accepted difference between receptive/passive and directive/active imagery described as follows:

- Receptive or passive imagery (sometimes referred to as spontaneous imagery) comprises the mental images that arise into conscious awareness. These could either take the form of spontaneous images (such as memories or fantasies) or images that are deliberately elicited through guided imagery instructions. An example of the latter would be a client producing a metaphoric image of a prison cell when asked to produce a mental image representing a feeling of depression. Receptive or passive imagery is generated by the imaginal perspective.
- Directive or active imagery, on the other hand, comprises consciously manufactured or produced mental images (such as visualising oneself performing certain actions) or conscious deliberate modifications made to receptive mental images. An example of the latter would be suggesting to a depressed client who has produced an image of being inside a prison cell that they could visualise a key that could unlock the door. Directive or active imagery is created by the rational perspective.

Therapeutic procedures that are designed to employ both types of imagery are sometimes referred to as interactive or dialogic imagery techniques. These terms highlight the way that mental images operate as a means of communication between the rational and imaginal perspectives. A vestigial transtheoretical model can be detected in framing these techniques as a dialogical process. Yet, in this basic form, it is obviously too elementary to provide a useful framework for the wide range of practices and approaches that have been developed by different schools and clinical innovators.

Identifying some common functions of mental imagery in therapeutic practice

In order to identify a locus for integration I decided to carry out some research to see if it was possible to identify any more specific commonalities in its practice that could move beyond the simple distinctions discussed in the previous section. I designed a research study in which I analysed a sample of published clinical vignettes from peer-reviewed journals containing reports of working with mental imagery. These vignettes were chosen from a range of different therapeutic approaches. The grounded theory analysis of the data disclosed some common ways in which imagery operates in therapy (interested readers are referred to Thomas [2011] for a detailed description of the research project). The following section describes these findings in detail.

Six functions were provisionally identified in the use of mental imagery in a therapeutic context as follows: diagnostic; monitoring; processing; reparative; process management; and framing. In the descriptions below, the distinctions between each function have been sharpened in order to identify and articulate the essential operational characteristics. However, in practice, these functional differences are not so clear-cut and there is considerable overlap between them. In other words rather than providing absolute categorical distinctions these six functions have fuzzy boundaries.

I use the same convention for each of the six identified functions beneath; i.e. each one is given a short descriptive title followed by an explanatory statement with some clinical illustrations (taken from the original reports used in the research). In particular I aim to offer ideal examples for each category. The discussion includes some indication of the way different schools have understood and utilised the particular function. An attempt has been made to make the titles of the particular categories as generic and transtheoretical as possible.

Readers will note that some of the examples given for specific functions could also serve as an example for another different function. This functional overlap is due to a particular characteristic of the therapeutic use of mental imagery, i.e. one mental image can be used for more than one function at the same time. I will return to discuss this important multi-functional aspect in the following chapter.

The reparative function

Definition: Repairing/improving/restructuring maladaptive responses or dysfunctional states.

The reparative function is the deliberate use of imagery to promote a specific positive change or improvement in a presenting issue. As Shorr notes, 'Another function of imagery that has special relevance to psychotherapy is the fact that images can be transformed, re-experienced and reshaped in line with a healthier self-concept' (1983: 464). There has been an emphasis on this function in CBT; right from its inception, reality-based imagery has been commonly used in covert modelling procedures where clients are encouraged to imagine someone else performing the action that the clients experienced as problematic (discussed previously in Chapter 3). The premise is that through imagining a better outcome or a more skillful action this will lead to improvements in the actual behaviour of the person; examples of this can be seen in sports psychology applications. However, it is important to note that imagery rehearsal is not restricted to this school – other approaches recognise that, '... maladaptive reactions can be changed, first in the imagination, then in reality' (Desoille, 1966: 7).

More recently, cognitive therapies have recognised the importance of working directly on autobiographical memory in order to treat intrusive imagery. A good example of this kind of reparative work can be seen in rescripting techniques where mental imagery is employed to make changes to traumatic memories and thereby help clients manage them more effectively (see the example of Smucker *et al.*'s [2002] clinical work summarised in Chapter 3).

The reparative function is not restricted to reality-based or autobiographical imagery. Sophisticated integrations of metaphoric and reality-based imagery are possible as a memory-restructuring technique as the following example demonstrates. In a case study of interpersonal therapy (drawing on attachment theory), the therapist (Thomas, 2005) shows how intentional use of imagery can help clients with histories of childhood sexual abuse. The premise of his approach is that abuse survivors need to develop effective internal images of protection. His client had been in psychotherapy for two years but, despite discussing her sexual abuse in detail, she felt it still interfered with her ability to feel safe in intimate relationships. Thomas encouraged her to return to the memory of the abuse and visualise a figure that could protect her. The client imagined the figure of Wonder Woman and the therapist guided her through a process of picturing this figure standing between her and her abuser. In his report Thomas stated that the work his client did on restructuring her memories led to a new sense of confidence and strength as well as improvements in her relationship.

Finally, another example of the reparative function used with metaphoric imagery would be symptom relief. This is commonly used for psychosomatic issues such as tension headaches. An example of using imagery to restore a healthy sleeping pattern is given by Hall *et al.* (2006). A client was experiencing anxious racing thoughts that were interfering with her sleeping. When asked to produce an image for these racing thoughts she reported visualising a large basket full of balls of wool that had become tangled together. The counsellor encouraged her to untangle the wool and rewind it into separate balls. The client made the connection between the tangled state and her anxious muddled thinking. She reported later that by recreating this scene in her imagination before going to sleep had helped her gain some control over her internal processes.

The process management function

Definition: Actively managing and promoting therapeutic processes.

In this function, imagery is employed in various ways to actively manage an ongoing therapeutic process or to foster positive changes. This deliberate use of imagery bears some resemblance to the reparative function. However, there is an important difference in that the process management function does not aim to create a specific outcome – instead it is a means of facilitating more general positive processes.

A classic imagery application that demonstrates this function in operation is the use of imaginary dialogues between aspects of the self often symbolised as figures.

This technique has been a popular use of imagery because not only can it make inner dynamics more concrete for the client, it also offers an accessible means of working with these dysfunctional states. A current instance where imagery has been used in this way can be found in schema therapy, a contemporary CBT approach. In the following example taken from Bamber's (2004) clinical work, he presents a treatment plan for agoraphobia that is informed by schema theory, i.e. dysfunctional inner dynamics that are operating between four aspects of the self. The client is instructed to imagine his four operating modes as figures and to help them interact in a more balanced way. These operating modes are conceived of as: child mode; maladaptive coping mode; maladaptive parent mode; and healthy adult mode. The client viewed his child mode as a defenceless child and his maladaptive coping mode as a black knight. The client reported that the job of the black knight was to prevent his defenceless child experiencing pain, and this showed up as a fear of going out into the world. Over the course of the therapy the therapist helped the client build up the strength of his child mode and develop an image of a healthy inner adult that could challenge the power of the black knight.

This function comes to the fore in image-based therapeutic approaches – understandably, as mental imagery is the main means used to facilitate therapeutic processes. An example can be seen in Tajima and Naruse's (1987) 'Tsubo' imagery therapy. As described earlier in Chapter 3, in this approach the client is directed to imagine containers (tsubos) that hold within them the client's problematic material; with the aim of providing a safe way to explore difficult psychological states. The process management function is operating through the creation of a specific mental image that gives the client some control over their engagement with their repressed material.

Humanistic therapies deliver many examples of the use of imagery to manage helpful therapeutic processes. Assagioli (1965), in particular, developed a number of influential imagery methods that made extensive use of this function. In one technique, clients are instructed to discover images representing conflicting forces within themselves and then allow these images to interact: by using a combination of first and third perspectives (by taking on the role of each image in turn and also by viewing the conflict from a detached observer position) the client develops more insight into their conflict.

In a more general way, the process management function is also implicit in the way that guided fantasy in psychotherapy is structured to promote positive and effective therapeutic processes. A good example of this is Leuner's (1984) motif of the forest, which he uses to help clients begin to identify and relate to cut-off parts of the self. Clients are directed to imagine they are standing at the edge of a dark wood and they are told in advance that figures, either humans or animals, will sooner or later step out of the woods. Leuner believes that the figures and animals are dynamic structures representing the unknown 'shadow' parts of the self. The client is encouraged to actively engage with these frightening forms by giving them food. Leuner acknowledged that he was drawing from fairy tales that prescribed food as a means of pacifying and controlling threatening animals. This deliberate use of imagery is intended as a general means of promoting more integration of split-off aspects of the self.

The framing function

Definition: Providing generic templates or predetermined starting points for specific therapeutic purposes/work.

This function refers to the way that mental imagery processes can be deliberately and purposively shaped through the use of predetermined starting points or templates. The choice of the imagery frames the ensuing therapeutic process along certain deliberately chosen lines. This is a very common therapeutic function of mental imagery in counselling and psychotherapy. It will be noted that several of the examples given for other functions also display the framing function in action at the same time – I will be going on to discuss the multi-functionality of mental images in the following chapter. A range of different terms have been used for this function in the literature. In the European waking dream tradition, Desoille (1966) refers to specific 'triggering images' that he uses to initiate the client's exploration of a particular psychological theme whereas Frétigny and Virel (1968) term these starting points 'inductive images'. Shorr (1983), who draws on Rorschach's work, calls them 'projective devices'.

However, no matter how it has been termed, this function operates in the same general way: it initiates a therapeutic process that is structured along particular lines. Leuner provides a clear description of its use:

> Suggesting the idea of a fantasy to a patient provides a structured field of experience (at first empty of content) in a mild state of relaxation, even when the request to imagine something is deliberately given quite vaguely by the therapist.
>
> (1978: 127)

He elaborates further, 'The vague suggested motif serves as a crystallization point, with the purpose of stimulating a projective process in the realm of visual fantasy' (1978: 128).

Structured fantasies or guided imagery processes are one of the most common uses of the framing function and the literature provides many examples of different types of scripts to use in practice. Here the predetermined image is delivered as a series of imagery instructions with a specific goal or focus in mind. The following example shows how guided imagery scripts are approached within the humanistic school. Hall *et al.* give the following rationale for a particular script:

> The use of a waterfall in itself can be used creatively for clients who find themselves at turning points, crossroads or decision times in their lives. The natural energy contained in the flowing water seems to be capable of inspiring and revitalising even the most depressed.
>
> (2006: 41)

They then describe how a series of directions can be used for particularly passive and/or depressed clients. First, clients are instructed to visualise a waterfall in all its detail. Then they are instructed to imagine a cave behind the water where it is safe for them to stand. When they are ready, they are asked to imagine that they can step forward and stand in the waterfall itself. The clients are encouraged to experience the water flowing over them as fully as possible before stepping back out into the sunshine.

The example above deals with the structuring of an unfolding experience. Sometimes the framing function is restricted to just the production of an initial image. In the following example taken from a case study of psychoanalytic work with a depressed patient (Chestnut, 1971), instead of waiting for the client to produce a spontaneous image, the analyst suggests a type of image. In this case, the patient had had a previous experience of therapy where she had found herself becoming unable to relate or talk to her therapist. After the initial phase of therapy, Chestnut realised that this pattern was being replayed with him. All attempts on his part to help her break through the impasse did not work. He told his patient that he felt there was an invisible barrier operating between them and his patient agreed. He suggested that she could try closing her eyes and visualising a wall. His patient reported a high smooth wall that made her feel secure. Chestnut then encouraged her to begin to see him within the image and, after some initial reluctance, the patient was able to accomplish this. Chestnut reported that over time this allowed a more collaborative way of working with the patient's anxiety.

The diagnostic function

Definition: Delivering information about the presenting issue particularly with regard to factors implicated in the cause or maintenance of the problem.

The diagnostic function refers to the way that clients' mental imagery can operate as a means of generating insights into the condition or issue that is brought to therapy. All therapeutic approaches that accept the client's imagery as meaning laden would acknowledge this function, either implicitly or explicitly as Leuner does in the following statement:

> We have referred to this freely developed imaginal landscape as the 'catathymic panorama,' which can be roamed in all directions. As I will show you in the following, this panorama is of great diagnostic value and within a short time gives the therapist a relatively broad view of the patient's predominant conflictual constellation.
>
> (1984: 17)

This diagnostic function does not depend on how the image is produced. The image might have arisen spontaneously for the client in the course of the session (or the image might have been brought to the session by the client as something meaningful). Or it could have been deliberately elicited either through helping clients translate their presenting issue into a representative image or through using a guided imagery script pertinent to their presenting issue. An example of the latter would be the purposively diagnostic procedures developed by Shorr, (mentioned in Chapter 3) – he instructs his client to imagine two different animals (people, things, etc.) compare them and have them interact. He believes that this process reveals the client's internal conflict. It is clear how much importance that Shorr attributes to this function when he asserts that, 'A person's imagery, more than any other mental function, indicates how he organises the world' (1983: 463).

No matter how the image arises, it is deemed to carry information that, on further exploration and unpacking, will shed light on the presenting issue or themes the client is bringing. It is important to note that by using the medical model term 'diagnostic' this is not meant to imply that particular images have a fixed and universal meaning. Counselling and psychotherapy recognise to a greater or lesser extent that meaning and experience is symbolised or encoded in images in different ways. For instance, images can condense a range of aspects and meanings into one symbol. Or another example would be symbolic transposition, i.e. the process by which an important figure or event is represented in another symbolic form. Furthermore, people's imagery is shaped by individual, social and cultural conditions and contexts (matters of interpretation are discussed at length in the second part of this book).

This function does not determine how meaning is extracted from the mental image. Depending on the therapeutic approach espoused by the therapist the image may be approached in different ways. In classic psychoanalysis, the analyst would approach the client's mental image or fantasy with a particular view. Here the surface image is generally viewed with suspicion as it may be defending against the exposure of repressed material. The analyst will view the image through a particular interpretative framework seeking its latent meaning. Humanistic therapies, on the other hand, view the process of making sense of the image as led by the client. However, Hall *et al.* issue the following caution, 'Even some of the systems that suggest the counsellor should allow the client to interpret their own imagery have implicit forms of interpretation contained within the model' (2006: 54).

More recently, some contemporary CBT approaches have become interested in this diagnostic potential; clients' mental imagery is starting to be viewed as an emotional bridge that offers a means of tracing back to the source of current difficulties. A simple example of this would be the therapist asking questions to determine the historical cause of distressing intrusive imagery. And, as discussed in a previous chapter, there is more openness to the imaginal perspective as a source of valid knowledge in its own right. Butler and Holmes (2009) in their discussion of the use of drawings in working with childhood trauma comment on the way that clients make meaning from their images. This leads them to identify one of the functions of imagery is linking things up or making connections between thoughts and feelings.

The following example illustrates the diagnostic function in action. This illustration is taken from Silverman's (1987) innovative clinical work with mental imagery. Although he worked from a psychoanalytical perspective, he argued that it was important for psychoanalysis to develop a wider understanding of the therapeutic operation of imagery and to not limit itself to its narrow focus on latent meaning.

In his report of clinical work with a 'neurotic' client he describes one session when she complained that she felt emotionally 'dead'. After spending the first half of the session unproductively analysing her defences and transference, he asked her to allow an image to come to mind. She reported visualising an image of an electric chair; and as she did so, she made an immediate connection with an abortion she had had five years previously. In addition, she was also aware that this was linked with a recent miscarriage that she had been discussing in her therapy. The mental image allowed her to understand that this miscarriage was unconsciously associated in her mind with murder and this association led her to cut off her feelings. Silverman reported that this understanding allowed his client to move beyond the impasse created by the emotional block.

The monitoring function

Definition: revealing developments or otherwise in the presenting issue through changes in the representational mental image over time.

If mental imagery is utilised at the outset of a therapeutic process then returning to that image at a later stage can deliver insights regarding the progress (or lack of progress) of the represented issue. Changes in the original image can indicate where and how developments are occurring. This monitoring function is very similar to the diagnostic function in that it is predicated on the notion that imagery is a consistent and reliable source of information issuing from the imaginal perspective. This function is designated as a separate category because it is more concerned with accurately tracking a process unfolding over time rather than diagnosing factors implicated in the original presenting problem. In their discussion of the use of drawings for childhood trauma, Butler and Holmes (2009) explicitly identify one of the functions of imagery as a means of illustrating processes. They give a clinical example of a client who represented his abuse as pieces of a puzzle that slowly came together into a whole picture over the course of therapy.

Generally this function is something that is noted rather than deliberately applied. This is because re-engagement with the original image will often happen naturally as part of the unfolding therapeutic process. Generally, if there are any changes to the original imagery, this is viewed as a commentary on the therapeutic progress. Shorr notes this in relation to his exercise of using the dual imagery process to reveal inner conflict (described earlier), stating that after clients have resolved these inner dynamics, ' . . . the dual imagery situation will not appear as radically bipolarised – the essential difference between the two images may be minimal' (1983: 286).

A good illustration of the monitoring function in action can be found in Malamud's (1973) case study of guided imagery. In this example, the differences in the client's image operated as a confirmation of the positive changes undergone by the client over a one-year period. Malamud employed a guided imagery script featuring a bird in a cage to help his client identify the interior dynamic operating between two aspects of herself, i.e. the introjected parent (represented by the cage) and the child aspect (represented by the bird). During the first experience of using this script, the client produced an image of a hostile cage that wanted to destroy the bird inside it. The client realised from this that she had a hostile mother introject. This helpful insight indicated where the focus of the therapeutic work should be. One year later Malamud employed the same bird in a cage script again but this time the client's imagery had changed: she reported that she was picturing a party going on in the room and the bird wanted to fly among the guests. She imagined the cage saying it would be better if the bird stayed inside because otherwise she would get trampled. The scene unfolded with the bird disregarding this advice and flying out, whereupon the cage called out that it missed her and wanted her to come back. The bird asked the cage if it would let her out when she wanted to and the cage agreed to these conditions. The guided imagery episode completed at the point when the bird said it would return because it loved the cage. Malamud helped the client make links to the changes in the imagery. She realised that she had worked through some of her issues concerning an introjected hostile mother and the cage now represented her current relationship with her husband. The change in the imagery helped Malamud's client recognise her ambivalent feelings towards her husband – although she loved him she experienced his neediness as a trap.

Although the use of the monitoring function is usually implicit, there are some examples in the literature of its deliberate use particularly within the image-based approaches; one example being Leuner who noted the accuracy of mental imagery for measuring change. He developed an imagery method in which he instructs his clients to represent their therapy as a new building project – they are encouraged to view the progress of the building works as an indication of their progress in therapy. Another example would be Desoille's procedure where clients are directed to imagine carrying a sword (a symbol of the masculine aspect) or a vessel (a symbol of the feminine aspect) up a mountain and then examine these symbols carefully as, 'Any changes to the image are important' (1966: 5). Another example, this time of purposive monitoring, can be seen in Shorr's exercise of reverse time imagery. In this procedure he directs his client to create an imaginary situation, e.g. a field, and then build something in it. The client is then asked to imagine what the imagery would have been five years ago. Shorr goes on to comment on the usefulness of this type of deliberate monitoring, 'If verified by other elements in the patient's development, reverse time imagery provides a viable rule of thumb for measurement of the person's change' (1983: 286).

The processing function

Definition: Providing a conduit for the release of repressed material.

One of the characteristics of mental imagery that has long been recognised and exploited in psychotherapy is the way in which it can operate as a conduit for the (often rapid) release of repressed material. This material usually comprises emotional states but can also have cognitive and somatic components. In general this material has been constellated around previous experiences that the conscious mind has not been able to assimilate or process. When the imagination is harnessed, either through deliberately eliciting an image that represents the current problem or by using a more generic imagery procedure, it can provide a route for re-experiencing blocked memories. The processing function calls to mind Ahsen's (1984) ISM model, discussed previously, where the mental image is regarded as a container that, as it rises into consciousness, opens up and releases stored material. The facility with which a mental image can unlock blocked emotional material is generally attributed to its capacity to bypass conscious defence mechanisms. Shorr's psycho-imagination therapy provides a classic example of how this material can come to the surface spontaneously and begin to be experienced. He uses one of his standard imagery procedures of asking his client to imagine telling a secret to a stranger on a train that he will never see again. Shorr then goes on to describe how his client responded:

> He answered "I'll tell him that I am a mama's boy. I'm indulged. I'm not masculine and I want to masturbate." Then without a word from me, he began to re-experience a traumatic incident of his mother sexually stimulating him and making him her "man".
>
> (1983: 39)

As might be expected, this accessing of repressed traumatic experience is a common feature in the psychodynamic and humanistic approaches. However, not all repressed material takes the form of such clear episodic memory. In Suler's (1989) case study of psychoanalytic work with a young man diagnosed with a 'schizoid personality structure' the release of repressed material took a somatic form. Suler's client struggled to recall his earliest memories of his father who had died of a brain tumour two years previous to him seeking psychotherapeutic treatment. His mother had told him his father had been arrested on several occasions for exhibitionism. When the client complied with Suler's suggestion that he allow an image to arise to describe the relationship with his father, he had an instantaneous and dramatic physiological response. Suler reported that his client blanched and jumped up and began pacing the room whilst describing vivid sensations of choking, defecating and anxiety. From this powerful reaction, Suler's client realised that something important had been buried deep in his subconscious mind. In subsequent sessions his dawning suspicion grew that his father had sexually abused him.

Historically, within the CBT school there has been less attention paid to the processing function of mental imagery. Its use in this form has been mainly restricted to desensitisation procedures for treating phobias. Here, instructing the client to visualise the phobic object allows the client a manageable and controlled means of discharging the associated overwhelming affect. More recently, the explosion of interest in therapeutic applications of mental imagery has prompted the development of approaches that work for trauma. Methods such as imagery rescripting depend upon the processing function with regard to the reliving of traumatic experience combined with other imagery functions whereby deliberate changes or new elements are introduced into the memory. This function is identified explicitly by Grey when he states, with reference to the technique of updating trauma memories with imaginal reliving, 'This method has a number of functions, which may be seen as "processing" the memory' (2009: 177).

It is important to note that the processing function does not always result in a rapid release of repressed experience – it can also operate in a slower, less dramatic manner. In a more general way, mental images can allow a means for hidden parts of the self to arise into conscious awareness. These aspects are not necessarily linked to traumatic experience, instead they can take the form of inner dynamics that are implicated in dysfunctional behaviour and psychological states. The mental image provides a conduit for the understanding and assimilation of these parts of the self or patterns that have been denied to awareness. In other words, rather than an immediate reliving of experience, the mental image symbolising the unconscious pattern discharges its contents over a period of time. An example of this type of processing can be seen in Hall *et al.*'s work. They describe using mental imagery with a client who was experiencing increasing social isolation. His condition was linked to a fear of exposure that caused him to triple-check every thought before speaking or taking action. When asked to produce an image for the isolation, the client reported a seductive dark figure shrouding him from the outside world. Through repeated engagement with the image the client was able to gain more understanding of how his behaviour operated as a defence and he was, ' . . . daring to let it go very gradually and emerge from the safety of his isolation' (2006: 98).

Conclusion

Apart from Singer's (2006; Singer and Pope, 1978) work, discussed briefly in the preceding chapter, there has been little interest within counselling and psychotherapy to identify commonalities in the therapeutic application of mental imagery across the different schools. The basic operating and descriptive distinctions that are generally accepted in the field appear self-evident and have arisen out of observations from clinical practice. However, by themselves, these distinctions are too broad to offer an inclusive framework for the practice of mental imagery. The next step in a more theoretically robust endeavour would be to establish a locus for integration and therapeutic function seems promising. The six different functions that have been identified in my research study appear to offer a starting point for thinking about the use of mental imagery across the different schools. In the following chapter, I discuss how these six functions together offer a potential model for inclusive practice – one that captures some of the complexity of using mental imagery in clinical practice and allows the practitioner to draw on a wide range of approaches to imagery in a coherent and effective way.

References

Ahsen A. (1984). 'ISM: The Triple Code model for imagery and psychophysiology', *Journal of Mental Imagery*, 8, 4: 15–42.

Assagioli, R. (1965). *Psychosynthesis*, New York: Hobbs, Dorman & Co.

Bamber, M. (2004). '"The good, the bad and defenceless Jimmy" – a single case study of Schema Mode Therapy', *Clinical Psychology and Psychotherapy*, 11: 425–438.

Butler, G. and Holmes, E. A. (2009). 'Imagery and the Self Following Childhood Trauma: Observations concerning the use of drawings and external images', in L. Stopa (ed) *Imagery and the Threatened Self: Perspectives on mental imagery and the self in cognitive therapy*, 166–180, London: Routledge.

Chestnut, W. J. (1971). 'Directed Imagery: A means for dealing with patient defensiveness', *Psychotherapy: Theory, Research, Practice, Training*, 8, 4: 325–327.

Desoille, R. (1966). *The Directed Daydream*, New York: Psychosynthesis Research Foundation.

Frétigny, R. and Virel, A. (1968). *L'Imagerie Mentale*, Geneva: Mont Blanc.

Grey, N. (2009). 'Imagery and Psychological Threat to the Self in PTSD', in L Stopa (ed) *Imagery and the Threatened Self: Perspectives on mental imagery and the self in cognitive therapy*, 137–165, London: Routledge.

Hall, E., Hall, C., Stradling, P. and Young, D. (2006). *Guided Imagery: Creative interventions in counselling and psychotherapy*, London: Sage.

Leuner, H. (1978). 'Basic Principles and Therapeutic Efficacy of Guided Affective Imagery (GAI)', in J.L. Singer and K.S. Pope (eds) *The Power of Human Imagination: New methods in psychotherapy*, 125–166, New York: Plenum Press.

——. (1984). *Guided Affective Imagery in Short-term Psychotherapy: The basic course*, New York: Thieme-Stratton Corp.

Malamud, D. (1973). 'Self-confrontation Methods in Psychotherapy', *Psychotherapy: Theory, Research, Practice, Training*, 10, 2: 123–130.

Shorr, J. E (1983). *Psychotherapy through Imagery*, 4th edn, New York: Thieme-Stratton Inc.

Silverman, L. H. (1987). 'Imagery as an Aid in Working through Unconscious Conflicts', *Psychoanalytic Psychology*, 4: 45–64.

Singer, J. L. (2006). *Imagery in Psychotherapy*, Washington, DC: American Psychological Association.

—— and Pope, K. S. (eds) (1978). *The Power of Human Imagination: New methods in psychotherapy*, New York: Plenum Press.

Smucker, M. R., Weis, J. and Grunert, B. (2002). 'Imagery Rescripting for Trauma Survivors with PTSD', in A. A. Sheikh (ed) *Therapeutic Imagery Techniques*, 85–94, Amityville, NY: Baywood Pub.

Suler, J. (1989). 'Mental Imagery in Psychoanalytical Treatment', *Psychoanalytical Psychology*, 6: 343–366.

Tajima, S. and Naruse, G. (1987). 'Tsubo Imagery Therapy', *Journal of Mental Imagery* 11, 1: 105–118.

Thomas, P. (2005). 'Dissociation and Internal Models of Protection: Psychotherapy with child abuse survivors', *Psychotherapy: Theory, Research, Practice Training*, 42, 1: 20–36.

Thomas, V. (2011). *The Therapeutic Functions of Mental Imagery in Psychotherapy: Constructing a theoretical model*, Unpublished DPsych. thesis. Held in Middlesex University e-repository available at: http://eprints.mdx.ac.uk/10561

Chapter 6

Developing a more inclusive model of mental imagery in therapeutic practice

I still recall the excitement during my research project when I realised that the group of functions identified through the analysis of the data had the potential to deliver a more inclusive model of mental imagery. This realisation happened when I noted something glaringly obvious: the six functions divided into two groups that mapped onto the commonly accepted distinction in clinical practice between directive and receptive imagery.

In this chapter I describe this mapping in more detail and I go on to explain how the six identified functions model the way that mental images operate as an interactive communication process between the rational and imaginal perspectives. The chapter concludes by offering some thoughts on the advantages of this model as a more inclusive framework for practice and also acknowledges its limitations.

A description of the model

The model proposed in this book captures two fundamental aspects of the way that mental images operate in therapeutic processes. First, it differentiates the ways in which mental images operate as a means of communication between the rational and the imaginal perspectives. Second, it clarifies how one mental image can operate in different ways in the context of therapeutic work. In this section I explain in detail these two aspects and finally present a diagram of the resulting model.

How the different functions relate to each other

In the previous chapter I identified and described in detail six different functions of mental imagery in therapeutic application. These functions can be further classified along basic operational lines into two main types. In very general terms the mental image either:

1 Provides a conduit for delivering communications from the rational to the imaginal perspective. This would include the **reparative function** whereby the rational perspective instructs the imaginal perspective to make specific

changes to a dysfunctional behavioural pattern or maladaptive response. The **process management function** also falls into this category as this is the way that the rational perspective instructs the imaginal perspective to provide predetermined forms that can be employed to promote a therapeutic process. Finally, the **framing function** belongs to this group because here the rational perspective is instructing the imaginal perspective to shape its productions and communications along predetermined lines.

2   Or it provides a conduit for delivering communications from the imaginal to the rational perspective. This would include the **diagnostic** and **monitoring** functions as both of these functions deliver information from the imaginal perspective. It would also include the **processing** function as this refers to the way that repressed material and/or experience coded in or stored within the imaginal perspective can be delivered into the awareness of the rational perspective where it can be re-experienced and consciously integrated.

The two basic categories identified above bring to mind the main operating distinction generally accepted in clinical practice, i.e. between directive and receptive imagery, as follows:

1   Directive imagery comprises mental images deliberately created by the conscious mind for specific therapeutic purposes (the **reparative**, **process management** and **framing** functions).
2   Receptive imagery comprises mental images that arise spontaneously and are received by the conscious mind (this would also include images that are elicited, but not predetermined, by the conscious mind) (the **diagnostic**, **monitoring** and **processing** functions).

In other words the six functions appear to map onto and further differentiate out a generally accepted common distinction in therapeutic practice with mental imagery (although it is worth noting that although the functions are equally balanced between directive and receptive, this is an early stage of developing the model and this symmetry might not hold in future versions). In the following sections I will be explaining how this further conceptualisation of the differences between directive and receptive imagery can lay the foundation for a sophisticated modelling of the therapeutic application of mental imagery.

The multi-functionality of mental images in therapeutic practice

When I analysed the data from the vignettes of clinical practice in my original research study (Thomas, 2011) I was struck by the way that the same mental image could show up in more than one function category. In some respects this multi-functionality is quite straightforward and it would be expected that one mental image can operate in different ways through the course of therapeutic work.

A simple example of this would be the monitoring function that often follows a diagnostic use (in the following discussion I will be referring back to the case material used to illustrate the different functions in the previous chapter). Malamud's (1973) use of the 'bird in the cage' guided imagery is a case in point. The initial image of the bird in the cage is used diagnostically. One year later, when the client is directed to visualise the bird in the cage again, the image is being used to monitor the progress in the client's therapy. An example of using the monitoring function following a different function can be seen in Bamber's (2004) case study of schema therapy with an agoraphobic client. Because the client is instructed to visualise his four operating modes as figures and to help them interact in a more balanced way, this would represent the process management function. Towards the end of this therapeutic process, it is noted that there are changes in two of the images and this is taken as a commentary on the client's progress in therapy (the black knight – the figure representing the client's maladapted coping mechanism – appeared to have died). In other words the image is being used later on in its monitoring capacity.

Another different example of one image being used in more than one way over time can be seen in Chestnut's (1971) case study of psychoanalytical work with a depressed patient. His work provides an example of the framing function when he initially asks his patient to visualise the barrier between them as a wall. Then, with the intention of helping the client begin to break down an old defence, Chestnut used the reparative function. He directed his patient to make a change to the image, by suggesting she should incorporate an image of himself sitting on top of the wall.

However, what is less obvious is that this multi-functionality is not just sequential: a mental image can display more than one function at the same time. Taking the same case study by Malamud as an illustration, right from the onset, the mental image of the bird in the cage is functioning in two different ways. There is a framing function operating, i.e. the bird in the cage is given as a template to shape the imagery production. This image is also, at the same time, functioning as a diagnostic tool, i.e. the nature of the image produced by the client is viewed as delivering significant information about her current difficulties. Another example of two functions operating at once can be seen in Shorr's (1983) clinical work, which I used to illustrate the processing function in the previous chapter. His standard imagery procedure (of asking his client to imagine telling a secret to a stranger on a train that he will never see again) is another example of the framing function. When the client used mental imagery as directed he re-experienced a traumatic memory – the processing function in action.

In the examples given above, it can be seen that one mental image can display a range of functions both simultaneously and sequentially. The therapeutic functionality of mental imagery appears dynamic and complex. The helpful binary distinction between active and receptive functions is not a rigid either/or state. One image can be display directive and receptive functions at the same time such as Shorr's example where the framing and processing functions are operating at the same time. Or this can be sequential – a client can produce a spontaneous image that initially is used diagnostically and then changes might be made to the image for reparative ends and so on.

This dynamic process appears to be shaped by two factors. First, dependent on the orientation of the therapist, certain functions may be favoured over others. Examples of this would be a tendency within CBT towards using directive functions and a bias towards the receptive functions that can be seen in psychodynamic practice. However, from an integrative perspective, it would seem that this process is more generally shaped by therapeutic requirements. Through the course of therapeutic work, particular functions come to the fore dependent on different therapeutic needs. At one stage the task might be to use imagery to help clients gain more insight into their presenting issues (diagnostic function); later on the image may be used to monitor the client's progress. Initially, an image may arise that provides a rapid release of repressed material (processing function), later on it might become apparent that this image requires some reshaping for curative ends (reparative function). Somewhat tangentially, this brings to mind another inclusive model, i.e. Clarkson's (2003) five relationship framework. Here, it is understood that there is the potential for different relationships operating between client and therapist that are informed by a particular intersubjective perspective. Different types of relationship come to the fore dependent on what is happening within the therapy. Clarkson's framework allows a means for integrative psychotherapists to draw on a wide range of different theoretical perspectives on the nature of the therapeutic relationship.

The 'interactive communicative' model of mental imagery

In the preceding section I have made a case that it is possible to differentiate out the basic distinction between directive and receptive imagery into a range of operations. Six functions have been identified so far that appear to comprise some of the main ways that mental images operate as bidirectional agents of communication between the rational and imaginal perspectives. Based on this case I am proposing an interactive communicative model of mental imagery that, I would argue, captures some of the complexity inherent in therapeutic practice with mental images. This model is represented schematically in Table 6.1.

Some comments on the advantages and limitations of the model

The main advantage of the proposed interactive communicative model of mental imagery is that it is transtheoretical: it is not grounded in one particular counselling or psychotherapy approach; neither is it informed by a particular psychological model of the self. The model itself builds upon generally accepted clinical observations regarding therapeutic practice with mental imagery. On these grounds I would assert that this model can provide a more inclusive framework for practitioners to think about how they are using mental imagery in their own practice.

Table 6.1 The interactive communicative model of mental imagery

Interactive communicative model of mental imagery

Rational to imaginal (directive)	Imaginal to rational (receptive)
The *reparative function*: Repairing/improving/restructuring maladaptive responses or dysfunctional states.	The *diagnostic function*: Delivering information about the presenting issue particularly with regard to factors implicated in the cause or maintenance of the problem.
The *process management function*: Actively managing and promoting therapeutic processes.	The *monitoring function*: Revealing developments in the presenting issue through changes in the mental image over time.
The *framing function*: Providing generic templates or predetermined starting points designed for specific therapeutic purposes.	The *processing function*: Providing a conduit for the (often rapid) release of repressed material.

This model will be of particular use to two types of practitioners: integrative psychotherapists and counsellors, and therapists who use mental imagery as a primary means of facilitating therapeutic processes. In terms of the former, this transtheoretical framework provides a structure for drawing on mental imagery practices across a wide range of therapeutic modalities or eclectic approaches. And specifically, it offers a coherent way for practitioners to utilise imagery according to the changing requirements of ongoing therapeutic work. In terms of the latter it offers a transtheoretical model for therapeutic work that employs mental imagery as the main means of communication and integration between the rational and imaginal perspectives. As discussed previously, clinical innovators who develop mental imagery work are prone to create idiosyncratic theoretical blends informed by pre-existing therapeutic approaches. This proposed framework does away with this by offering a locus of integration that is functional. Furthermore, it supports an interactive dialogic process between the rational and imaginal perspectives without privileging one over the other.

Hopefully, it also offers a way for therapists with affiliations to particular modalities to engage with the use of imagery from a more inclusive perspective. The interactive communicative model can be used to broaden out clinicians' understanding and use of mental imagery without violating the basic principles of their espoused therapeutic approach. In other words, this model offers a possibility of bridging the gap between empirically informed and phenomenologically informed practices with mental imagery.

However, it is important to bear in mind that all models are inherently limited; by representing knowledge of a system or process in a usable form, they simplify reality and do not include everything. Therefore, notwithstanding the potential usefulness of such a model, it is just as important to consider its disadvantages. First, it has to be acknowledged that the interactive communicative model is descriptive.

It does not offer an explanation for the therapeutic efficacy of mental imagery; instead, it delivers a modelling of the process. It does this by identifying particular functions operating in the therapeutic use of mental imagery and clarifying how one image can operate multi-functionally. However, although it lacks explanatory power, this does not detract from its usefulness. It is worth noting that another descriptive model in mental imagery, i.e. Ahsen's (1984) image/somatic/meaning model (ISM) of mental imagery discussed earlier, has proved to be a helpful way of understanding mental imagery in practice.

Second, one model cannot capture the totality of a complex phenomenon. Just as conceptual metaphors structure thinking along particular lines, so too does this model as it highlights particular aspects of the therapeutic use of mental imagery. In this case it brings to the fore one particularly important aspect, i.e. how mental images function as a means of communication between the rational and imaginal perspectives. In so doing, it casts into the shade other dimensions of therapeutic work with mental imagery. Therefore, even though it is proffered as a more inclusive framework, it can only ever be partial.

Finally, it is important to add a caveat: although the ground of this model appears to be valid and its basic structure displays coherence, the different functions identified here must be provisional. They have arisen out of the findings of one research study. Although these functions appear to capture the ways that mental images operate to communicate between the rational and imaginal perspectives, over time I would expect them to be refined and further conceptualised by other clinicians and theorists. One advantage of the model is that its structure does allow for an expansion or reduction or reconceptualisation of the functions without it being undermined or losing its internal coherence.

Conclusion

This transtheoretical model builds on and further develops simple distinctions generally observed in clinical practice. By so doing it appears to capture more of the complexity involved in the therapeutic use of mental imagery; particularly in relation to the way that images operate as potent communication agents allowing a productive and interactive dialogue between the rational and imaginal perspectives. Although in its early stages of development, its base and structure appear to be sound and it has the potential to offer a helpful more inclusive framework for practice. However, the test of a model's usefulness lies in its application to therapeutic practice. In Part Two I will discuss the contribution this model can make to more inclusive practice.

References

Ahsen A. (1984). 'ISM: The Triple Code model for imagery and psychophysiology', *Journal of Mental Imagery*, 8, 4: 15–42.

Bamber, M. (2004). '"The good, the bad and defenceless Jimmy" – a single case study of Schema Mode Therapy', *Clinical Psychology and Psychotherapy*, 11: 425–438.

Chestnut, W. J. (1971). 'Directed Imagery: A means for dealing with patient defensiveness', *Psychotherapy: Theory, Research, Practice, Training*, 8, 4: 325–327.
Clarkson, P. (2003). *The Therapeutic Relationship*, 2nd edn, Hoboken, NJ: Wiley-Blackwell.
Malamud, D. (1973). 'Self-confrontation Methods in Psychotherapy', *Psychotherapy: Theory, Research, Practice, Training*, 10, 2: 123–130.
Shorr, J. E. (1983). *Psychotherapy through Imagery*, 4th edn, New York: Thieme-Stratton Inc.
Thomas, V. (2011). *The Therapeutic Functions of Mental Imagery in Psychotherapy: Constructing a theoretical model*, Unpublished DPsych. thesis. Held in Middlesex University e-repository available at: http://eprints.mdx.ac.uk/10561

Part II
Towards more inclusive practice

Chapter 7

An introduction to the model in practice

In Part One of this book, I considered the wider historical and cultural contexts of mental imagery as a healing modality and the theoretical dimensions of developing more inclusive frameworks: now in Part Two the focus turns to how theory can translate into more inclusive practice. This chapter presents an introduction to how the interactive communicative model of mental imagery can be used to inform therapeutic practice. I begin by discussing the main principle that informs the application of the model, i.e. maintaining a dynamic balance between the rational and imaginal perspectives, and the implications of this for therapeutic work. Other important aspects of therapeutic work with mental imagery are also considered, including: the induced relaxation state; how both the therapist's and client's attitudes towards imagery influence the work; and issues of imagery interpretation. The second half of the chapter goes on to introduce and provide a context for the next three chapters in this part of the book; all three deliver guidance on using three particular framing images that represent important aspects of the self.

The main principle of the model in action

Generally, in the practice of mental imagery, clinical pioneers and theorists of different persuasions have tended to privilege either the rational or the imaginal perspective rather than treating them equally. One-sided approaches can be limiting. An over emphasis on the rational perspective can produce a therapeutic practice that is harnessed to the limited instrumental vision of the ego or conscious personality. Whereas an over-reliance on the imaginal can create ungrounded confusion because, as the anthropologist Price-Williams bluntly notes, 'The mythopoetic function can produce drivel as well as wisdom . . . ' (1992: 261). The interactive communicative model of mental imagery explicitly supports a balanced position, by viewing both perspectives as equally important. A more inclusive practice informed by this model aims to use imagery to facilitate an interactive productive communication process between the two perspectives taking care not to privilege either one.

A commitment to this principle should not result in holding a rigid position; applying it effectively requires insight and flexibility. How can the rational and imaginal perspectives work together – the rational with its curative and reparative agenda, and the imaginal with its hidden purposes that are revealed in the unfolding experiential processes of life? It is a dynamic balance; sometimes the requirements of one perspective needs to be foregrounded, at other times an over emphasis on one perspective needs to be challenged. There cannot be any prescriptive rules for this. It requires an ongoing responsive sensitivity to the requirements of the process.

This important principle of balance will be made evident throughout Part Two in the emphasis placed in this work on encouraging the client to engage in an ongoing dialogue between the two perspectives. This process is supported through therapist-facilitated inquiry. Standard examples of this would be: if the client reports changes to the image the therapist asks what this might be related to in the client's life; or if the client reports a significant change of mood, the therapist asks how this is represented in the imagery. In other words the client is encouraged to always consider the presenting issue from both perspectives.

One of the main implications of this principle in practice is that the therapist needs to actively work on behalf of maintaining the dynamic balance. This will involve having to advocate for the neglected perspective. Examples of this would be: if the client wants to impose ill-considered changes on the mental image, the therapist would urge further inquiry and reflection; or if the client wants to develop the imagery without reflecting on how this connects to their experience, the therapist would encourage making links between the two.

The conscious relaxation state

No work on the clinical application of mental imagery would be complete without addressing the issue of procedures for inducing relaxed states. It is generally acknowledged in the literature, '. . . . that one key to helping a patient capture the imagery experience is a state of relative relaxation' (Singer, 2006: 170). The everyday waking mind state is not regarded as conducive to consciously accessing the imaginal mind. Early pioneers recognised that there was a particular state of mind that allowed images to emerge; Happich (1932) called it the 'meditative zone'. This site where rational and imaginal perspectives meet, interact and communicate is an intermediate state where images can arise and be viewed, experienced and, if need be, worked with. The link between the two perspectives is explicitly acknowledged in some of the terms used for image-based psychotherapy, such as 'waking dreams'. In keeping with the deliberately transtheoretical position of the inclusive model, I will be using the term 'conscious relaxation state' throughout the practice section of this book. As this term implies, it is taken to mean a deliberate, purposive and conscious accessing of a receptive state of consciousness.

However, it is important to note that this intermediate zone is not a clearly marked and boundaried position but more a place on the continuum of consciousness between the rational and imaginal perspectives. The far end of the rational continuum would be abstract analytical reasoning and the far end of the imaginal being the dreaming mind during sleep. Initially, part of the therapist's job, when working with mental imagery, is to help clients to access this midpoint of the continuum where both perspectives meet and to stabilise their attention there. This task is often difficult for people at first and takes practice. Furthermore, another level of difficulty is posed by the additional demands made on the client; as, in this intermediate zone, they are also required to hold the two different perspectives at the same time. Engaging with the imaginal perspective, the person is required to not only symbolise outer experience but also open up to experiencing the embodied nature of imagery in the form of other sensory modalities, e.g. physical sensation and emotion. In other words clients need to experience the imaginal landscape or symbolisation as if it were actually happening to them, i.e. from a first-person perspective. And, at the same time, engaging with the rational perspective, clients are required to hold a third-person perspective and view the imagery experience as a phenomenon that they are actively exploring and interpreting. An example would be the building image presented in the following chapter. Here, clients are asked to visualise a representation of their psychological structure in the form of a building. They are then required to imagine themselves standing in front of the building and to experience it as if they are actually in the landscape. As they explore the building they are also being asked to maintain a detached perspective that understands the image as a symbolisation of themselves.

Accessing this zone in talking therapies is usually, but not always, facilitated through an initial relaxation procedure. This is because there appears to be a relationship between types of conscious states and degrees of physical relaxation. Closing the eyes and relaxing mind and body allows the point of conscious attention to shift towards the intermediate zone. The degree of relaxation determines where the attention is positioned on the continuum between the two perspectives. Leuner elaborates further:

> Precise observation has shown that there is a close functional correlation between the state of relaxation and the stimulated motif in the fantasy. As the fantasy becomes more active, the state of relaxation deepens; this, in turn, renders the fantasy increasingly more lively and colourful, which brings about a further deepening of the relaxation state.
>
> (1978: 127)

Working with both perspectives in this intermediate zone of consciousness requires a balanced access to both. However, this balancing act is dynamic, fluid and ever-changing. Attention moves back and forward, along the continuum, as therapeutic needs shift and change through the course of the work. Sometimes a deeper access to the imaginal realms is operating when a mental image is functioning as a conduit for the rising up into consciousness of repressed experience. At these points the client can display signs of being deeply engaged with and immersed in the contents of the imagery. Sometimes a much more detached relationship with the image is operating as the client is accessing the rational perspective to consider the nature and meaning of the image. This can be seen, for example, when the client is considering how to use the reparative function and make an appropriate alteration to the imagery. Part of the therapist's job will be helping the client manage this dynamic state of conscious relaxation in order to best facilitate therapeutic processes. This is a complex area of practice and requires experience and skills. Issues arising in working with conscious relaxation states are addressed further in Chapter 12.

The therapist's attitude

It is inevitable that the therapist's attitude to imagery will influence the work. Reading some of the historical literature on mental imagery in therapeutic work from a postmodern perspective, one cannot help but notice how little attention was paid to the wider contexts that influence subjective experiences. We are more sophisticated now, in this regard. At the level of the images themselves, it is important to understand that our own unresolved issues, blind spots and unreflected cultural conditioning will help to shape therapeutic processes. If the therapist's ego identifies with particular characteristics and values, this will impact on the approach to the client's images. Some images may be judged as sickly or ugly. Furthermore, some of the received ideas that therapists rely on in this work may be faulty. A pertinent example is given by Watkins (1984) who notes that a common reason for using techniques to increase ego strength is based upon the idea that frightening images arise because the ego is weak. She points out that it could just as easily be that images are frightening because the ego is too strong and this is the only way for the imaginal to get the message across.

At an even more fundamental level, the therapist will also have an attitude towards the imaginal itself and this will determine how the imagination is used. As discussed in earlier chapters, historically Western culture has devalued the imaginal. This has led to an unbalanced view with the likelihood that most Western-influenced people will automatically over-privilege the rational perspective. Watkins consistently warns against subjugating the imaginal to the will of the conscious personality. Both she and Hillman (1975, 1979) highlight the danger of viewing the imaginal from the ego's perspective. Examples of imposing particular agendas informed by the rational perspective can be seen in the work of some of the influential clinical innovators. Both Desoille (1966) and Leuner (1984) recommend procedures for bringing the productions of the imaginal under the control of the ego. Desoille explains what to do when clients produce fear-inducing imagery, '. . . I encourage the patient to subdue the beast or tame it with the powers of a magic wand (this suggestion is perfectly acceptable to most people)' (1966: 5). While Leuner recommends other strategies for when the client encounters frightening figures in their imagined landscapes – as discussed previously, he believes these figures represent cut-off aspects of the self such as the shadow and they can be pacified through offering them food.

Experience itself in working with mental imagery is another way of understanding our own attitudes towards imagination as well as providing insight into the nature of imagery processes. I agree with Shorr who emphasises that it is important for the '. . . expanding awareness of the therapist, he asks himself the same questions and imaginary situations that he proposes to the client' (1983: 246). Therefore it is strongly recommended that therapists who want to develop more inclusive imagery practice, particularly with the type of work presented in this book, engage in a programme of creative reflective practice to prepare themselves. Although no claims are made that the imagery work presented in this book is a new method, there is one feature in particular that marks it out from standard imagery approaches, i.e. the use of particular images as sites for ongoing work. The framing images presented in the following three chapters represent fundamental dimensions of human experience and, as such, can operate as long-term therapeutic process containers. It is important to gain some personal experience of how these images can operate and evolve over a period of time.

The client's attitude

There are two people in the therapeutic space: the client also brings a particular attitude to mental imagery that will have been shaped according to cultural and personal experience. These attitudes are likely to make themselves apparent as soon as the therapist introduces the possibility of using imagery as part of the therapeutic work. Most clients in Western clinical contexts will privilege the rational perspective. This position can often entail a somewhat defensive attitude towards the contents and productions of the imaginal perspective. Clients will often resist the notion that images are carrying information from a different part of the self, and will have a default setting of 'imaginary equals false'. Sometimes this resistance shows up in attempts to censor the arising images. At other times it will be revealed in the common question, "How do I know that I am not just making this up?" Although, it is important to note that clients' resistance to mental imagery could also be a form of fear – that in allowing a door to be opened, the person will come face-to-face with unmanageable emotions and realisations (see further discussion in Chapter 12).

Sometimes, but more rarely, the bias will operate in the opposite direction where the imaginal is privileged over the rational perspective. This entails a resistance to viewing the productions of the imaginal with discernment and discrimination. Sometimes, this can be associated with a naive engagement with New Age or esoteric practices that leads people towards over emphasising the role of the imaginal in their world. This bias can result in resistance to viewing the arising mental images from a detached viewpoint. Attempts by the therapist to introduce more of a rational perspective can be interpreted by clients as an attempt to disenchant their world. In these cases, it is important to advocate for a more balanced view as although everything can be read symbolically, this does not mean that everything should be taken as primarily symbolic. Sometimes this resistance to the rational perspective is a manifestation of escapism. I noted this tendency in my work with substance misusers. Some clients, particularly those who had a predilection for hallucinogenic drug use, initially responded enthusiastically to the idea of using imagery. However, enthusiasm would cool when it transpired that the work would involve the use of imagery to explore their relationship with the real world. It is also important to note here that imagery work is contra-indicated for people who find it difficult to distinguish between their own imagery productions and the real world and this will be discussed in more depth in Chapter 12.

Finally, there are other cultural perspectives on imagery that could also impact on the work. There is an overlap between therapeutic use of imagery and the use of mental images as spiritual and religious symbols. Clients with strong religious or spiritual affiliations will view therapeutic work using imagery through a particular frame of reference. Christian sects with fundamentalist leanings would offer an example of this as they tend to view working with symbols outside those specified within their tradition with suspicion. Clients with a non-Western heritage may identify this way of working as similar to indigenous traditional healing or shamanic practices and this may evoke fear. It goes without saying that it is important to respect different cultural, religious and personal views on the imaginal. Using mental images to foster an interactive communicative process between the rational and imaginal perspectives is not suited to everyone. Sometimes resistance to using imagery is an unconscious attitude that can be rectified simply through providing information and exploring the resistance. Sometimes the resistance needs to be respectfully accepted as an indication that this is not an appropriate method.

A matter of interpretation

Interpreting mental imagery is a contentious issue. Although, on balance, interpretation or making meaning of the image is generally regarded as part of the therapeutic work, not everyone would support its necessity. The oneirotherapists (Frétigny and Virel, 1968), for example, take the view that making connections between the images and daily life, although useful, is not necessary or sufficient for a cure – instead the cure arises through getting in touch with symbolised material and moving more freely within it.

How matters of interpretation are approached vary widely in terms of who does the interpretation and what is used to inform the interpretation. There are also differences in relation to whether the image is viewed as important in its own right, i.e. meaning-laden or is viewed merely as a symptom of something else. For example, historically in CBT approaches, intrusive imagery has been seen as just a symptom of a pathology. Only very recently have clinicians and researchers begun to consider whether the image is meaningful in its own right through providing an emotional bridge to the original cause. Approaches also differ regarding the emphasis placed on the latent or manifest content of the image. However, despite these significant variations, the three main schools discussed in earlier chapters of this book do agree on one fundamental point: that the images produced by the imaginal perspective can be understood as forms of communication.

A more inclusive approach to imagery interpretation would attempt to synthesise an interpretative approach from across the range of strategies and positions adopted by different schools and clinical innovators. In order to do this the client is regarded as the person best placed to understand the image. However, the therapist also has a role to play in terms of expanding the client's interpretative repertoire. Therefore, interpreting imagery is viewed as a collaborative process.

In order to support a more inclusive approach to making sense of the client's mental imagery, I would argue that there are three general levels of interpretation that need to be taken into account and these comprise the personal, cultural and universal dimensions of human experience. All of these dimensions need to be considered in the meaning-making process. These levels are defined as follows:

1 **The personal level**. The mental image is a personal individual representation that is unique to the individual and draws on personal memories, individual experience and personal beliefs.
2 **The cultural level**. The mental image is shaped by a wider cultural/historical context. The culture in which the individual lives will have a set of pictorial representations and symbols with particular meanings assigned to them. A good example of this is the different meanings assigned to colours – in the West, death and mourning are associated with black, whereas in China, the colour white is linked to funerals and bereavement.
3 **The universal level**. The meaning of the image is self-evidential without reference to the personal or the cultural. This level of interpretation is based on the understanding that there are some images (or aspects of imagery) that would have the same general meaning for everyone. Examples taken from the three framing images presented in the following chapters would be: a building that is collapsing indicates an unstable self-structure; a crossroads indicates a time of decision; and a plant that is blossoming indicates a time of positive self-expression and the beginning of a new cycle of growth.

How these levels of interpretation interrelate and operate in practice can be seen in case study illustrations and further discussion in the following chapters.

Furthermore, the model's focus on a balanced interactive communication process between the rational and imaginal perspectives is mirrored in the interpretative process. Any move towards understanding or decoding the communications delivered through mental images would aim for retaining a balance between the two perspectives. The commitment is to find a way to enhance the communication process between the two perspectives without distorting either one; one of the best descriptions in the literature can be found in the following account given by Watkins:

> Integration between the ego and the image may be seen more as a system of fine silk threads that pull both into connection and relation without destruction, without losing the nature of the image. In this sense interpretation is

not a reductive process, but more an attempt to pull into relation gently and through the dimension of time. Our associations to the image then do not lead us away but rather form the threads that bind the consciousness of the imaginal more closely to the real, the real to the imaginal. Interpretation in this way does not destroy and betray the image. It tries to aid the metaphor in continually placing the material and the imaginal side-by-side, with their own natures retained. By keeping both elements of the metaphor together, the interpretation allows for the material to be seen in relation to the imaginal background that couples it.

(1984: 139)

In practice, a more inclusive approach to interpretation would involve paying equal attention to both the imaginal and rational perspectives. In terms of the former, an interpretative strategy would be to allow the mental images to unfold on their own terms without conscious interference (sometimes termed the 'amplification of imagery'). In terms of the latter, the interpretative process would involve cognitive meaning-making informed by the client's experiential understanding and the therapist's considered questioning.

Introducing the imagery work presented in this book

Although this model can be applied to working with mental imagery in general, I am using the opportunity to present a particular type of work – one that I believe is particularly suited to showing the full range of the inclusive model in action. This clinical work is characterised by two main features. First it employs mental imagery as a primary means of facilitating therapeutic processes, a characteristic it shares with all imagery-based therapeutic approaches. Second, the mental images used here are representations of aspects of the self: these then become sites for ongoing work and are regarded as an integral part of the totality of the therapeutic process. This section introduces the following three chapters, each of which offer a detailed guide to working with specific representational images.

In this work the framing function of imagery is a means of providing both a starting point and also an ongoing reference point for therapeutic work. The clinical work employs particular framing images that are deemed to represent fundamental dimensions of human experience. Furthermore, these framing images are theorised as conceptual metaphors. The set of conceptual metaphors referring to the self that are presented in this book comprise: PEOPLE ARE BUILDINGS; PEOPLE ARE PLANTS; and LIFE IS A JOURNEY. In essence, conceptual metaphors are viewed as deep level schemas or 'experiential gestalts' that cognitively structure the individual's perception of self and self in relation to the environment; and, as discussed previously in Chapter 4, there is growing support for the possibility that these underlying schemas can be accurately represented by mental images. It would follow, then, that eliciting imagery representations of conceptual metaphors is a means of gaining information from the imaginal perspective regarding the way in which the individual's sense of self is shaped.

These mental images can provide a means for ongoing engagement with non-conscious cognitive processes. Once the procedure for employing the framing image has been undertaken, the image then offers a site for a productive interactive dialogue between the rational and imaginal perspectives. This image can be used through the course of the therapy as a way of both containing and tracking the client's therapeutic process over time. How this process unfolds and is managed is discussed at length in Chapter 11.

It is important to add that the guidance offered in this book is informed by a generally accepted principle in the field that it is important to embrace the embodied experience of imagery. It is worth noting that recent research into cognitive approaches to mental imagery seem to confirm the importance of first-person perspectives. Hackmann *et al.* conclude from the findings of a recent study, 'that to become happier, people need to use imagery from a first person ('field') perspective as if it is really happening to them, rather than a third person ('observer') detached perspective' (2011: 41).

The three framing images

The three framing images presented here, i.e. the building, the plant and the path, represent a body of work formulated from many years of clinical experience. When I began using them I was unaware of conceptual metaphor theory. They arose within the context of working with substance misusers who presented in crisis with complex needs that required immediate attention. I discovered that these basic framing images could provide a clear overview of the client's current state, indicating where the immediate therapeutic focus should be. And more than this, these concrete representations appeared to make sense to the clients; giving them a way to understand their predicament. It was very rare for me to need to explain how these framing images might map onto their experience. This ease of comprehension also lends weight to the argument that these images are conceptual metaphors arising out of embodied experience of being in the world.

As acknowledged in the introduction to this book, my clinical experience has inevitably shaped the work presented here. My formative clinical experience with complex traumatised clients can be detected in the focus on the importance of stabilisation and containment (as well as the fact that a significant proportion of the vignettes are taken from clinical work with this client group). Readers may also note a psychoeducational tendency in this work. Right from the start, it seemed important to me to convey to the substance-misusing clients that paying attention to their mental imagery could be a helpful resource for their recovery. The potential therapeutic benefits of training clients in imagery skills have been noted by other clinicians, such as Singer (2006). Over time, this notion of imagery as a tool has evolved into a general aim in my clinical work, i.e. to help the client become more able and skilled to see the real and the symbolic at one and the same time.

The structure of the three chapters on framing images

The following three chapters are all structured the same way: each one is designed to be a manual and reference text for working with a particular framing image. Furthermore each chapter is used explicitly to demonstrate the application of the interactive communicative model of mental imagery in practice. The chapters are organised along temporal lines. Different stages of the process are considered, starting with a detailed account of the initial diagnostic procedure, and then moving onto how the mental image can be developed and used in ongoing therapeutic work. In addition, specific functions of imagery are identified as especially pertinent to particular stages of the work. It is important to read these three chapters in conjunction with the more general guidance given on practice issues in Chapter 12. Each chapter is copiously illustrated mainly in the form of short case vignettes. Although it is important to note that these illustrations foreground the clients' imagery and are therefore only partial accounts of what happened in the therapy. It is understood that there are other factors, beside the use of mental imagery, that are implicated in helpful therapeutic processes.

Although these guidelines to practice are presented in a somewhat formulaic and prescriptive way, this work is unique to each individual and more fluid and flexible in practice. The guidance needs to be adapted to each individual client and the therapist's way of working. How this type of imagery can be integrated into ongoing work, as well as issues that can arise around its practice, are addressed in later chapters.

References

Desoille, R. (1966). *The Directed Daydream*, New York: Psychosynthesis Research Foundation.
Frétigny, R. and Virel, A. (1968). *L'Imagerie Mentale*, Geneva: Mont Blanc.
Hackmann, A., Bennett-Levy, J. and Holmes, E. A. (2011). *Oxford Guide to Imagery in Cognitive Therapy*, Oxford: Oxford University Press.
Happich, C. (1932). 'Das bildbewusstsein als ansatzstelle psychischer behandlung', *Zentreblatt Psychotherapie*, 5: 663–667.
Hillman, J. (1975). *Re-visioning Psychology*, New York: Harper & Row.
——. (1979). *The Dream and the Underworld*, New York: Harper Perennial.
Leuner, H. (1978). 'Basic Principles and Therapeutic Efficacy of Guided Affective Imagery (GAI)', in J.L. Singer and K.S. Pope (eds) *The Power of Human Imagination: New methods in psychotherapy*, 125–166, New York: Plenum Press.
——. (1984). *Guided Affective Imagery in Short-term Psychotherapy: The basic course*, New York: Thieme-Stratton Corp.
Price-Williams, D. (1992). 'The Waking Dream in Ethnographic Perspective', in B.Tedlock (ed) *Dreaming: Anthropological and psychological interpretations*, 246–262, Sante Fe, NM: School of American Research Press.
Shorr, J.E. (1983). *Psychotherapy through Imagery*, 4th edn, New York: Thieme-Stratton Inc.
Singer, J.L. (2006). *Imagery in Psychotherapy*, Washington, DC: American Psychological Association.
Watkins, M. (1984). *Waking Dreams*, 3rd revised edn, Dallas, TX: Spring Publications Inc.

Chapter 8

The building image

Buildings, usually in the form of a house, have been used in many different cultural traditions as ways of representing the self. A classic example from the Christian canon would be the biblical parable of the House on the Rock. The distinction made between the wise people who build their houses on solid ground and the unwise people who build on sand is intended to convey a message about the positive impact on the self through basing one's life on Christ's teachings. Another example from a different tradition would be the Chinese geomantic system, feng shui, where the physical house is viewed as a concrete symbol of the self (interested readers are referred to the American architect, Marcus [2006], who discusses this notion in depth from a Western perspective).

There are many references to the building or house image in the psychotherapeutic literature and they display a range of ways in which this image has been utilised in therapeutic work. Very early on, Freud (1900) considered the possibility that his patients' personalities were represented in the images of houses they reported from their dreams. His influence can be detected in Leuner's (1984) image-based psychotherapy. Leuner uses the building image as one of his main motifs; particular areas of the interior are emphasised such as the kitchen, which he theorises as revealing oral needs, and the bedroom because of its presumed correlation with sex. Jung (1969) was also particularly interested in this symbol: for him, the levels of the house represent the way that the structure of the individual self emerges out of the bedrock of the collective unconscious. His ideas were developed through his own personal experience of physically constructing a symbolic building on the shore of Lake Bollingen. Later on, humanistically informed clinicians drew on Jung's insights into house imagery and adapted some of his approaches in practice. However, their emphasis on the creative potential of images has resulted in a less structured approach to working with this image. For example, Hall *et al.*'s (2006) report that the main focus of their clinical work with the house image has been creative exploration of the objects found inside the house, some of which might include childhood toys or memorabilia.

As previously mentioned, in the clinical work presented here, the framing image of the building is understood as a pictorial representation of the conceptual metaphor, PEOPLE ARE BUILDINGS. There are many common linguistic metaphoric expressions in English that are generated by this conceptual metaphor. Examples would be: 'On hearing the dreadful news, she crumbled.'; 'He is cracking up under all that pressure.'; and, somewhat humourously, 'All the lights are on, but no one's at home.' According to conceptual metaphor theory (Lakoff and Johnson, 2003), a particular metaphor of the self will illuminate some aspects of the total phenomenon and hide others. In this case it brings to the fore structural aspects of the self. It can give some indications as to how the personality and ego structure formed up in relation to early life conditions and how subsequent life experience impacted on the adult self structure. Other aspects of the self such as agency and the cyclical processes of growth and development are obscured (these aspects are illuminated by different conceptual metaphors presented in the two following chapters). Because of the power of this framing image to disclose fundamental structural issues, the focus in the therapy tends to be on the building itself and not on it as merely the container for dynamics or objects. In this chapter I will identify the main principles and guidelines for working with this structural representation including an overview of some of the main features of this mental image. Some indication is given throughout in the discussion and the clinical vignettes of the ways that the different functions of imagery are used to facilitate therapeutic work.

Overview

Early on in my clinical work, the image of the building presented itself as a means for getting more understanding of the psychological condition of substance misusers entering a crisis intervention unit. Inevitably, these clients had become destabilised through chronic substance misuse and the building images they reported usually revealed structural damage. One of the advantages of using this framing image was that it offered not only a concrete mapping of their difficulties but also revealed where the reconstruction work needed to focus. As I broadened out to use this framing image with other client groups, it continued to be a very valuable means of delivering insights into clients' presenting issues as well as a way to facilitate ongoing developmental and therapeutic processes.

The building images that clients produce are as individual as the people themselves. However, despite the wide range of types of buildings, this framing image will give some immediate indications about the person's psychological stability and containment; for example, collapsing buildings and broken-down walls would be self-evidential signs of serious psychological problems in this regard. The image can shed light on two aspects of the person's psychological structure. First, it can show how the personality structure formed up through early life experience. Difficult formative conditions such as childhood trauma and a lack of early emotional security can show up as distorted building structures. Childhoods where the parents were psychologically or physically missing can be represented as incomplete houses. Second it can also show the impact of later life experience, both positive as well as negative, on the person's psychological structure. Common examples of the former would be extensions to the building or refurbishments.

Examples of the latter would be some of the common patterns seen in substance misusers' representations of abandoned and derelict buildings indicating chronic self-neglect.

General guidelines for working with the building image

As the building image is a representation of a fundamental dimension of the person's self, i.e. psychological structure, stability and boundaries, it requires careful and skilful handling. The following points have arisen out of clinical observation and practice and are offered as general principles to guide practice.

- **Ensuring and promoting the stability of the structure.** This is the main principle guiding the work. The focus must always be on ensuring the stability of the building. Parts of the building may appear to be in a precarious condition such as collapsing walls or subsiding foundations. If this is the case, it is important to work with the client to create reinforcing imagery to temporarily stabilise the structure. Any major reconstruction work is a long-term project that requires a clear plan that takes into account the importance of containing the therapeutic process. A rash intervention can further destabilise conditions.
- **Damage limitation.** If there are problems or damage to the structure that, if left, will result in deteriorating conditions then it is important to use reparative imagery interventions that will temporarily limit the damage. Examples of this would be large holes in the roof that can be temporarily covered up with a tarpaulin, or abandoned houses that can be secured with a metal safety fence (these procedures are described later in detail).
- **Clarity about what can and cannot be achieved.** The type of structure (such as different kinds of buildings, their basic size and shape) is a given and needs to be accepted. There are occasions when radical changes take place to the type of structure, for example after sustained transformational personal development; however, these are rare and they go beyond the remit of this book. Distortions in the structure nearly always represent early formative experiences and conditioning, and these need to be approached with great care. Any work here will inevitably activate very problematic psychological material for the client. It is best to avoid any work on fundamental structural problems unless the person is equipped to deal with this and is familiar with the process of therapy and has a lot of support in place. The guideline to observe here is to only intervene at this level if the structure of the building is threatened and requires some temporary stabilisation (as indicated earlier).
- **Construction not destruction.** It is important that no work is engaged with that involves any destruction of pre-existing features of the house. The building operates over time as a container of the self and making rash alterations to it, in particular, destroying any aspect of it, will have unforeseen and possibly

negative consequences for the person. It is important to dissuade clients from attempting to destroy features of the building they may not like. The building can begin to display alterations but this tends to happen in ongoing work and it reflects changes that are happening to the person (see the case vignettes for examples of this process). The process of improving or developing the building is a synthesis between the rational and imaginal perspectives. Conscious considered reparative interventions are integrated with the emerging requirements of an unfolding creative process not subject to the control of the ego.

- **Emphasising/maintaining the boundary between the exterior/interior of the structure.** There is an obvious distinction between the outside and the inside of the building. The exterior deals with the basic containment of the self and how it is positioned in terms of its relationship to the external world. There are three aspects involved. First, there are the basic features of the self-structure, e.g. size and type of building, condition and structural stability. Second, there is the presentation of self, e.g. defensive (fortified building), open/closed (windows and doors), false persona (when the façade is significantly different to the rest of the building). And third, it can show the relationship to the environment, such as embedded in a social matrix (e.g. terraced house), or self-sufficient and independent (e.g. detached house). In other words the exterior is the publicly perceived self-structure. However, the inside of the building represents the interior domain of the person's psychological structure, in other words, the private self. I believe it is important to respect this distinction in therapeutic practice. When clients are viewing their representational building image while in a conscious relaxed state, it can become more difficult for them to hold boundaries. If the therapist suggests going inside the building, the client might not be able to refuse. This is particularly relevant to working with clients who have a history of abuse. Therefore I would usually wait until the client initiates an exploration of the building interior (although, occasionally, if appropriate, I might suggest a halfway measure such as looking through a window).

The first stage of the work

In order to use the building image effectively it is important to gain as detailed an image as possible. The first step is to use the framing function of imagery that will allow the client to map their psychological structure onto the given template of a building. Clients can then be facilitated in some initial exploration of the meaning of their image. This diagnostic procedure will usually take up a whole session and it will lay the grounds for ongoing work.

Bringing the building into view: using the framing function

The following procedure is designed to elicit a clear and detailed initial picture of the exterior of the building. Before commencing, it is best to discuss with clients the concept of translating their sense of themselves into a picture of a building or house. It is important to explain the reason for doing this, i.e. because it can give a very clear overview of their current inner state and reveal where the therapeutic work needs to focus. Sometimes people might think that this method sounds too complicated so it is a good idea to reassure them that this is a simple process. I would usually emphasise that the aim initially is to gain a picture of the outer structure just to see what condition it is in and if it needs any particular attention. It is also important to let clients know that they can stop the procedure at any time if they are feeling uncomfortable (for further elaboration on preparing the client for imagery work please see Chapter 12).

Adapt the following procedure to the individual client. When instructions are followed by bracketed terms, this indicates that you will need to select one that is suitable for your client. Suggested verbatim instructions or questions are given in quotation marks.

1. Make sure the client is sitting comfortably with uncrossed legs and both feet on the floor. Ask them to close their eyes. Then take them through a simple relaxation procedure of your choosing.
2. Ask them to imagine that they are standing somewhere outside with their feet firmly on the ground (if they imagine being inside a building ask them to come outside as it is much more difficult to survey the structure from within). Suggest to them that it is neutral territory and that for the time being the surroundings are unclear. It is not an environment they recognise. Make sure they are imagining themselves actually being there, i.e. not viewing themselves from a third person perspective. I will say something along the lines of: 'Be in your body. Imagine you can sense the ground under your feet.'
3. Instruct them to silently ask their subconscious mind (inner self, etc.) to begin to show them a house or building directly in front of them that represents their inner psychological structure or, put in simpler terms, what they would look like in the form of a building. Tell them not to worry if it is vague at the beginning because you will help them to see it more clearly. Tell them to accept the first picture that comes and not to censor it. Give them a couple of minutes to begin to get a sense of the building.
4. Tell them you are now going to ask some questions to get a clearer picture of the building. Reassure them at this point that they are not to worry about getting it right but instead just to allow their imagination to produce the image. Adapt the following questions as required to elicit a basic picture.

'Does the building seem big or small?'
'Does the building feel modern or old?'
'What kind of building does it seem to be? Is it a house or a different kind of building?'
'Does it appear lived in or uninhabited?'
'Is it by itself or with others?'
'What kind of landscape is it in?'

90 Towards more inclusive practice

By the end of this stage, clients will usually have produced a reasonably clear picture of their inner representational building. However, this is not always the case. Sometimes clients may produce a picture of a house that exists in reality, e.g. their childhood home. If this is the case, it could be one of two possibilities. You will need to very gently explore the significance of this. First, it could be that a very important emotional attachment or trauma is being indicated here that will require therapeutic attention. This issue needs to be addressed and any work on a representational image of the internal structure postponed until this is dealt with. In this case, the rest of the survey procedure should not be followed. Another possibility is that the imaginal perspective has selected this image of a known building because it works as a symbolic expression of the person's inner structure. In this case you can continue with the rest of the survey. However, using an image of a real house does complicate matters, as it can be confusing for the person to undertake imagery work with a picture of a building that exists in reality.

Something else that might occur at this stage is the complete absence of an image of a representational building. Again there are two possibilities. The first is that the inner structure cannot be symbolised by a conventional structure. Gently inquire if the client is getting hints of a very different kind of structure but is dismissing it because it does not fit with the general idea of a house. Help them focus on this and bring it more into view. Then adapt the following survey appropriately. The other possibility is that there is strong internal resistance to visualising a representational structure; in this case I would usually gently suggest that we abandon the procedure for the time being.

5 Finally get some sense of the client's initial response and main emotional response to the structure. As a prompt it can sometimes be helpful to remind them that this image represents them. This step is important because it will indicate the fundamental attitude clients are holding towards themselves.

6 Suggest to the client that they are going to have a closer look at their building in order to see it from all angles and to note what condition it is in. Reassure them that whatever they see will be useful information. Direct the survey in the following order, but adapt it as appropriate if the structure is radically different from a house.

- Look at the front of the building and check the fabric of walls for holes and cracks or any unusual features. Where is the main entrance to the building – what form does it take? Where are the windows and what condition are they in?
- Go all around the outside of the building checking the condition of the sides and back. Take note of any unusual features. Sometimes clients report that they cannot gain access to a part of the external structure, e.g. they might not be able to get around to the back. In such cases it is important to accept that there is some kind of resistance operating and to

just work with as much of the building that can be visualised (see Chapter 12 for a more detailed discussion about not over-riding the client's defences). Note if there are significant differences between the back and the front of the building.
- Check the structure and state of the top of the building. In order to do this I might suggest that clients imagine themselves floating up above the building and looking down on it. Get them to clarify if the roof covering is solid or if there are holes or gaps.
- Take note of any unusual features. There might be outbuildings or extensions to the building for example. If so ask the client to include these in the initial survey to get a clear picture.
- You can ask clients if they can get a sense of what the foundations of the building are like. But don't press this because it is unlikely to be apparent in a pictorial representation of the outside of the building.
- If appropriate, it is also worth asking clients if they get any sense whether the building appears to be inhabited or not.

7   At this point, if appropriate, it can be useful to ask clients what aspect or feature of the building stands out for them or is drawing their attention. This will usually indicate an aspect of the self that needs attention or exploration. There are many possible responses to this question ranging from quite general feelings that are evoked by the building through to noticing quite specific concrete features such as a very small door or a damaged roof. In these latter cases it can be helpful to get clients to begin to make some links between this particular feature and themselves. I would try some general questions along the lines of: 'What do you think that . . . . . . is connected to in your life?'; 'Can you get any sense of how long that. . . . . . has been like that?'; or 'How do you think that. . . . . . shows up in your current life?' Bear in mind that this is a challenging task as you are asking someone to hold both the rational and imaginal perspectives at the same time and make connections between the two. Therefore if the person struggles to make these links it is best to postpone this until a discussion can take place after the initial diagnostic imagery procedure is over.

8   When the basic survey is complete, advise the client that the process is coming to a close. Ask them to stand in front of the building. It can be useful to give them a minute or so visualising the front of the building. Then instruct them to turn around with their back to the building and create a blank screen.

9   Instruct clients to switch their attention back to their physical body and let them know that you are going to bring them back into their everyday state of mind. Then use a simple standard procedure for bringing their awareness back to everyday consciousness.

10 Finally, at the completion of the procedure, it can be helpful to summarise their account of the building as a preparation for discussion of the experience.

Starting to work with the building: the diagnostic and reparative functions

After the initial survey has been undertaken, the first steps in the work with the image will involve making meaning of the building in relation to the client's self. In other words there will be an emphasis on the diagnostic function. The reparative function may also come to the fore if there are any significant problems identified in the external structure that either need immediate attention or some longer-term repair or rebuilding work.

In this section I will discuss the ways in which clients can be facilitated in using the building image as a means of increasing self-understanding as well as how to use the image as a site for therapeutic work. This discussion will include a consideration of common aspects of the exterior illustrated by case vignettes. Some self-evident interpretations are suggested for these common aspects although these are offered only as potential starting points for meaning making. As I have noted previously, interpretation of mental imagery is a complex process that needs to take into consideration the personal, cultural and universal dimensions of human experience.

This section starts with the important matter of the client's attitude towards the building as this will impact on therapeutic work and process. It then goes on to offer some general comments on the potential range and variety of building images before focusing in more depth on some common issues that can require attention and therapeutic work.

Attitude to the building

The attitude held towards the self shows up clearly when getting a client to view the building image. Initially, there is often a degree of surprise expressed at what they visualise or some difficulty in accepting the image as an accurate representation of the self. However, this response is not usually reflective of clients' attitudes towards themselves but, instead, reflects a lack of trust in the truth of their imagination. This common reaction is the reason why I usually wait until part of the way through the procedure of eliciting the building image before I directly ask clients how they are responding to the building. By this point, the initial culturally constituted disbelieving response has often faded away. As might be expected, a wide range of attitudes towards the building can be reported, from outright rejection to warmth. The degree to which clients report acceptance of their building image is directly correlated to their engagement with the therapeutic work with the image as illustrated in the following vignette, titled *Resisting the Building*.

> Julia, a highly intelligent and determined woman in her early forties, initially came for counselling because she had experienced bullying at her workplace over a number of years and this had undermined her self-confidence. She reported two building images: one was a 'beautiful' spacious white building that was floating high in the sky; whereas the other one was an 'ugly', damaged

brick building on the ground. It soon became clear that the white building represented an idealised self with the perfect life that Julia hankered after. The brick building was the self that had felt rejected as a child and had been further damaged through her recent work experience. It took a considerable amount of persuasion on my part over the course of a year to help Julia refocus her energies on the real building and begin the process of self-acceptance. Little by little, she worked on re-establishing firmer foundations based on self-acceptance and rebuilding her sense of self that had been damaged over the previous years. This was difficult work and required her to relive painful childhood experiences and process the accompanying release of uncomfortable emotions. However, her commitment to allowing repressed memories to resurface began to pay off in her day to day life as she reported an increasing sense of serenity. This progress was reflected in her building as, bit by bit, the foundations were reconstructed and the top of the walls were rebuilt. However, for a long time, the image of the white building still remained, floating tantalisingly out-of-reach and, in times of stress, Julia would often return to her wish to escape from her self and find a new life and way of being somewhere else.

General comments on the building image

As mentioned earlier, a very wide variety of possible building images can be reported. In addition, all aspects of the building image offer the potential for further exploration and developing more insight into the self. It is impossible to predict if any of these features will be an important focus for the client – the unfolding process of work with the building is unique for each individual.

There are some more general aspects of the image that would usually be noted in the initial discussions. One of these would be the size of the building. I have observed a range from very small shacks through to very large complex structures such as castles. Leuner suggests that large buildings such as mansions are expressions of unconscious wishes and this equates to narcissism. However, this interpretation does not accord with my own clinical experience. In general, when clients have reported large buildings they have usually expressed surprise and often questioned these representations as real reflections of themselves.

How the building is positioned in its surroundings can also display a wide range of possibilities. At one end of the spectrum are buildings that are clearly closely related to others such as terraced houses and at the other end are buildings standing by themselves isolated in otherwise empty landscapes. The self-evident interpretation would point to the way in which someone experiences themselves in relation to the surrounding society.

Different types of buildings are reported, although, in my experience, the domestic house is the most common representation. Naturally, these domestic dwellings reflect cultural origins. Working with clients from different cultures requires the therapist to check out if their clients' building representation reflects common features found in their own culture or whether it departs from this norm in any particular and significant way. When the building image departs from a standard dwelling place, such as tower blocks, industrial buildings, lighthouses, offices, etc. (these are some examples I have seen) it is worth at some point exploring with the client the potential meaning of this. Heavily fortified buildings, such as castles, would be an example. In these cases it would seem that a defensive self-structure formed up in response to conditions that threatened the developing self in some way. This representation would also have implications for the therapeutic process as clients who report such images often perceive attempts to explore the building as potentially threatening. Sometimes the age of the building is significant. Quite often I have noted that clients produce buildings that belong to the decade of their actual birth. Sometimes buildings from earlier periods are associated with a strong ancestral influence on the person or an influential figure such as a grandparent.

The condition of the building

An important question to consider in regards to the initial survey of the building is its condition particularly with regard to stability and repair. Working with substance misusers in crisis, it was common for me to receive descriptions of buildings in a very poor state of repair and, in some cases, with nothing but ruins remaining. Such extreme depictions are less likely in the general client population. However, other experiences and different types of chronic conditions can also have detrimental impacts on the condition of the building.

The most important question when the client reports damaged or poor conditions is whether this requires immediate reparative intervention. If the building appears stable an assessment can be made of work that could be undertaken at some point if appropriate. The following section discusses the state of the building in the light of this question. It begins with highly structurally compromised buildings and then moves on to consider issues with the state of different parts of the exterior of the building.

Highly-compromised buildings would include all building representations that are in parlous states and are uninhabitable in their current condition. If clients report such a compromised building they are also likely to be presenting significant levels of anxiety and self-reported instability. It is often a shock for people to have their intuitive sense of their poor state confirmed in such a concrete way. As a rule of thumb, ruins indicate long-term neglect, collapsed buildings suggest a psychological breakdown and half-complete buildings suggest interrupted or arrested childhood development. If a client produces an image of a highly compromised building an assessment needs to be made regarding the suitability of imagery as a therapeutic method. Sometimes, if the client's core issues are linked to very early formative conditions, other approaches would be indicated such as long-term psychodynamically informed therapy. These assessments all depend on the therapist's skill and judgment. To emphasise the importance of therapist expertise, I am including an example of what can happen if imagery is used without a good enough understanding of psychotherapeutic processes. In the following vignette, titled *The Incomplete House*, I made a mistake very early on in my clinical work with imagery when I underestimated the power of defences laid down in childhood.

James was a talented and articulate man in his early forties who had been a heavy drinker and heroin user for the previous ten years. He described his life as having been successful and exciting in his twenties when he worked as a musician. However, when he was thirty his life had gone downhill after the ending of a long-term relationship. He had entered the rehabilitation programme because he wanted to get his life back on track. He described his inner building as an unfinished terraced house from the 1960s: the shell of the building was there but there were no doors or windows or interior rooms. He made the link between work stopping on the building and being sent into care as a young boy when his parents split up. He was very interested in this image of the incomplete house and said that he was ready to do the necessary psychological work to begin to complete it. However, after an initial and enthusiastic start, it slowly became clear that the work on the house was triggering problematic emotional processes for James. As he paid attention to the building image, he started to re-experience repressed memories of going into care (an example of the processing function of mental imagery in operation). One of the main stumbling blocks in the work was his resistance to accepting his feelings of rage towards his parents. His engagement with the visualization work became half-hearted and, meanwhile, his unconscious anger expressed itself more and more in a refusal to comply with the rehabilitation programme. I was sorry but not surprised when he left the rehabilitation unit halfway through the programme.

On reflection I can see now that I had been lulled into a false sense of security by both the apparent straightforwardness of the image of an incomplete terraced house and also by James's initial determination to work on completing it. I had underestimated the extent of the buried rage that would arise. I also did not fully take into consideration what completing the house might actually mean: he would lose the false security of being incomplete and, in essence, would have to let go of his infantile attachment to his parents. The only thing that can be said in favour of this piece of work is that by the time he left he had created an interior structure with dividing walls within the originally empty shell of a house which indicated to me that some development had taken place.

Although the example above illustrates the importance of caution with regard to therapeutic work with highly compromised buildings, there are some immediate interventions that are safe to use. These strategies are described in detail in the later section on the process management function. They include:

- helping clients increase their sense of stability and containment by visualising a simple temporary inhabitable structure next to the compromised building;
- helping clients feel more secure by visualising some form of protection around the compromised building, e.g. a temporary security fence.

Uninhabited buildings are often damaged or in poor repair. I recall this was a very common theme in the building images produced by my clients who were chronic opiate users. These uninhabitable deteriorated structures eloquently convey the experience of chronic self-neglect. Very often the initial therapeutic task was to persuade these clients to take some responsibility for their structures. Even if they did not want to repair the damage (this often equated in outer world experience of refusing an offer of a place in a rehabilitation programme) I would try to persuade them, at the very least, to visualise some kind of safety fence erected around the structure to keep it secure for the time being (this particular process management intervention is described in a later section).

In the general client population it is far less common to see such deteriorated structures. However, the theme of abandoning the self may still be operating. This is why I usually check with clients in the initial diagnostic process if they get a sense whether their building is inhabited or not (although sometimes this does not become clear until the person goes inside; see the vignette, titled *The Light in the Hallway*, presented later in the chapter). The following vignette, titled *The Abandoned Victorian House*, illustrates this theme.

> June, a resourceful woman in her mid-sixties, originally came to therapy because she had recently ended a difficult relationship with a substance-misusing partner. She wanted to look at her pattern of attracting abusive men and find a way of developing more self-confidence. June had had periods of long-term therapy and possessed considerable insight into the origins of her presenting issue – an unhappy childhood in a home dominated by a controlling alcoholic father followed by the suicide of her mother when June was a young teenager. Her building image was a large detached Victorian house that was showing signs of long-term neglect: there were holes in the roof and the brickwork needed repointing. Rainwater had come in through the gaps and the inside of the building was damp. However, apart from that, the building appeared to be structurally sound. June believed that the neglect had begun very early on when she was a baby – her earliest memories were of trying to look after her very depressed mother. When I inquired how long the building had been uninhabited, she had a very emotional response and replied that it dated back to the day her mother had died. The sense of having been abandoned appeared to be the dominant emotional theme of June's life.
>
> Yet, the building image itself conveyed something positive; despite the abandonment and neglect, it was still structurally sound and solid. June resonated with this more hopeful perspective and made links to her strength and resilience. She had brought up two children who were settled and happy, and furthermore, despite chronic depression, she had not repeated the family history of alcoholism and drug dependency (her brother had been dependent on heroin for many years). She agreed that the building could be repaired, and she visualised scaffolding being erected around the outside walls. She made a link between the scaffolding and her intermittent spiritual practices and she acknowledged that she needed to discipline herself to a daily regime of meditation and yoga. However, despite feeling more

hopeful, June was under no illusions of how difficult it would be to finally accept her mother's death and she was convinced that she would never be able to get beyond this defining trauma of her adolescence.

Roof damage is not unusual. As mentioned in the preface, my observation that crack cocaine misuse was associated with a pattern in the building image of roof damage confirmed for me the self-evident interpretation that the roof relates to the head and/or mind. In these particular drug misuse cases, a chronically over stimulated mind starts to break down leading to negative mental states such as paranoia (a common symptom of crack cocaine misuse). Stimulant misuse is not the only cause of roof problems. Any physiological trauma to the head or traumatic psychological experience that impacts on the person's mind will also leave its mark in a similar way (see the vignette above). However, no matter what the original cause, holes in the roof are problematic because, left unattended, they can lead to deteriorating conditions within the building due to the interior being exposed to the elements. A simple reparative intervention of getting the client to visualise a tarpaulin covering the roof can be a very helpful strategy. This intervention is illustrated in the following vignette, titled *The Damaged Roof*, of the impact of abusive parenting in early childhood.

I worked with Amelia, a sensitive and perceptive woman in her mid-thirties, over a period of several years. She was the only child of a very controlling father and a passive mother. Her father had focused all of his energies on molding his child to fit his notion of a perfect daughter. Amelia reported that as far back as she could remember she had been locked into a battle of wills with her father who attempted to control every detail of her life. This had taken its toll on my client who had experienced bouts of anorexia and a lengthy stay in a unit for personality disordered patients. A lot of our work together was focused on strengthening and repairing her sense of self. Her building image was a large fortified mansion that had originally shown up as deserted and uninhabitable. Part of the roof was missing and Amelia equated that to the mental damage she had experienced from not being able to express her real self in any form that would be acceptable to her father. This damage was experienced as a disturbing confusion or a gap in her mind. Although she had good intellectual skills, in challenging circumstances she would find it difficult to apply her mind in any constructive way. In the early stages of our work together Amelia agreed to temporarily cover the damaged roof with a blue tarpaulin. This protected the building while she focused on dealing with her overwhelming emotional states. When she had done enough work to be able to regulate her emotional self, she was ready to confront the way in which her mind had been damaged in her childhood. At that point, several years later, she felt ready to attend to the repair of the roof.

NB: Two further extracts taken from Amelia's work are presented later on (*The Sad Little Girl in the Basement* in this chapter, and *Three Framing Images* in Chapter 11).

The front and back of the building are significant aspects of the person's structure. The self-evident interpretation would suggest that the front of the building is the façade (or persona) that we present to the world. If this is so, then the back of the building would represent, conversely, the more private self. I have noted that it is not unusual for clients to report that the back of the building was not quite what they would expect from viewing the front. These differences may or may not be a focus for exploration. However, sometimes the mismatch between the public and the private self is so great that it becomes an important focus of the therapeutic work as illustrated in the following vignette, titled *An Imposing Façade* – a highly condensed account of in-depth work carried out over three sessions on a complex structural distortion. I must emphasise that I had already established a good therapeutic relationship with this client during previous admissions to the crisis intervention agency and was familiar with his life story. He had also been through two therapeutic treatment programmes and had a good understanding of his emotional issues.

> James, an articulate and charismatic thirty-five-year-old man from the North of England, had been misusing crack cocaine and benzodiazepines for many years. He was admitted to the crisis centre when a recent relapse had turned into chaotic poly-drug misuse and a suicidal state of mind. I was concerned about the depth of his despair and therefore suggested to him that it might be time to look at the stability and solidity of his internal psychological structure. His first view of the inner house took the form of an imposing villa fronting onto a main street of what, initially, appeared to be a 19th-century mid west American town. The building had a front porch with two pillars and a coat of arms above the portico. However on closer inspection the house seemed to be just a façade and the entire street was an artificial construct just like a film set. It was impossible to walk through the main door of the front of the building and James was nervous about going around the back to see what lay behind it. James related to this façade and described his awkwardness with people who appeared to be impressed by his 'front' and his inability to let people in to the real person for fear they might reject him. When he overcame his initial reluctance to inquire any further, he plucked up courage to see what, if anything, lay behind the façade. When he did so, he discovered another building hidden behind the film set – his grandmother's house where he had lived on and off from the age of eight (he had been sent to live there due to family problems). He reported that he could see his eight-year-old self with his grandmother inside the house, and this evoked difficult emotions from that time leaving him feeling exposed and vulnerable. He agreed that unresolved psychological problems resulted from those early experiences, and the inner house clearly demonstrated to him how he had created a façade to protect himself.
>
> Yet, this left him in a quandary because, in this state, the house was not inhabitable. Early conditions had created a structural distortion that could not be easily changed: the façade could not be dismantled because he would

be too exposed and the inner structure of his grandmother's house was not suitable for his adult self. James said that he felt this was a very clear symbolisation of his current state and that, even though he had done a lot of therapeutic work on his childhood, he had never felt able to grow and develop. I discussed with him the implications of undergoing work on a distortion in the structure and how important it was that he prepared himself for the very difficult emotions that would inevitably arise.

Bearing in mind James's fragile psychological state, my main concern at this point was to help him increase his sense of security and stability. Therefore, I suggested to him that it might be helpful to create a temporary structure near his inner house that would serve as a secure holding place where he could then, over time, begin to come to terms with the events of his childhood.

NB: An account of how James created and made use of a temporary structure is given in another vignette (titled *The Gate Keeper's Cottage*) towards the end of this chapter.

The foundations of the building represents the base on which the whole structure stands and the self-evident interpretation would link this to early formative conditions. It is very unusual in my clinical experience for an initial survey of the building to clearly identify problems with the foundations. In most cases, the reality is that some kind of base has formed up that allows a structure to build on it. If there have been problems in the foundations this appears to be reflected in a compensating structural distortion. Doing any work on the foundations needs to be very carefully considered for similar reasons to the caveats given regarding highly compromised buildings. Directive interventions at this foundational level are likely to be experienced as disturbing and destabilising. However, this is not to say that changes cannot happen at this level and I will return to some consideration of how work on the foundations and structural distortions can unfold in the later section on developing work with the building.

Windows are linked to the person's capacity for perception. Of course, windows operate in two directions also allowing others to look in. This link is reflected in common expressions such as, 'The eyes are windows to the soul.' I always pay attention to the state and condition of the windows as well as their size and position in the building. Sometimes a simple reparative intervention can be made such as cleaning dirty windows. Sometimes the size and structure of the windows change over time. When the latter happens it is usually indicative of changes happening to the way the person is perceiving the world. In the following vignette, titled *The Cracked Window*, the damaged state of a window indicated how a traumatic event had altered the way the client perceived the world.

Graham was a stoic and resilient man who had taken on the role of looking after his two young children at home while his partner went out to work. His elder daughter had a chronic illness and she required a great deal of physical care. He sought psychotherapy because, due to anxiety and stress, he was finding it increasingly difficult to regulate his emotional states. His building image took the form of a large four-storied mansion block set at the corner of the street. Although structurally sound, there were holes in the roof and it was uninhabited. Graham also reported that one of the windows on the ground floor was damaged. He felt that it had been broken for a while and made an immediate connection with the 'shattering' experience of receiving the diagnosis of his daughter's serious health condition shortly after her birth. He said that this experience had changed the way he viewed the world and that this was a contributory factor in the emotional difficulties he was currently experiencing. However, although the window clearly needed attention, both of us agreed that a more pressing issue was the damaged roof that needed repairing. I suggested that he might consider covering over the window as a temporary measure – a reparative intervention aimed at reducing the disturbance he was feeling. Graham visualised the window being boarded up. He commented that although this spoiled the aesthetics of the facade, it did give him a sense of more security and protection. He also felt more reassured that he would be able to return to mend this broken window when the time was right.

The door or doorway is particularly significant. It will show, in general, how people manage the boundary between their private interior self and the outer world. If the door is broken or missing it will require immediate attention in the form of a reparative intervention to secure the building. Without a functioning door, there is the potential for the person to be invaded, sometimes literally by other people or more subtly by other external influences. As a matter of interest, anecdotal reports from colleagues suggest there may be a pattern emerging that is connected to excessive use of social media. In these cases clients have been producing building images where recent changes have occurred to the entrances – once solid doors have either become flimsy curtains or they have vanished leaving completely open doorways. This imagery representation appears to be capturing one of the potential detrimental consequences of indiscriminate digitally mediated communication, i.e. an erosion of a clearly managed boundary between self and the external world.

More specifically, the door of the building can deliver insights into how someone communicates, particularly verbally. The following vignette, titled *The Tower Block with a Side Door*, illustrates how useful it can be for clarifying difficulties with communication.

> Jenny, a young woman in her early twenties, was making a determined effort to recover from a steadily increasing heroin dependency. She came across as spirited and feisty; however, it was also clear that underneath this tough exterior lay confusion and sadness. Jenny described her inner building as a tower block that had been deserted for five years since the death of her father. Although the general condition of the building had deteriorated somewhat due to neglect, no major structural problems were evident. There was,

though, one unusual feature present – the main entrance door was not positioned at the front of the building where one would naturally expect it to be, instead it was round at the side.

As Jenny talked about her upbringing over the next few sessions, the odd position of the main entrance to her building began to make more sense. Her father and mother divorced when Jenny was a child and her mother remarried shortly afterwards. The contrast between Jenny's father and her stepfather was pronounced. She described her father as a rebellious unconventional man who treated her as a friend: her stepfather was a 'bully' who ruled the home. During her teenage years she would stay with her father in Germany for the summer holidays enjoying his somewhat chaotic heavy drinking lifestyle, and then she would return to the authoritarian regime of her stepfather. This had left her with a deep conflict towards authority. She said that she was always rebellious towards authority figures but, at the same time, she also felt intimidated. This paradox was apparent in her reactions to the authority of the rehabilitation centre staff. It is a tribute to her determination that she was able to keep herself in the programme as she oscillated between rebelliousness and fear. She was able to make links between the position of the door in the tower block and her problems with communicating, particularly with anyone in authority – she felt she could never be upfront and straightforward because of her history.

NB: I return to give an account of what happened next in a vignette (titled *The Repositioned Door*) later on in the following section.

Developing the work with the building: monitoring and processing functions

After the initial diagnostic stage has been completed, the building image is available as a potential site for ongoing therapeutic work. This section examines ways in which this work can be developed and looks at how interactive imagery processes can facilitate and support the therapy. The work builds on the initial diagnostic stage, i.e. the procedure of bringing the exterior of the building into view, and then moves inside the building to explore and work with the more interior dimensions of the self. Finally it discusses how two functions, in particular, may come to the fore in ongoing work, i.e. the processing and monitoring functions. It is important to note that it needs to be read in conjunction with Chapter 12 that deals in more depth with the process of integrating inclusive imagery work into ongoing work.

Although the processing function of imagery, i.e. the way that imagery can operate as a conduit for the release of repressed material, can function at any time, it is more likely to operate after the initial diagnostic stage. As discussed in Chapter 5, one of the characteristic features of the processing function is the way in which mental images can trigger an almost instantaneous reliving of the experiences that they symbolise. However, in the case of the building image, the processing function usually operates in a more controlled way. This is understandable as this image represents the self structure, which by its very nature is inherently stable. Even though different features, aspects and, in particular, compensating structural distortions symbolise repressed experiences these have now become integrated into the person's psychological structure. Therefore, the act of viewing a particular aspect of the building image does not automatically trigger the processing function (although there are always exceptions to this rule – see the vignette, titled *The Light in the Hallway*, presented later in this chapter).

However, if the client consciously and deliberately engages with an aspect of the building image then the processing function can be activated. This activation can take place over a period of time and will usually involve the client reliving the original experience. If the client is able to withstand the release of this repressed material and integrate it more consciously, associated changes will happen to the building image (I discuss these processes in more detail in the later chapter on integrating imagery work into ongoing therapy).

The building image as with the other framing images considered in this book can offer a very valuable commentary on the client's therapeutic processes. As a general rule, the building image will reflect any significant permanent changes in the client's way of being whether these are behavioural, emotional or cognitive. I am aware that I draw on the monitoring function very regularly in ongoing work with this image. Clients become used to me requesting a quick visit to the building for a check-up particularly when they report having experienced a change in an old pattern. In the following illustrative case vignette, titled *The Repositioned Door*, I return to the story of what happened when Jenny worked on changing her attitude towards authority symbolised by the side door to her tower block.

> The crisis came for Jenny when she was told that she had an official interview for a place in a second stage residential unit. She became very anxious at this prospect, as all of her issues with authority returned with a vengeance. She experienced a fear that she would be rejected and at the same time felt rebellious towards a system that she believed was making her jump through hoops. We undertook a preparatory session to help her find a more balanced way of approaching the interview. She used all the support that the rehabilitation centre could provide, and the following week to her delight she was accepted for the place at the second stage residential unit.
>
> In our final session together, we looked again at her inner structure and it was clear that her building was much brighter and cleaner, confirming for her all the hard psychological work she had done in the previous three months. There was, however, one unexpected alteration to the tower block – the main entrance door was now at the front of the building rather than round to the side. Jenny linked this change to her experience of attending the interview two weeks previously. She explained to me that it had been the first time she had ever been able to express herself directly and calmly to someone in

a position of authority and, since that point, she had noticed that all of her communication was becoming more direct (this had been also remarked upon by members of staff). I was very pleased that all of her hard work had paid off for her. The change in the building image appeared to confirm that an old distortion had been released and she was in a better position to communicate in a more direct way and thereby reclaim her own authority.

Work on the building becomes an ongoing unfolding process

Although initially, the therapeutic work (informed by the initial diagnostic procedure) might appear to be quite clear-cut in terms of what interventions might be required, ongoing work on the building is not so predictable: it unfolds according to an inner logic. This is particularly the case with structural issues and the foundations of the building. Through experience I have come to the conclusion that nothing should be initiated in terms of attempting any kind of intervention with such fundamental aspects of the building image (apart from the two process management strategies that I discuss at the end of this chapter). Instead it is important to wait and see if and how ongoing work with the building begins to facilitate changes in these areas spontaneously. For instance, it is not unusual for the client to be drawn to the foundations during a period of intensive reflection on the origin of problematic behaviours and note that some work appears to be taking place. In terms of structural issues, likewise, it often happens that suddenly a client notices an issue with the structure at the same time as having insights into earlier formative experiences. It is as if the building opens itself up to the exploration and discloses further dimensions of itself. The following case vignette, titled *A Repaired Building Needs Work on its Foundations*, illustrates both features.

> I worked with Maria, a sensitive and resilient woman in her late thirties, over a period of eight months. She originally came for therapy because she was experiencing mounting anxiety that interfered with her ability to work. Maria proved a very willing and able practitioner of imagery work. Initially, she visualised a big white building, dilapidated on one side, with a back windowless wall. She was shocked to discover that part of the roof had been damaged a long time ago and she made a link with a confusing period in her life when she was sent by her parents to live with her aunt. Despite her fears of exploring the damaged interior, Maria persevered and realised that part of the hole in the roof had been repaired over time. At that point she suddenly grasped that her building had a double structure: the modern white building she could see from the outside had been built around the original little damaged house. This discovery made sense to Maria as she reflected on the way she had been striving since she was a teenager to create a proper life for herself. This had included leaving her village, going to university and then emigrating and establishing herself in the UK. The results of all her efforts

were symbolised by the way that a new building had been built up like a containing shell around the original damaged house. Maria was very keen to engage with further exploration and work with her building – she could see that parts of the dilapidated walls needed repairing. After a few more sessions, followed by a short break when she returned to visit her family in Eastern Europe, her attention spontaneously turned to the ground around the building. She was dismayed to realise it was strewn with rubbish and that this rubbish also formed part of the foundations of the house itself. After time reflecting on its nature, she came to the conclusion that this detritus represented all the negative beliefs that were part of the cultural fabric of her village background. This insight initiated a process of consciously examining the ideas she had absorbed from her background and as she did so she visualised herself slowly and patiently clearing out the foundations of the building. During this process, Maria felt that she was working on traces of traumatic experiences lived out long ago but still preserved in the collective memory of the people in her village.

Exploring the interior of the building

Initially the focus of the work is usually on the outside of the building. However, later on, the work is likely to move into its interior (although, sometimes, clients will find themselves inside the building right from the start because this is where their pressing concern is represented). As mentioned earlier, I believe that the decision to enter and explore the building needs to be initiated by the client. Furthermore, it is important that the therapist refrains from the temptation to point the client in a particular direction. I would never suggest that, for example, locked rooms should be opened up, or that certain parts of the interior should be explored. Neither would I make suggestions that certain objects might be found within the building. But, this does not mean to say that the role of accompanying the client's exploration is a completely passive one. On the contrary, I would be actively encouraging clients to deepen their exploratory process through asking phenomenologically oriented questions throughout. I would also be prompting clients to make links between their imagery and their experience; in other words I would be asking them what the imagery might be representing. Usually entering the building is a straightforward process, but in some cases resistance and difficulties are immediately encountered as the following vignette, titled *The Light in the Hallway*, demonstrates.

George, a newly-qualified teacher in his early forties, had come to counselling in order to address some difficulties which he believed were associated with physical abuse at the hands of his mother during his childhood: he found it difficult to manage conflict. When he looked at the exterior of his building image, he reported that it was a medium-sized house that appeared to be in good condition apart from looking a little bit old. He was drawn to go inside and explore the interior. However, on imagining opening the door and stepping into the hallway he reported a strong light in the ceiling switching on and he experienced a rising fear. His initial reaction was to come back out of the house but instead he withstood his mounting anxiety and started to explore the interior. To his surprise he gained the impression that his house had not been inhabited for twenty or so years and he made a connection to this being the time when he stood up to his mother and left home. He realised that the electric light in the hallway represented the fear from childhood that had effectively sealed off his interior world from development and exploration. By allowing himself to re-experience his fearful reaction he had gained access to himself.

NB: The next part of George's exploration can be read in the vignette (titled *A Fire Is Lit*) presented towards the end of this chapter.

General comments about the interior

Although it is important not to be prescriptive about the exploration of the interior, it is possible to make some general comments concerning what may be encountered. In this section I consider some general features of the interior of the building and some common areas of exploration. I will conclude by offering some caveats.

It is important to note that one would not expect there to be known figures within the building. Important formative influences on the person's life are usually represented in the structure itself (as in the previous vignette, titled *The Tower Block with the Side Door*, where the impact of the authoritarian step father is shown in the unusual positioning of the main door). But, I have sometimes witnessed more explicit references, particularly to significant family members, often in the form of portraits on the wall (see the later vignette, titled *A Fire Is Lit*). When clients, on the rare occasion, report that they are encountering known figures who appear to be occupying their building this will need further exploration. It can signify an unhealthy dependency or that the client is being psychologically controlled by another person.

The interior of the building is usually divided up in some way with interior walls and ceilings – representing the different parts or aspects of the self. But this is not always the case, and occasionally the interior is an open space. Sometimes this might indicate that the person's next developmental task is to differentiate out parts of the self, but it could also reflect the opposite, i.e. a highly individuated way of being, as illustrated in the following vignette, titled *One Big Space*.

> When I first encountered Jean, a very creative woman in her early fifties, she was in remission for cancer. Her building image took the form of an unusual modern structure with floor to ceiling windows on one side overlooking a lake. Inside was one large space, empty apart from some furniture. When I queried the lack of different rooms, Jean was very clear about its meaning. She said this was an accurate representation of the way in which all aspects of her life were creative and there was little distinction for her between the way she earned her living, teaching craft and building skills to young unemployed people, and the

way in which she had designed and built the furnishings of her actual home. She said that the empty space in her building image reflected that creative centre of herself. Furthermore, she added that if it were subdivided into distinct rooms her creative energy would be diminished in some way.

Different parts of the interior have a history of being linked to particular areas of the self. In general, my clinical experience has confirmed some of these obvious self-evident interpretations and I discuss some of the most common ones below.

The basement appears to be the storage area for repressed aspects of the self such as painful experiences or unaccepted emotions. When clients report that they are being drawn down to the basement this is usually accompanied by feelings of anxiety and resistance. The first stage in this work is usually just to get a sense of what might be stored down there. Sometimes there are images of objects connected to the past, sometimes the basement contains a significant amount of material that needs to be processed over a period of time as the following vignette, titled *The Sad Little Girl in the Basement*, illustrates. This is a further extract from Amelia's work presented earlier (in the vignette titled *The Damaged Roof*).

> Unsurprisingly, given the difficulties in her upbringing, the basement in Amelia's mansion was extensive – a complex area of the building with different compartments and contents. The whole area was dominated by a very large spider that evoked fear and disgust in Amelia (see note below). Most of the early part of the work with the building involved Amelia finding a way to manage her responses to the spider and gain more insight into what else the basement contained. The most significant discovery that she made was a figure of herself as a sad abandoned child. This was a powerful emotional experience for Amelia as she made links with the part of herself that had been buried during her battle to survive her emotionally and mentally abusive upbringing. Over a period of time she was able to strengthen that part of herself and place it in a different part of the building where it could develop and flourish with her conscious attention.

NB: The spider is a common symbol in many cultures that is freighted with a range of complex ambivalent interpretations. Part of our work together did involve reflecting on its association with the idea of fate as this was a particular area of interest for Amelia.

The attic, similarly to the basement, appears to be another important storage area in the building image. The self-evident interpretation of the attic suggests a link to old memories or forgotten experiences or parts of the self. However, the contents are not usually as disturbing to the conscious mind as those of the basement.

Bedrooms are self-evidently linked to the person's sexual expression and experiencing of intimacy. In my experience, clients have not been drawn to explore this part of the building unless there have been particular explicit difficulties in this area of their life. One example from my casebook would be the experience of a cancer patient who disclosed a history of repeated sexual abuse by her step father. Her mother had also been sexually abused as a young girl within the family. Without any prompting from me, she realised that she needed to visit the bedroom in her building image. She reported that the bedroom walls were not solid and she made the link to the way in which her sexual boundaries had been violated. As noted earlier, Leuner considers that it is important to focus on this part of the building. Furthermore, he suggests that the therapist can initiate an exploration of the bedrooms. I don't agree because as I stated previously, I think it is important that the exploration of the interior of the building is led by the client.

The living room is often one of first areas of the building that opens itself up to initial exploration. Self-evident interpretation would link this to the part of the self that is consciously inhabited and identified with. The furniture or furnishings are often a fruitful source of meaning-making as these can represent the person's consciously chosen or unconsciously inherited cultural values or beliefs. I have noticed a common report from clients that the living room furniture is old-fashioned in some way. Sometimes the living room will also contain a fireplace which is self-evidently linked to the person's energy. The following vignette, titled *A Fire Is Lit*, illustrates how changes began to take place when the living room was explored. It is a further extract from George's work presented in an earlier vignette (titled *The Light in the Hallway*).

> After George entered his building, he noticed that the hallway led to a staircase and on the landing was a collection of old-fashioned children's toys. As he explored this part of the interior he experienced memories of playing alone in his room as a way of escaping from the tension and potential violence in the home. He realised that this habit of escaping from difficulties was being played out currently in the way he would spend hours alone on the internet and watching films.
>
> On the ground floor was a living room. George noticed a portrait of his father on the wall that conveyed a particular negative attitude that he remembered from childhood. In one corner of the room stood a television set that was broadcasting images of his mother continuously speaking. On the sofa sat a skeleton that he believed represented himself and was a warning of what would happen if he did not change. This was a disturbing representation that created anxiety for George. However, he was determined to do the work needed to break through his psychological impasse and he set himself the task of trying out new assertive behaviours in conflict situations. One month later when he returned to check up on the living room, he reported that a fire had been lit in the fireplace. This was an emotionally liberating experience for George as he realised that he now had the possibility of taking down the controlling image of his father and consigning it to the fire. His determination had paid off: change was now possible. He accepted the self-evident interpretation that he had got his 'fire' back.

It is not the purpose of this chapter to present all aspects of the interior of the building but rather to give some idea of the way in which self-evidential interpretation can be a useful starting point for exploration and meaning-making. Thus the bathroom because of its function and associations can be a commentary on how the person processes emotions; or the kitchen, likewise, shows how the person nurtures themselves. In the end it is the cumulative experience of working with a wide range of building images that develops expertise in facilitating the client's meaning-making process.

The process management function

The process management function of mental imagery may or may not be used in the course of the work with this particular framing image. In this section I discuss two particular procedures employing this function that have evolved over the course of my work. The first way makes use of a common technique in mental imagery, i.e. using figures (or sometimes animals) to represent parts of the self which can then be used in an interactive way to facilitate a therapeutic process. Because the focus in this work is on the structure rather than on internal dynamics, I have generally restricted my use of this technique to visualising potentially helpful impulses arising within the self. Therefore, particularly when the client appears to be focusing on rebuilding or developmental work with the building, I might suggest that the client imagines helpful figures such as an architect (to advise on design and planning), and builders (to erect scaffolding and implement the work). On occasion, when clients have reported unprotected or unsecured buildings I have suggested imagining a security fence around the property that is patrolled by a guard dog.

However, over time, I have noticed that perhaps the most significant use that I have made of the process management function is in the creation of temporary structures. I began developing this procedure early on in my clinical practice with substance misusers who often visualised buildings that were so deteriorated that they were uninhabitable. These representations were usually accompanied by clients reporting feelings of extreme vulnerability and exposure. I started to suggest that in such cases clients could visualise a simple temporary structure in the vicinity of the main building. The purpose of this was to help to lessen the person's feelings of insecurity and to provide some containment. Over time this procedure has evolved and I will suggest this to clients in other circumstances as well, such as when their building is undergoing structural repair, rebuilding or developmental work that is making it temporarily uninhabitable. This visualisation procedure seems to help to contain someone who is going through a period of inner change. It allows them a means of anchoring themselves in a perspective on change rather than feeling over-identified with and overwhelmed by the process of change. When I suggest the idea of creating a temporary containing structure I would recommend that the client produces something simple such as a static caravan or a site hut. However, as always, in therapeutic work with mental imagery, it is important to adapt to the clients' individual requirements. In the following vignette, titled *The Gatekeeper's Cottage*, the client spontaneously produced a more permanent structure that indicated he would not be ready to work on his inner house for quite a long time. This illustration is a further extract from James's work presented in an earlier vignette (titled *The Imposing Façade*).

> James agreed that it would be helpful to have some way of containing himself whilst work could take place on his building. Despite my recommendation of imagining a simple temporary shelter, he visualised a gatekeeper's cottage made of thick, stone walls. He explained that he needed the security and solidity offered by a stone building and, furthermore, it seemed more real than the filmset. This was important to him because it offered protection without giving a false image to the outside world. Initially he felt it was a little austere and cold, but he imagined a fire in the hearth and was reassured by the warmth he felt spreading through the house. He said he felt a sense of relief that he could create a place inside himself that felt more secure.
>
> When I met up with James two years later at the crisis agency where he had been admitted after a short relapse, we returned again to check his inner structure. He reported that he could see the little gatekeeper's cottage again, but it was now furnished and comfortable. He made links between this solid and stable structure and his experience of being drug free and maintaining a disciplined lifestyle where he had had sole responsibility of looking after his young child. During this period he had also been able to undertake short courses at a local college. He was also clear that, even though the childhood issues symbolised in the original building with the façade had not been resolved, this temporary structure could hold him until he was ready to address them. He felt that his recent relapse was connected with stress and he was pleased that he had been able to correct it without too much damage.

Longer-term work with the building

It is beyond the remit of this book to discuss in any detail how the building image operates in longer-term work apart from making some general observations. Once the building image has become established in the clinical work as a site for therapeutic work, I will continue to monitor it with the client. How the therapeutic work with the building image unfolds depends on the individual client's process. Usually, the image becomes something that the client starts to own more and to use independently as an ongoing reference point.

Working consistently over a period of time with the building image has revealed some consistent themes (see further discussion of changes in imagery after long-term work in Chapter 11). In general, the image appears to become more and more responsive and can start to display positive changes. These changes go beyond the resolution of an earlier structural distortion such as the one described in the earlier vignette (titled *The Tower Block with a Side Door*). Instead they can begin to display the characteristics of new developments, as illustrated in the following vignette, titled *A New Conservatory*. This is a further extract from Maria's work presented in a previous vignette (titled *A Repaired Building Needs Work on the Foundations*).

Towards the end of our eight months together, Maria agreed that her original issue of paralysing anxiety at work had lessened to the extent that she was able to manage her workload and professional interactions much more easily. When she returned to her building image she was very surprised to note a new development; a conservatory had appeared on the side of the house. After investigating it and reflecting further she said that this extension was an accurate representation of a new optimism and an emerging sense of self-belief. She was in the middle of arranging her wedding and she was noticing also that some thoughts were arising about developing her own business. She identified the function of the conservatory as a place within her that now could nurture new developments.

Conclusion

In this chapter I have indicated the scope and potential offered by the use of the building as a framing image in therapeutic work and offered some guidance on its application in clinical practice. The image of the house has a long history of being used as a symbol of the self in counselling and psychotherapy. However, the particular work presented in this book is unusual because it focuses explicitly on the structural dimensions of the building image rather than its contents. By so doing, the interactive communicative process that is facilitated by mental imagery concentrates directly on the individual's psychological structure. Initially, the image can offer helpful insights into this fundamental dimension of the self and it can then go on to provide a productive site for ongoing work which, in my experience, often generates significant positive change and development for the client. In Chapter 11 I will be returning to discuss further how working with the building image can be integrated into ongoing counselling and psychotherapy practice. In particular I will be discussing how the building image combined with two other framing images offers a powerful multi-aspected vehicle for therapeutic processes.

References

Freud, S. (1900). 'The Interpretation of Dreams', in J. Stachey (ed) (1962) *The Standard Edition*, vols 4 & 5, London: Hogarth.
Hall, E., Hall, C., Stradling, P. and Young, D. (2006). *Guided Imagery: Creative interventions in counselling and psychotherapy*, London: Sage.
Jung, C. (1969). *Memories, Dreams, Reflections*, London: Fontana Library.
Lakoff, G. and Johnson, M. (2003). *Metaphors We Live By*, 2nd edn, Chicago: University of Chicago Press.
Leuner, H. (1984). *Guided Affective Imagery in Short-term Psychotherapy: The basic course*, New York: Thieme-Stratton Corp.
Marcus, C.C. (2006). *House as a Mirror of Self: Exploring the deeper meaning of home*, Lake Worth, FL: Nicolas-Hays Inc.

Chapter 9

The path image

This chapter presents the framing image of the path as a means of representing the living of a purposeful life; this would include goal setting and life choices as well as how the individual deals with challenges and obstacles. This metaphor of the path or journey has often been used in different cultures and historical periods to express ideas related to living a purposeful life; examples from the world's spiritual traditions would be the Buddhist concept of the eightfold path and *The Pilgrim's Progress* (Bunyan, 1974) from the Western Christian canon.

Curiously enough, although there are plenty of examples in the literature of the client's interior experience being represented as a landscape, the path metaphor or image is nowhere near as prevalent as the building or house symbol. One example that relates directly to the notion of a journey can be found in Leuner's (1984) work with the motif of the meadow. He suggests to the client particular features in this landscape to explore, such as following the course of a brook back to its source – the brook symbolising the journey of the self from birth to death. Other clinicians have used the idea of travelling through a landscape in a variety of different ways – usually the nature of the landscape is predetermined, such as climbing a volcano. These types of landscapes are believed to represent universal themes that, through exploration, promote therapeutic processes and allow clients to develop self-insight. Elements in the landscape are often viewed as symbolisations of parts or aspects of the person. An example of this is Hall *et al.*'s (2006) discussion of using the theme of climbing a mountain, where they present a Gestalt-informed experiential technique of having the client identify with the mountain itself. They suggest that through such procedures clients can reconnect with buried qualities of strength and persistence.

In the work presented in this chapter, the framing image of the path is theorised as the conceptual metaphor LIFE IS A JOURNEY. As previously discussed, conceptual metaphors (Lakoff and Johnson, 2003) are understood to structure cognition and perception along certain lines and in this case the journey metaphor highlights the dynamic processes associated with living a purposeful life. I have used the term 'path' rather than 'journey' for this framing image because the former expresses this metaphor in more concrete terms. Ungerer and Schmid (1996) note that metaphoric expressions that deal with movement through space are among the most foundational conceptual metaphors. The conceptual metaphor LIFE IS A JOURNEY is a particular application of our embodied experience of movement to a more abstract concept of engaging purposively with life. It generates linguistic metaphors in English such as: 'She's lost her way in life.'; 'He's back on track.'; 'It's a hard climb to get to where I want to be in life.'; 'I feel like I am walking through treacle.'

In this chapter I will identify the main principles and guidelines for working with this particular framing image including an overview of some of its main features. This discussion will then address some common themes that clients bring relating to living a purposeful life such as: feeling lost or trapped and needing to make a decision.

Overview

I began using the framing image of the path early on in my work with substance misusers. This starting point was prompted by very common reports from these clients that, as a consequence of their drug habit, they had lost their way in life. Sometimes they expressed this idea as being trapped somewhere or having lost their connection with reality. Getting a picture of where they were appeared to be helpful – it provided a concrete way of expressing their predicament. Furthermore, it also illuminated what steps could be taken to move in a more positive direction.

As I began to work with nonsubstance-misusing clients the framing image of the path continued to be a very useful way of understanding how people are leading their lives. The path image can be a useful diagnostic tool. Although it is common in clinical work for clients to make use of linguistic metaphoric terms that relate to this aspect of life (such as a very common expression, 'I feel lost') this does not give the kind of clear detailed information that is produced by an image. Representing the state as a mental image will usually reveal clearly and immediately the imaginal perspective's view on their situation. It can indicate if someone is in immediate danger (I have seen examples of clients who are very close to a cliff edge or clinging precariously to it) or where someone is expending effort that is, in fact, exacerbating their current difficulties (see the case vignette titled *Stumbling Along in the Desert*). It can also be helpful in illuminating how clients' circumstances are impacting on their experience of making progress in life. I will usually ask clients how long they feel they have been in the place they visualise and if they can make any connection between the image and to what was happening in their life at that point.

Apart from obvious indications that this might be a useful framing image to employ, e.g. the client's linguistic metaphoric expressions regarding difficulties experienced on life's journey, I have also found that it can be a helpful way of working with states of self-reported depression. It was only later on in my practice that I found some corroboration in Rowe's account of the ways in which her clients pictured their depression, which included landscape images similar to the ones I have noted in my own work. Her depressed clients reported:

... images of empty landscapes, waterless deserts or frozen wastes or images of boundless oceans. The person sees himself trudging alone towards an empty horizon or caught in a violent storm, or sitting helplessly immobile on a burning rock or a melting ice floe.

(2003: 2)

Due to the common experience of clients presenting with depression, it seems a good place to begin this chapter on the framing image of the path. In the following vignette, titled *Sinking into a Swamp*, the landscape imagery was particularly helpful in showing how a depressive state was being maintained.

Jane, a sensitive woman in her early twenties, had been struggling with severe depression for over two years. When she arrived at the community counselling service where I was working she appeared to be very withdrawn and she told me that she did not see any way in which she could regain her former cheerful self. When I suggested she could represent her depression as a place on her journey through life, she reported finding herself in the middle of a swamp sunk up to her knees – every time she struggled to move, it felt as if she was sinking further into the mire. On further exploration of the circumstances that linked to the onset of her depression, Jane told the story of how her family had become involved in a very stressful protracted court case. Her mother had been a witness to a serious crime and had agreed to give evidence but, in so doing, she herself had become a target for bullying and intimidation by the criminal gang. This was a very disturbing and frightening time for everyone in the family. Although the court case was successfully concluded, Jane had not been able to move on from that experience. Initially, and somewhat to my surprise, Jane was resistant to any reparative interventions I proposed such as getting her to imagine a concrete link to the edge of the swamp in the form of a rope. She wanted to stay where she was. It then became clear that the swamp was operating as a form of protection and as long as she stayed out of reach in the middle no one could hurt her. In other words, at some level, even though she found her depressed state unbearable, it was functioning as a defence. We only started to make some progress when I assured Jane that the process was completely under her control and that I would not be pressurising her to leave the swamp. At that point she began to accept the possibility of making some minor changes to her picture: she visualised a block of wood in the middle of the swamp that could be used as a platform to support her. She equated this with her group of close friends. Over the course of the therapy Jane was able to lay out a path made of blocks of wood that could lead her out of the swamp of her depression; each block of wood representing a particular strategy that she could use to help her manage her return to the world of interaction with people. By the time she imagined laying down the final piece of wood, she felt strong enough to return to work. She recognised that her depressive state had been a form of protection and that it had given her the time and space to recover from a very stressful experience.

General guidelines for working with the path image

The following points have arisen out of clinical observation and practice and are offered as general principles to guide therapeutic work with this particular framing image.

- **Ensuring safety.** The principle of ensuring the safety of the client overrides all other principles in this work. Therefore if clients visualise themselves in a clearly precarious situation, e.g. clinging to the edge of a crumbling cliff, or sinking further and further down into a quicksand, it is important to offer an immediate reparative intervention in order to establish a temporary holding position (see case vignettes for examples of this type of intervention in action).
- **Respecting the right to stay put.** It is important to convey to clients that by identifying exactly where they are, this does not mean that they will be pressured into moving on from this position (see the previous vignette titled *Sinking into a Swamp*). Visualising the landscape is a means of collecting information as to their whereabouts and helping them prepare for the time when or if they are ready to move on.
- **Keeping contact with the ground.** It is best to encourage clients to stay in contact with the earth in the form of keeping their feet on the ground. In general, contact with the ground appears to ensure that the process of life is being fully lived out. There are exceptions to this, for instance, when people find themselves located in a body of water rather than on land. See the following section on floating and/or drifting for further discussion.

The first stage of the work

The following diagnostic procedure is designed to get a clear initial picture of where clients situate themselves on their journey through life. Before starting, it is best to discuss with clients the reason for doing this, i.e. because this procedure can show them quite clearly where they are and also give some indications about how to approach difficulties or obstacles in their life that may be impeding their progress.

Bringing the landscape into view: using the framing function

The concept of life as a journey seems quite easy to accept for most people. This is usually the case for linguistic metaphors that are generated by conceptual metaphors. But, there are some technical aspects of bringing the inner landscape into view that seem to require more explanation. From experience I have found words along the following lines to be an effective introduction. They can be adapted appropriately to the individual client as follows:

> 'I am going to help you to get a clearer picture of where you are on your journey through life. This is quite simple and straightforward. I will ask you

where you feel you are, at the moment, on your journey and you will respond in the form of a simple picture or a feeling. For example I might ask other people this question and they could come up with answers such as: standing at a crossroads, fallen down a hole, up against a brick wall, or they might not be able to give it a picture as they just feel lost somewhere. Don't worry if you think you are just imagining this – just allow yourself to create a picture. Then, when you are ready I will ask you to be in that landscape in order to get more sense of where you are.'

It is also important to let the client know that they can stop the procedure at any time if they are feeling uncomfortable (for further elaboration on preparing the client for imagery work please see Chapter 12). Adapt the following procedure to the individual client. When instructions are followed by bracketed terms, this indicates that you will need to select one that is suitable for your client. Suggested verbatim instructions or questions are given in quotation marks.

1. Make sure the client is sitting comfortably with uncrossed legs and both feet on the ground. Ask them to close their eyes. Then take them through a simple relaxation procedure of your choosing.
2. Ask them the following question, 'Where do you feel you are at the moment on your journey through life? How would you sum it up for a stranger like myself?' There are two possible general responses to this question: either clients will pull up a metaphoric image; or they will report that they do not know where they are, because they are either completely lost or they cannot visualise anything. If it is the latter this will need further clarification before you can move onto the next step. Do this by using questions to elicit the following basic information if possible. Establish if clients feel that they are standing on some kind of solid ground and, if so, what kind of ground. If they feel they are floating, get them to sense what they are floating in. If it is air, how far above the ground are they? If they can't see anything, ask them if this is because it is dark, or are they inside something such as a fog or a cave. Persist with gentle questioning until clients have some kind of image of their situation, however sketchy this might be.
3. Help the client connect more deeply with the metaphoric landscape using the following instruction, 'Now let yourself actually be in this landscape instead of just looking at it like a picture. Be in your body inside this landscape. See if you can get a bit more detail of your surroundings.' As discussed previously, it is important to make sure that clients are viewing the landscape from a first-person perspective (and not just viewing themselves within the landscape from a third-person perspective). Then ask them to describe what they are seeing.
4. In this next stage, you are going to help clients gather more information about their current situation. Help them clarify their position, and, if appropriate, ask the following question, 'How long do you feel you have been in this place?' It is helpful to know if the landscape represents a long-term situation or a

place where the person has recently arrived. Another useful question would be, 'How do you feel about being in this place?' People will have a range of responses to their landscapes. Their emotional reactions and attitudes to where they find themselves will have an important bearing on the therapeutic work.

5   It is useful to begin to get clients to make some clear links between their inner landscape and their outer life circumstances. Asking the following question can help them do this, 'How does this place show up for you in your outer life?' However, this is quite a challenging task if the person is inexperienced in using imagery. Therefore if they struggle to make these links, it is best to postpone this until a discussion can take place after the initial diagnostic imagery procedure is over.

6   When the client has gathered a clear enough picture of their landscape, advise them that the process is coming to a close. Do not, however, bring clients out if they have found themselves in a precarious position in their inner landscape. By precarious, I mean a situation that self-evidently requires immediate intervention, e.g. clinging to the edge of a precipice or sinking in water, etc. In such cases it is important to offer an immediate reparative intervention that will create a temporary halt to this situation, such as creating a rope to hold the person in place or a lifebuoy to prevent the person from going under the water (see following section for a range of appropriate strategies).

7   Instruct the client to stop seeing the picture of the landscape and to switch their attention back to their physical body. Let them know that you are going to bring them back into their everyday state of mind. Then use a simple basic procedure designed for this purpose.

8   Finally, when clients have completed the procedure, it is helpful to summarise their account of the landscape as a preparation for a discussion of their experience.

Starting to work with the path: the diagnostic, reparative and monitoring functions

Similarly to working with the other framing images, all the therapeutic functions identified in the inclusive model can come into play at various stages of the work with the path image. The most significant difference between the path imagery and the other two framing images is that, in general, the processing function is less evident. The building and the plant images are far more likely to contain repressed material in a symbolised form as they represent structural and developmental aspects of the self. Because of this I attend to the processing function in a separate section at the end of the chapter.

General comments on the path image

The imagery of the landscape and path has the potential to change over a period of time in a more radical way than the two other framing images of the building and the plant. This is understandable, as the path image is the symbolisation of a dynamic process. The current obstacles and conditions experienced as someone progresses through life will be revealed in the imagery of the landscape. This framing image represents how clients are currently drawing on their own resources in the process of responding to and interacting with the challenges of leading a meaningful and purposeful life.

One of the great advantages of this framing image is that it can operate as a very clear commentary on clients' progress over a period of time, thus giving them an invaluable tool for tracking and monitoring the direction their life is taking. This monitoring function is important as the journey through life takes many forms: sometimes, it is a leisurely stroll and, sometimes, it is a very challenging process of overcoming difficult obstacles; occasionally, the way ahead seems impossible and we backtrack, and at other times, we are paralysed by indecision; sometimes we lose our way and at other times we reach important staging posts. It is important to note that by using the conceptual metaphor, LIFE IS A JOURNEY, this does not imply that the focus is on arriving at a final destination (in reality there can only be one final destination for everyone in this life, which is death). Instead the focus is on the journey itself. There is an individual rhythm to each person's journey; there are times when the person needs to rest up and times to push on. Working with the path imagery can be a very good way of helping to develop more insight into the balance required between agency and receptivity on life's journey – the dynamic balance between the conscious goals set by the rational perspective and the different requirements of the imaginal perspective. Problems in life often arise when there is an imbalance between the two.

Clients can bring a variety of difficulties in relation to their sense of leading a purposeful life. This section discusses some of the main themes (such as being lost or encountering obstacles) presented by clients and how these can be represented in their landscape imagery. A range of potential reparative interventions are also discussed for some of the more problematic landscapes such as finding oneself in a deep hole. In general, interpretation here is mostly self-evident.

Lost

No matter how lost clients feel, the diagnostic procedure will usually locate them somewhere – even at the most basic level of sensing whether their feet are on some kind of surface or not. Articulating where they are in relation to a landscape presents a more concrete place to begin to understand how they have become lost and how to reconnect with a more meaningful direction in life. In my experience there are usually two main ways in which people represent themselves as lost: either they cannot see where they are or they picture themselves in an undifferentiated landscape with no indication of a direction to follow.

In the former case, the first step is to help clients identify why they are unable to visualise anything. This is often because the place they are in is dark or their vision is obscured in some other way. Reparative interventions could take the form of suggesting a torch (representing insight) to shine a light onto the surroundings. One of the basic things to establish at this initial stage is whether clients think they are inside something or not. Sometimes people report that there is a fog or cloud around them. These conditions are often associated with confusion. A useful intervention is to suggest to clients that they are wearing X-ray glasses that allow them to see through the fog or mist. An important thing to establish is whether this fog is a temporary state that will vanish of its own accord, or whether it is a more permanent feature of the landscape and that the person needs to find a way through it. Some of the questions outlined in the diagnostic procedure should be helpful in this regard, particularly the ones that aim at eliciting a sense of how long the person has been at this point on their journey and what this may be connected with.

The second possibility is that someone might be able to visualise their surroundings but these environments are undifferentiated spaces. Common examples of such landscapes would be clients reporting that they are in the middle of a forest, in a desert, out in the middle of the ocean or standing in a vast featureless plain. What all these landscapes have in common is that there is no clear path or direction to follow. Quite often, people report that they feel they have been in these spaces for a long time never really knowing if they are heading in a productive direction or just wandering around in circles. In these situations it seems to be important to get more sense of the landscape in order to establish a direction. Over time I have developed a general method for gaining a wider perspective on the current situation. In this procedure I guide clients through a process of imagining themselves rising up above the landscape to get a bird's-eye view. An example of offering this intervention can be seen in the extended vignette (titled *Traversing the Dark Woods*) presented at the end of this chapter. As a result of doing this, people will usually begin to identify a feature in the landscape that they can head towards – something that will operate as a clear objective or reference point. When I bring them back down to their original starting point I often suggest that they visualise a compass that can be used to orient themselves in their landscape and help guide them in the right direction. It is important to ask them to identify what this inner compass might represent; examples could be: following the advice of a trusted person; following gut feelings or specific spiritual teachings; and listening to one's conscience, etc.

Struggling

It is quite common, in my clinical experience, to encounter clients who feel that they are struggling to either achieve something specific or to get to a particular place that they might conceptualise as an emotional state, e.g. feeling more secure, happy, confident or fulfilled. Very often they report that it does not matter how much energy they invest or how much willpower they apply, they are not getting to where they want to be. The path image can be very useful diagnostically because it can shed light on the nature of the struggle which, I have noticed, is often caused by a conflict between the rational and imaginal perspectives. In other words, the person is attempting to impose a set of conscious goals that is not in harmony with other processes operating in the person's life. An example of this can be seen in the path image produced by Julia whose work has been previously presented in Chapter 8 (in the vignette titled *Resisting the Building*). Julia's aim was to rebuild her confidence after a damaging experience of being bullied at work. She believed she would achieve this desired state if she found another job. However, the main thrust of the work we undertook together over a period of two years focused on her becoming more conscious of the negative impact of her early childhood on her sense of self. Nevertheless, throughout this period Julia continued to invest a great deal of her energy in a frustrating and fruitless quest for employment. The conflict between her rational and imaginal perspectives showed up in the image she reported of her journey through life – struggling to move through an enormous shallow box containing a jelly-like substance. This image remained exactly the same until Julia completed her work on the foundations of her building and reported a new sense of inner confidence. I will return to how her path image changed in the following section on monitoring the image (in the vignette titled *Released from the Jelly*).

The following vignette, titled *Pulling a Heavy Truck*, is an example of trying to continue with a goal despite fundamental changes occurring in the person's life.

> James, an insightful and engaging man in his early forties, came for counselling because, after the death of his father, he found he was no longer able to manage his day-to-day life. He said that he found it very difficult to cope with the way in which he had changed from a dynamic and self-motivated businessman to someone who could not manage all the competing demands on his time. In the assessment session he explained to me that his coaching business relied on helping his clients create and realise very clear goals in both their business and also in their personal life. He was very concerned that his own goal-setting strategies were not working.
>
> James's landscape revealed his struggle – he reported that he was pulling a heavy truck and that he needed to get through a dense wood in order to reach a fairy-tale castle. It was clear to James that this picture showed that he needed to stop trying to force himself to achieve his goals but instead to take some time to understand what the truck contained. Over the course of three sessions James investigated the truck and began to understand how it seemed to be linked to a relationship that he had experienced as damaging and destructive. As he gained further insights into the way that this relationship had mirrored his early life circumstances of being an adopted child, the image of the truck began to change: the wheels fell off and it sank down into the mud. Furthermore, he also had the liberating realisation that he could leave the truck behind and he was also able to let go of the ropes that had harnessed him. In our final session together James said that he felt calmer and had more clarity about how to manage his life. He believed he had done

enough work so he could now move on. In his inner landscape he reported that an open green pathway had formed up, and, interestingly, the image of the fairy-tale castle had faded away.

Trapped, stuck or blocked

Another quite common theme reported by clients is the sense that their progress has been halted in some way. I recall extreme versions of this theme in my work with substance misusers who often found themselves at the bottom of a deep hole. In these situations clients usually expressed their shock and dismay accompanied by despair because they could see no way out. Over time I developed some reparative procedures that could be used to help instill hope and engage the client's agency to reconnect with a sense of direction and purpose. These would take the form of importing helpful elements into the landscape such as ladders and climbing equipment that could be used to extricate them from their predicament. Less extreme experiences of finding ones progress blocked are expressed in common linguistic metaphors such as: 'hitting a brick wall' or 'I've reached a dead-end'. In these anxiety-provoking situations people will often default to their automatic reactions. These responses commonly take unhelpful forms such as falling into despondency and helplessness or, the other end of the continuum, attempting to overcome or break through the block using force. Sometimes the automatic response can manifest as a rigid mental position that is characterised by either/or thinking and an attempt to impose a decision rather than allowing a process to unfold. The path imagery can be very helpful in these situations because it offers another possibility, i.e. a more conscious exploration of the block and how to resolve it. As a general rule, paying attention in the landscape allows the imaginal perspective an opportunity to convey more insights into particular features. In the following example, titled *An Unexpected T Junction*, I present a further extract of George's work seen previously in Chapter 8 (in the vignettes titled *The Light in the Hallway* and *A Fire Is Lit*).

> George had spent three years on a professional training course and had high hopes for his first post. Unfortunately he soon discovered that he had been recruited into a poorly functioning workplace with a rapid turnover of staff. He arrived for our eighth session in a state of shock – that morning he had been summoned for a meeting with the management and had been fired. I suggested that it might be helpful to orientate himself by looking at a representation of his journey. George reported that he found himself standing on the green verge of a tarmac road that had come to a T junction. On the other side of the junction was a high brick wall that appeared to be impassable. He had no hesitation in interpreting the landscape as an accurate representation of what had just happened; he had been traveling on a clear professional path and, out of the blue, the way ahead was suddenly barred, forcing him to turn either to the right or to the left. He said he was trying to make some kind of

sense about what he could do next. The loss of his job was leading him to consider radical and unwelcome possibilities of abandoning his dreams of establishing himself in his new profession. The brick wall appeared insurmountable. He found himself oscillating between feelings of hopelessness and dejection and an impulse to make an immediate decision in order to calm his understandable anxiety about money and security.

I urged him to explore the image further through turning it into a drawing. As he drew a bird's eye view of the T junction, he realised that the wall only extended a short distance in both directions. In fact, it appeared to be an outside wall enclosing a rectangle of ground and buildings. The road running left and right at the T junction also curved around each end of the perimeter wall. As he reflected on the drawing he said he felt calmer and he realised that maybe there was an alternative to his initial either/or thinking. In the following session he reported that he was starting to be more hopeful that he could find a way around this obstacle and continue to develop his professional career.

Drifting or floating

Interestingly, unlike some of the other themes discussed in this section, clients are far less likely to explicitly identify problems with floating or drifting through life. This is probably because they do not experience these conditions as pressing difficulties. It is usually others who make these observations as evidenced in common linguistic metaphoric expressions used somewhat pejoratively such as, 'He's just a drifter.' This lack of concern is usually mirrored in people's responses to where they find themselves in their landscapes. A starting point for therapeutic work will usually focus on a discussion regarding the long-term implications for the client of continuing to float or drift. In this section I will be offering some guidance for two common imagery manifestations of this theme – floating in the air and drifting out at sea.

It is not unusual for clients to report that their feet are not on the earth. Usually people feel that they are hovering just a little way above the ground. These conditions suggest escapism or resorting to fantasy. This self-evidential interpretation is supported by the way in which associated metaphoric expressions of 'not being grounded' are used to convey the idea that someone is not dealing with reality. It is helpful to establish with clients some idea of how long they feel they have been floating. Sometimes this is a representation of a personality characteristic, in particular, a tendency to live in fantasy. Sometimes it represents the response to a life event (as the following case vignette titled *Orbiting the Planet* illustrates). I am usually quite explicit with clients in this situation about the importance of some kind of grounding. Sometimes people who are very close to the surface of the earth will be able to land and engage more fully with the ground. However, other clients may have different responses including a disinclination to come down to earth. One of the guiding principles for work with the path image is respecting the right of clients to choose to remain where they are. Over time I have developed a reparative intervention that accommodates the range of potential responses to grounding the self more fully (including the possibility that someone might choose to continue to float). In this procedure I offer the possibility of visualising some form of connection with the ground below usually in the form of a silver-blue rope tied to a suitable anchor. Clients can then imagine that the other end of the rope is tied around their waist. I would emphasise that this is a temporary holding position. This intervention is usually acceptable because, although at one level it holds the person in place, it also allows some freedom of choice. Clients can decide if they want to use the rope to pull them down to earth or not. The rope also allows them to control the speed of their descent. This is particularly important when there are complex factors involved in returning to earth as illustrated in the following case vignette, titled *Orbiting the Planet*.

> I encountered Lee, a determined and thoughtful man in his mid-thirties, when he was beginning to address his long-term crack cocaine habit. Lee talked about the damage and despair caused by his chronic drug misuse and he struck me as highly motivated to change his life. Over two therapy sessions, we explored Lee's current position on his journey through life.
>
> He was surprised at first to find himself floating out in space orbiting the planet, particularly as it felt to him that he had been there a long time. I immediately made the connection with his crack cocaine use. Lee, however, was not convinced by my interpretation, explaining that his sense of dislocation had been present before his serious drug habit had begun. As he explored this picture in more depth, he realised that it was linked with a big change that had occurred in his adolescence. At the age of fifteen, he had returned from a relatively enjoyable period in a boarding school on the south coast of England to live at his family home in London. He said that he had very quickly become involved in crime and drugs.
>
> However, he felt that now he had reached the end of his drug-using career and it was time for him to return to reality and a more normal life. When I suggested to him the imagery strategy of using a silver-blue rope, he responded enthusiastically and requested that the other end should be tied around a tree near his old boarding school. In the second session, Lee returned to this image and he reported that he had come down a long way and was now just above the south coast town ready to land. I was concerned that he might be coming down too fast and I discussed with him the dangers of being unprepared for such a rapid change. After some careful consideration, Lee decided to leave himself in this position for a little while longer; he was beginning to get in touch with some long suppressed painful memories of his childhood and he realised that he needed to take this process more slowly. The dangers of a too rapid descent were made clearer to me as Lee spoke about the physical abuse he had experienced at the hands of a violent father. We left the work at this point with Lee feeling clear about both where he was

and also, more importantly, the next step he needed to take in his process of recovery from his substance misuse. Although he had always been skeptical about the necessity for therapy (he believed that willpower combined with motivation should be sufficient to break a drug habit) he was beginning to accept that he would need considerable therapeutic support to come to terms with his childhood experience.

The other general variant of being disconnected from the earth is when people report that they are floating in a body of water. The element of water is not the problem as such – it is the lack of agency that just floating would indicate. People can find themselves in a wide range of situations in relation to this scenario: they could be struggling to keep afloat; they may be drifting in a damaged boat; they could be close to the shore; or they may be way out in the middle of the ocean. Depending on their situation there are some possible reparative interventions and strategies that can be offered. The main principle to observe is ensuring safety.

In difficult situations, the first step is to help clients make their current position more tenable. Therefore, for people who are treading water I would suggest something that would keep them afloat such as a raft or a dinghy. If they report that they are in damaged boats then I would suggest some method of stopping up the hole and bailing out the water. I might also suggest the idea of dropping an anchor as a means of temporarily calling a halt to the drift. With all of these interventions it is important to help clients make links to what these images might represent in their outer world.

The next step is to discuss with the client the possibility of establishing a direction in which to head; in other words to recruit more agency in the way in which they are leading their life. People may well be ambivalent. One example, I recall, was a client who was highly resistant to returning to solid ground. He reported being in a well-equipped but somewhat storm-battered boat and he wanted to continue sailing about on the ocean. He felt he had been drifting for several years while he had been using heroin. It was only when, in response to my question, he said his boat was named *Nostalgia* that he started to reflect on his attachment to this aimless drifting and started to consider the possibility of landing his boat.

As an initial strategy I would usually suggest that people who have been out at sea for a while find somewhere, such as an island or shore, to drop anchor. This reparative intervention has a similar aim to the rope offered to clients who find themselves floating above the earth – it allows a temporary holding position. Whilst they are anchored close to the land they are then in a position to make choices about where they want to go. At the same time, they are not committed to disembarking. All of these suggestions need to be adapted to the individual requirements of each client's scenario. All kinds of variants are possible and some of the interventions suggested above will not be appropriate. Sometimes people are afloat in unusual containers that convey significant information about their situation. One client described herself floating out at sea inside a closed wooden box. My initial thought was that this sounded like a coffin. It seemed to me that this client was symbolising a dangerously passive attitude towards her life: she felt she had been like this for a year when her drug use had become chaotic. This imagery prompted some very delicate and gentle therapeutic work to help her take more responsibility. Eventually, she started to break open the top of the box so that she could see where she was more clearly.

Making a decision

The framing image of the path can be particularly useful when clients have reached a point in their lives when they are faced with a choice regarding their future direction. A range of factors may be implicated in the decision-making process including inner psychological changes as well as external events, such as the ending of an important relationship or project. Sometimes people are very clear about the process of making a choice and at other times they may experience considerable confusion and resistance. No matter how clients respond to decision making, the imagery of the landscape has the potential to offer some clear guidance. We have some common metaphoric expressions in English for such times of choice and classic examples would be: 'coming to a fork in the road' or 'being at a crossroads'. It is not surprising, therefore, that these expressions translate directly into the imagery clients report. In my early experience of using this framing image with substance misusing clients I can recall many instances of clients finding themselves at a crossroads where they had been waiting for a very long time. Their drug use had operated to keep them at that point of indecision. The following vignette, titled *Arriving at a Crossroads*, is an example of some of the classic imagery that arises when someone arrives at a point of change and choice in life.

> Alison, a vivacious woman in her early sixties, originally came for counselling to deal with her emotional reactions to the ending of a long-term relationship. She described it as a complicated and unusual relationship that had gone through different phases over two decades, in the last few years becoming a companionable friendship. When her partner decided to move on and find someone else, Alison felt bereft, even though at a rational level she had accepted the inevitability of this parting. After spending a few sessions exploring her thoughts and feelings she reported that she felt she was more peaceful and ready to accept a future without him. When I suggested she might look at where she was on her journey through life, she reported, somewhat to her surprise, that she was standing at a crossroads. She believed that she had only just arrived and this was linked to her acceptance the previous week that she was on her own. She said that although she could not read any directions on the signpost, she felt peaceful and happy to be in this new position. Alison contemplated the significance of finding herself at a crossroads: it was clear to her that the decisions she made now would determine the next stage of her life. When I asked her how long she thought this decision would

take she replied that it would last a year and would involve exploring all the possibilities that were open to her. I suggested that she might be interested in some kind of temporary shelter that would contain her through this period (see the later section that discusses process management procedures) but Alison replied that she did not want to be constrained in any way. We left her landscape at that point with Alison feeling happy to have arrived at such a clear calm point after the emotional turmoil of the preceding months.

Making a big effort

When clients are experiencing a time in their life that involves significant effort they often report imagery of climbing up steep slopes or mountain paths. These could be times when the external environment is particularly challenging or periods in life where a great deal of the person's energy is being harnessed to a significant goal or achievement. These periods are usually difficult but ultimately rewarding times of highly focused energy characterised by slow painstaking progress. Vigilance and careful planning is often required in order to avoid mistakes that could jeopardise the endeavour. This stage of the journey can take many different forms. However, no matter what stage someone is at, the framing image of the path allows clients a means of carefully considering each step of the way.

Sometimes people find themselves at the point when they are going to embark on a challenging task. I recall one client who saw himself standing at the foot of an almost vertical rock face with very few footholds. He immediately linked this with a very difficult decision he had to make concerning his children – he would have to involve social services to ensure their welfare. He knew that this action would inevitably trigger a confrontation with his volatile ex-partner. After some deliberation it was clear to him that there was no other viable option. However, he was very clear from the imagery that this was going to be a challenging process that was fraught with danger. Our work together focused on preparing him mentally and emotionally for the difficulties that lay ahead: one false move and he could lose his foothold, which he interpreted as the potential for losing access to his children.

Any form of climbing brings with it the danger of falling. The principle of ensuring safety is paramount here. At the end of a session where a client has been exploring and working with path imagery that represents making a big effort, it is important that the client is left in a tenable position. On precarious rock faces or mountain climbs, a secure holding place would be a ledge or a cave. Some potentially useful reparative interventions can be offered to clients who find themselves in these landscapes. Clients who report themselves as feeling ill-prepared for the scale of the challenges ahead could be offered the possibility of a rucksack containing useful equipment. The therapeutic work here could involve exploring how to increase clients' resilience, resourcefulness and determination in relation to what they may be facing. Clients often welcome suggestions that they could imagine symbolic objects such as: a torch that represents insight; or climbing equipment to represent the ability to manage particularly difficult parts of the climb. People may also want to visualise particular spiritual symbols to strengthen their faith. Sometimes these periods of great effort are short but sometimes people may experience significant stretches lasting years when all of their energy is required to make progress on their path. Amelia, whose work is presented in vignettes elsewhere (*The Roof with a Hole* in Chapter 8 and *Three Framing Images* in Chapter 11) is a case in point. During the first few years that we worked together, her inner landscape took the form of mountainous terrain. Her arduous journey represented the huge efforts that she had to expend on the process of establishing herself as an independent and self-reliant adult in the world. There were many difficulties on the path. At times she experienced the struggle as being overwhelming but she persisted. By the time she felt strong enough to operate in the world with a secure identity and the ability to regulate her emotions, she reported that the barren and precarious mountainous landscape was becoming greener with gentle slopes (I will be returning to discuss Amelia's process in more detail in Chapter 11).

Developing the work with the path: monitoring and process management functions

It should come as no surprise that the monitoring function plays a particularly important role when working with the framing image of the path. This is due to the fact that, unlike the other two framing images, the path is the representation of a dynamic process. The image offers a means of tracking someone's progress through life and can be a useful resource during periods of doubt and confusion. As I noted earlier in this chapter, it appears to be particularly helpful when important decisions and choices need to be made. It can also offer confirmation of the client's intimations that something subtle but important has changed. This is illustrated in another extract from Julia's work, titled *Released from the Jelly*, briefly referred to earlier in this chapter and also in another vignette (titled *Resisting the Building*) presented in Chapter 8.

> Julia had experienced a lengthy period of feeling that she was not able to make any progress in her external life. All the time that she was working on developing a stronger sense of inner security (represented in the rebuilding of the foundations of her house image), she felt frustrated because she could not find a new job. The imagery representing her journey through life did not seem particularly helpful for her – all she reported was a sense of herself struggling to make her way through an enormous shallow box containing a jelly-like substance. Although it made sense to me that the internal emotional work needed to be completed before she could fully engage with the outer world, Julia was not convinced and continued her fruitless quest to find suitable work.
>
> Towards the end of our work together on her building image, Julia announced that she believed she had finally established more self-confidence.

In addition to this, she had also had a realisation that because of this inner change she could now re-engage properly with the world of work. I suggested that she return and review her path image. She reported that, much to her surprise, her landscape image had suddenly changed. The enormous box containing the jelly had disappeared and, instead, she found herself standing in front of a two-dimensional painting of a landscape with a path in it. She felt that very soon she would be stepping into this picture and the little path represented a clear unimpeded direction. Although she was very surprised by the change in the imagery she agreed that it resonated with an inner sense that she was emerging from a long period of struggle and that she was on the point of being able to make a very big decision about where she was going to live and work.

NB: For another illustration of the way that the path imagery can be used to track a client's progress over time, see the detailed vignette (titled *Traversing the Dark Woods*) in the following section.

In general, the framing image of the path appears to provide less scope for using the process management function. However, there is one particular application of this function that has proved to be generally helpful – i.e. temporary shelters or structures that can be offered as potentially useful interventions at appropriate points. This procedure is very similar to the one described previously in the building chapter although it serves a somewhat different purpose. There are times when clients report that they need to stay in one place until they are ready to engage with the next stage of their journey. There could be a range of reasons for this including: the need for a period of recuperation; or time to prepare and plan; or a need to stop for a while and reflect. Sometimes these pauses represent a need for withdrawal from an active engagement with the outer world whilst the self undertakes a period of inner developmental and transformational work. At these points it can be helpful to offer the possibility of some kind of container in the form of a temporary shelter. Suggestions can be offered to the person in the form of tents, tepees, simple huts, tree houses or cabins. The client can design a suitable structure based on these suggestions. The main rule is that these need to be very simple structures and the interior should have the minimum requirements for the person's temporary needs. These interventions should not be pressed upon the client but instead offered tentatively. I have found from experience that people are quite clear in their responses (an example of offering this possibility and it being refused was illustrated previously in the vignette titled *Arriving at a Crossroads*). It is helpful to get clients to make some links between the temporary shelter and what this might signify in their external world.

These shelters appear to offer some containment for a short-term process and seem to be particularly useful as a means of managing transitions (an example of which can be seen in the detailed vignette, titled *Traversing the Dark Woods*, in the following section).

An example of the processing function in ongoing work with the path

As I mentioned earlier on in this chapter, the processing function is less evident in working with the path image than the other two framing images. In my experience, it is unusual for clients using this image to encounter repressed material that is explicitly symbolised in the landscape itself. However, there are occasions when the client's journey involves an active re-engagement with difficulties from the past. This is illustrated in the following final vignette, titled *Traversing the Dark Woods*, where I take the opportunity to present a more detailed account of some focused ongoing work with the path image.

> When I first met Mehmet, a sensitive and intelligent thirty-year-old man, he had been drug free for approximately two years and was struggling to cope with depression and chronic back pain. His will power was such that, even though in chronic psychological and physical pain, he had not relapsed. However, he was feeling hopeless about ever finding any personal happiness and fulfillment. I thought it might be helpful for him to get a sense of where he was on his journey and I suggested in our third session that I could help him translate his sense of being stuck into a landscape. He agreed to try it out although he admitted that he was skeptical about its usefulness. Predictably enough, Mehmet described a bleak picture – he saw himself standing in a derelict urban landscape that was encircled by a dense dark wood. He said that he had been there for ten years ever since his drug habit had become chaotic. Every now and then, he had made attempts to leave but after short forays into the woods he had felt defeated and had returned to his starting point. The only thing that had changed in the last two years was that he was drug free, otherwise he felt stuck in the same place. I felt moved by his stoic refusal to give into his cravings for heroin to relieve his pain but I was also concerned about how long he would be able to manage this untenable position. Over the next couple of sessions we discussed the possibility of his making another attempt to move through the woods. Mehmet believed that this feature in his landscape represented all the psychological problems that had built up from his formative experiences in a dysfunctional family. He knew he had to work his way through this but he did not feel confident that he could complete the task. However, as there seemed to be no other viable option, he agreed to make another attempt.
>
> Over the next three months, I saw Mehmet regularly and, bit by bit, he moved more deeply into the woods. This was a painful experience for him as he talked through the early difficulties he had experienced in his family. The main theme that dominated his memories was the experience of being humiliated and over powered by his father. It was clear to him that these early experiences at the mercy of a domineering parent were the source of his current feelings of inadequacy and powerlessness. However, the process of

expressing his thoughts and feelings was not making any tangible difference to Mehmet; his mood remained very low. My main focus during this period was to constantly remind him that making his way through dark woods was bound to feel heavy and oppressive. After three months, circumstances conspired to end our sessions together. Mehmet had some practical matters to attend to, so he took a break from the work and I, too, took leave of absence from the substance misuse treatment centre.

About nine months later I returned to the centre and met up again with Mehmet. I was very pleased to see him but I was concerned by how stressed he seemed – his skin looked grey with tension. He told me that events in his family had pushed him to near breaking point. His father had recently been charged with a serious and shameful criminal act and had gone into hiding. His mother, who had a history of mental ill health, was reacting very badly and Mehmet was doing his best to hold the family together. When he looked at where he was on his journey, he reported that he was in a very dense part of the woods. He felt very tense and trapped and he was not sure that he had the resources to survive. I believed that it was important to instill some hope into Mehmet and so I asked him to imagine rising up above the landscape in order to gain a wider perspective. When he looked down on the woods, he could see that he had reached its dark and dense heart and that this was the halfway point on the journey through to the other side.

Over the next couple of months, I saw Mehmet weekly as he moved through the crisis. Most of the time spent in these sessions involved emotionally supporting him as he struggled on a daily basis both with the testing external events and the exacerbation of his already stressed and depressed psychological state. In each session I endeavoured to get him to briefly revisit his internal landscape in order to concretise his perception that he was working through the core of his difficulties. Without this perspective I was concerned that he might lose hope. By the end of the two months, his father had received a custodial sentence, and Mehmet had assumed the role of head of the family, a role that he was anxious to exercise in a sensitive and appropriate way. The inner and outer parallels in this work are very striking; at the same time that Mehmet was working through his sense of having been psychologically imprisoned as a consequence of his father's abusive treatment, his father was in the process of being jailed. By this stage, the immediate crisis having passed, Mehmet felt emotionally exhausted and said that he needed some time out to rest psychologically and attend to practical matters.

Three months later, Mehmet returned to complete the work we had started together (I had let him know that I was going to leave my position at the agency). I was struck by how much more relaxed he appeared to be. He agreed that although still generally depressed, his condition had improved somewhat and that, every now and then, little glimpses of a brighter future were appearing. When we looked at where he was on his inner journey, he found himself, to his surprise, beginning to emerge on the other side of the dark woods. He peered out through the trees and reported a landscape of grassy fields and rolling hills. This was clear confirmation to me that Mehmet had successfully worked his way through some very difficult early psychological conditioning and was now ready to move on into a new stage of his life. Mehmet, however, did not embrace this idea with much enthusiasm and regarded any movement beyond the safety of the woods with alarm. This was understandable; the woods, although dark, had been safe and familiar. It was obvious to both of us that he would need some time to get used to the idea that a different future might lay in store for him. I therefore suggested to him that he create a temporary shelter at the edge of the woods that would act as a safe container while he prepared for the next stage. Mehmet visualised a tree house and he said that he would need about six months to get ready to move on. The final sessions were used to understand what this preparatory period would entail. Mehmet reported that he felt in a strange position: he was still depressed but he was also making plans for travelling in Southeast Asia. He said he knew that he had started to heal some of the wounds from his childhood but he was not convinced that he would be able to have a fulfilling life. However, he accepted that he needed time to come to terms with all that had happened and he felt secure enough to end the therapeutic work at this point.

Some caveats

Finally, there are some caveats to note in relation to working with this framing image. In this section I discuss two important ones: first, the potential for the spontaneous appearance of figures within the person's inner landscape; and second, the use of 'magical' interventions. Both of these are contentious issues and the literature displays the different approaches taken by innovators in the field. In this section I offer some guidance based on my own clinical experience and observations.

First, it has been my experience that every now and then clients will feel overwhelmed by experiencing themselves on their own in these inner landscapes. In order to ameliorate these feelings, they may well summon up known figures from their life, such as partners, children, parents or friends, to accompany them on their journey. However, as a general rule, I do not think it is a good idea to try to import actual representations of known figures into the framing images. In the case of the path image, it could indicate an over-reliance on others and a refusal to take full responsibility for one's own life (although, it is worth noting that other clinicians take different views on this practice – Desoille [1966], for example, promotes the importation of known figures into the client's inner landscape for specific therapeutic purposes). I would usually work with clients to find a compromise, one that will honour their feelings but also accord with the requirements of working with this framing image. I have usually found that suggesting that they could carry with them an object that symbolises the relationship – something that they can draw comfort and support from – is usually acceptable. This will often take the form of a locket with a photograph or some small personal memento.

Other types of figures can also spontaneously appear, although in my clinical experience these are rare. These figures (sometimes nonhuman ones such as animals and birds) might be completely unknown or they might be significant figures from the client's belief system or from the client's cultural repertoire, e.g. a cartoon image or figure from a folk tale. This is a complex area and I can only give my own thoughts here about how this matter could be approached. The main principle I would recommend is caution. Some preliminary investigative work needs to be done with the client to determine what this figure might represent. Usually this can be done through facilitating an interactive dialogue between the client and the figure if appropriate. Sometimes the figure can represent a part of the self that needs to be made more conscious. In other words, the client is at a point where some developmental work is required.

There is one possible manifestation that requires some further discussion: i.e. a figure, human or nonhuman, that explicitly announces itself as a guide. These ideas have become popularised in some of the Western self-help literature that draws on shamanic and premodern indigenous practices. In general, in the type of work presented in this book, guidance on the path is understood to arise out of an interactive process between the client's rational and imaginative perspectives. In other words, it is theorised as situated within the client's self. This conscious interactive process is facilitated initially by the therapist. As clients becomes more experienced in working in this way, they usually take more ownership of the process. When one element in the imaginal realm takes on the function of guidance there is a danger that the interactive process is becoming unbalanced. The figures purporting to be guides need investigation. They could represent parts of the self that have very different agendas to the conscious self. The world's folklore and fairy-tale traditions are replete with warning stories of mortals who followed false guides. There are other possibilities too depending on both the therapist's and client's view of the nature of consciousness. The secular Western materialist view of consciousness does not accommodate the possibility that a mental image can be anything other than a representational construct generated by the brain. However, other traditions (including Western esoteric ones), can and do accept the possibility that imagination is a way of contacting a nonordinary reality. These matters lie beyond the scope of this book and I would refer interested readers to the literature on transpersonal imagery such as Assagioli (1965, 2008), Jung and von Franz (1968), Rowan (2005) and Houston (1987).

Second, an important caveat concerns the use of 'magical' interventions. When clients find themselves in difficult or challenging circumstances, anything that offers an easy solution will be tempting. Such interventions could take the form of using magical means to either extricate themselves from a difficult landscape or to attempt to transform a problematic element of the landscape into something else. On the surface it might seem that using imagery in this way is just another example of using the directive functions in order to introduce new therapeutically productive elements into the landscape. However, magical interventions suggest to me that something potentially nontherapeutic is coming into play, i.e. an attempt to escape from difficulties and challenges in life. Other clinicians take a different approach. For example, in their account of using the guided imagery theme of ascending a mountain, Hall *et al.* (2006) suggest that clients can deal with an impasse by flying away and landing somewhere else. In general I am wary of interventions that have a 'magical' quality and I would not offer these kinds of interventions nor would I collude with clients who produce imagery that appears to me to be motivated by escapism. Difficulties in the landscape imagery need to be faced by the individual and therapy offers the opportunity to engage in a grounded process of working these through.

Conclusion

This chapter has provided an overview of the framing image of the path with some guidance to its application to therapeutic practice. Working with the path image is a creative process that aims to foster a more conscious approach to leading a purposeful and meaningful life. Once the framing image of the path is established, it can then continue to operate as a useful ongoing commentary on the person's progress through life. The landscape changes as the person moves forward – a never-ending accurate reflection of a personal journey through life with all its myriad twists and turns. In Chapter 11 I will be returning to examine in more depth how working with the path image can be integrated into ongoing counselling and psychotherapy practice. In particular I will be discussing how the path image combined with two other framing images offers a powerful multi-aspected vehicle for therapeutic processes.

References

Assagioli, R. (1965). *Psychosynthesis*, New York: Hobbs, Dorman & Co.
——. (2008). *Transpersonal Development*, revised edn, Forres, Scotland: Smiling Wisdom.
Bunyan, J. (1974). *The Pilgrim's Progress: From this world to that which is to come, delivered under the similitude of a dream*, Guildford: Lutterworth Press.
Desoille, R. (1966). *The Directed Daydream*, New York: Psychosynthesis Research Foundation.
Hall, E., Hall, C., Stradling, P. and Young, D. (2006). *Guided Imagery: Creative interventions in counselling and psychotherapy*, London: Sage.
Houston, J. (1987). *The Search for the Beloved: Journeys in mythology and sacred psychology*, Los Angeles: J. P. Tarcher Inc.
Jung, C., von Franz, M-L. (Eds.) (1968). *Man and His Symbols*, New York: Dell Publishing.
Lakoff, G. and Johnson, M. (2003). *Metaphors We Live By*, 2nd edn, Chicago: University of Chicago Press.
Leuner, H. (1984). *Guided Affective Imagery in Short-term Psychotherapy: The basic course*, New York: Thieme-Stratton Corp.
Rowan, J. (2005). *The Transpersonal: Spirituality in psychotherapy and counselling*, 2nd edn, London: Routledge.
Rowe, D. (2003). *Depression: The way out of your prison*, 3rd edn, London: Routledge.
Ungerer, F. and Schmid, H. (1996). *An Introduction to Cognitive Linguistics*, Harrow: Longman.

Chapter 10

The plant image

The use of plant metaphors as a means of representing more abstract human experience appears to be a nearly universal cultural practice. The world's literature contains many examples of plants used as symbols in this way: one example taken from the Buddhist tradition would be the lotus flower used to symbolise the development of consciousness. Accordingly, the counselling and psychotherapy literature also presents examples of this common practice of drawing on the metaphorical capacity of plants for concretely representing dimensions of the self. In terms of mental imagery, clinicians have developed a variety of procedures that are regarded as particularly suitable for the exploration of certain themes. These applications draw primarily on two aspects of plant imagery – first, specific types of plants lend themselves to particular aspects of human experience and, second, the stages of growth of the plant can be used to symbolise dynamic processes of human development. With regard to the former, the rose image is a common symbol that has been utilised in different ways. Assagioli (1965), for example, developed a guided imagery procedure where the client is instructed to visualise the blossoming of a rose to represent the development of spirituality. Leuner (1984), on the other hand, uses the image of the rose to represent sexuality. His guided imagery procedure of picking a rose is designed as a diagnostic test of a male client's attitude towards sex. Another plant image that is commonly used in therapeutic practice is the tree, probably because, as Hall *et al.* suggest, 'Clients have little difficulty in anthropomorphising the experience of being a tree, . . . ' (2006: 76). In their humanistically informed imagery work, the client is asked to draw a tree and the resulting picture is then used as a basis of self-exploration. Other modalities have also made use of this symbol – this image forms a component of one of the standard diagnostic assessment exercises used in art therapy, i.e. House-Tree-Person (Jolles, 1971) for measuring self-esteem.

Although the work presented in this chapter shares many common features with the work developed by the pioneers and clinical innovators mentioned above, it does differ in one important respect, i.e. it uses a more generic plant image rather than a particular plant type. In practice this less specific framing image appears to allow greater scope to the imaginal perspective to depict psychological and developmental issues pertinent and relevant to the individual. I note that clients have produced a very wide range of images in response to this starting point, from dormant bulbs through to mature trees (and this range will be evident in the clinical vignettes used to illustrate this chapter).

As with the other two framing images of the building and the path, the work on plant imagery presented here is informed by the theory of conceptual metaphor (Lakoff and Johnson, 2003). This theory asserts that the deep experiential gestalts that structure human cognition arise from embodied experience of the world. As people experience and interact with their environment, common features such as plants and animals contribute to shaping cognitive processes. This could explain the prevalence of plants as metaphors that has been noted by cognitive linguists. Kövecses (2002) argues that one conceptual metaphor, in particular, i.e. COMPLEX ABSTRACT SYSTEMS ARE PLANTS, accounts for the plant-related linguistic metaphors that are commonly used for a very wide range of abstract concepts including political and economic systems as well as social organisations. In the case of the framing image presented here, the conceptual metaphor is PEOPLE ARE PLANTS. There are many examples in English of linguistic metaphorical expressions that are generated by this particular conceptual metaphor. Some common examples would be: 'she is branching out at last'; 'he uprooted himself and his entire family and moved to another country'; 'she is blossoming in her new role.' As with the two other framing images, this particular image illuminates particular aspects or dimensions of the self and casts others into the shadows. In this case, personality traits and processes of growth and development are highlighted whereas other dimensions of the self are obscured.

This chapter begins with a general discussion of using the image of the plant form in counselling and psychotherapy. It then goes on to offer some guidelines for effective practice and presents the procedures for helping the client to generate a self-representation in the form of a plant. The main stages of working with this framing image are then discussed in detail.

Overview of the plant image

In the early days of my clinical practice with substance misusers, I experimented with a range of images to represent the self and I discovered that plant imagery was particularly helpful in shedding light on the person's psychological state. I observed that the clients were able to represent themselves as plant forms quite easily and that the image revealed the person's current condition and also symbolised earlier developmental issues. Not surprisingly, many of the plant images looked in poor states due to long-term neglect and required immediate reparative interventions. However, despite often revealing damaged conditions, the plant image also conveyed a hopeful perspective, i.e. no matter how damaged the plant, the image, by its very nature, also contained the possibility of regeneration. I believe that this is one of the reasons that the substance misusing clients seemed to find it helpful and acceptable to represent themselves in this way. Later on,

I continued to use this framing image with a wider range of clients and presenting issues, which allowed me to further develop and refine its use in therapeutic practice. My clinical experience leads me to conclude that the plant image can shed light on two important aspects of the self.

First, the type of plant form reported by the client can indicate the dominant personality traits or the characteristic way of being in and responding to the world. The imaginal perspective appears to draw on the available cultural, personal and self-evidential repertoire for an appropriate plant form to symbolise these characteristics; an example of this would be the self-representation in the form of an oak tree to convey the dominant trait of strength ('as strong as an oak' being a common expression in English). Another example would be a self-representation in the form of a cactus that highlights characteristic self-reliance – a self-evident interpretation.

Second, the plant image also represents processes of growth and development. This feature is a useful diagnostic tool because it can identify how and when these processes have been arrested. Furthermore, it can also offer a helpful corrective to an over emphasis, evident in contemporary Western culture, on the linear progressive dimension of development. In nature, development is cyclical – not only through the course of the life cycle of the whole plant but also through seasons of growth and dying away of parts of the plant, e.g. flowers on a tree. I have noted how helpful it has been for clients to have a non-pathologising way of viewing their life as going through natural cycles of expansion and contraction. Although in reality both the type of plant and its stage of development are interdependent aspects of one phenomenon, and cannot in truth be separated in therapeutic work, I have retained this distinction here as a means of structuring the presentation of the work in the following sections.

In general I would suggest the framing image of the plant to clients if they reported any of the following: a sense of unease, a feeling they were not flourishing, or struggling to thrive. Sometimes clients use clear metaphoric language that would indicate that the plant image could be helpful. When one of my clients said that she felt she was 'dying inside', I immediately suggested that she could visualise herself in the form of a plant. Her image of a drooping tree that was not gaining the right nutrients from the soil gave her a clear insight into the nature of her current difficulties. I also noted from my experience of many years of working in a cancer support agency that this was often the preferred framing image for the patients there. Therefore I would recommend this as a starting point if people are experiencing physical illnesses.

Main principles for working with the plant image

As the plant form image is a representation of a fundamental dimension of the person's self, i.e. the person's personality traits and psychological development, it requires a skilled and careful approach on behalf of the therapist. The following points have arisen out of clinical observation and practice and are offered, not as prescriptions, but as some guiding principles.

- **Ensuring the health of the plant form.** This is the main principle that should inform all aspects of working with this framing image. If the plant form appears to be compromised in any way, then the focus of the therapeutic work should attend to this. An important question would be how this negative state is manifesting in the person's life. Sometimes the condition is clear; for example, plants that are dying through lack of water or where plants are about to collapse because the main stem or trunk is damaged. In such cases, immediate reparatory interventions are required to halt the damage. In relation to the examples given, these imagery procedures would be: in the former case, visualising the plant being watered; and in the latter, visualising a temporary means of support such as tying the plant to a stake. Sometimes the plant form is compromised but stable. It has adapted to earlier damage and continues to grow albeit in a distorted form. In these cases immediate reparative interventions are not required. However, the compromised state of the plant indicates where the focus of ongoing therapy should be. An example of this would be a client who produced an image of a tree that had been felled when she was a child. There was a big root system under the ground that appeared to be still alive but above ground all that remained of the tree was a sawed off trunk. The therapeutic work focused over a period of years to help her recover from a very abusive childhood. During that time the tree trunk began to display some new shoots culminating in a fully grown tree by the end of the therapy.
- **Clarity about what can and cannot be achieved.** The type of plant form is a given and needs to be accepted. There are occasions when a plant form will change into another different type, but these are rare and I have only witnessed this happening either during long-term therapy or after sustained transformational personal development (see Chapter 11 for further discussion). The plant form symbolises the person's main personality traits as well as issues regarding inner growth and development, consequently, any changes that occur represent changes happening within the person. As with the two other framing images, the plant form provides a site for therapeutic work where the rational and imaginal perspectives can be constructively integrated. Alterations can be made to the plant form image but only if they are appropriate reparative or process management interventions. A person's inner growth and development is an unfolding creative process that follows an inner logic.

The first stage of the work

In the following process, the term 'plant' is used as shorthand for all possible kinds of plant forms, e.g. flowers, bushes and trees. It also encompasses all possible stages across the continuum of plant growth – one end being ungerminated states (e.g. seeds, bulbs, etc.) through immature stages (plant shoots, tree saplings, etc.) through to mature stages (e.g. fully grown trees, annual plants at the end of their growth cycle such as sunflower plants with seed heads, etc.).

Bringing the plant into view: using the framing function

The initial diagnostic procedure is designed to elicit a clear picture of the plant form. It is important to make sure that the person understands what this image is designed to represent. If the concept of psychological growth is a bit too abstract then I would use a question such as, 'If you were a plant, what kind of a plant would you be?' (for some more general guidance on introducing imagery work to clients, see Chapter 12). I would also reassure them that they will be in control of this process and that this is purely an information-gathering exercise.

Sometimes people might think that this method sounds complicated so it is a good idea to reassure them that this is a simple process. I would usually emphasise that the aim initially is to gain a picture of the plant form just to see what condition it is in and if it needs any particular attention. It is also important to let clients know that they can stop the procedure at any time if they are feeling uncomfortable (for further elaboration on preparing the client for imagery work please see Chapter 12).

Adapt the following procedure to the individual client. When instructions are followed by bracketed terms, this indicates that you will need to select one that is suitable for your client. Suggested verbatim instructions or questions are given in quotation marks.

1. Make sure the client is sitting comfortably with uncrossed legs and both feet on the floor. Ask them to close their eyes. Then take them through a simple relaxation procedure of your choosing.
2. Instruct them to imagine that they are standing somewhere outdoors. State clearly that it is neutral territory and that for the time being the surroundings are unclear. It is not an environment they recognise. Make sure they are imagining themselves actually being there, i.e. not viewing themselves from a third-person perspective. I will say something along the lines of: 'Be in your body, imagine you can feel the ground under your feet.'
3. Ask them to silently request their subconscious mind (inner self, etc.) to produce a picture of something growing such as a plant, flower, bush or tree (it is important that you specify the full range otherwise the instruction will restrict the scope of the response) that is a representation of their psychological growth and development. You can phrase this in more simple terms by asking them if they were a plant form what would they be? Suggest that this plant form will appear directly in front of them. Tell them not to worry if it is vague at the beginning, you will help them to see it more clearly. Recommend that they accept the first picture that comes and not to censor it. Give them a couple of minutes to begin to get a sense of the plant.

4   Tell them you are now going to ask some questions to get a clearer picture of the plant form. Reassure them at this point that they are not to worry about getting it right but instead just let their imagination work with it. Use the following as starting points to get a basic picture. Begin by clarifying the basic type of plant form, i.e. tree, bush, flower, plant. Usually this is a straightforward matter and most people will be able to identify the type. Although, there is a possibility that the person might produce an image that is difficult to categorise and will require some further exploration (one client, I recall, pictured what appeared to him to be stones in the desert – it took a while for both of us to work out that these were a form of cactus that looked like a stone until the flowering season when a brightly coloured flower emerges from the plant). Use the following questions – dependent on the type of plant form – to elicit a clear picture:

- If it is a tree, find out the following if possible: type of tree; stage of maturity; and what season it is in.
- If it is a plant, flower or a bush, find out the following if possible: type of plant; and what stage of growth or flowering it is in.

    Other clarifying questions if appropriate can be asked about its condition (is it healthy, neglected, wilting, damaged, etc.)
- Find out about its growing environment: ask if it is growing in the ground or a container – if the latter then elicit a description.

    By the end of this stage, clients will usually have produced a reasonably clear picture of their inner representational plant. However, this is not always the case.

    Sometimes people visualise plants that exist in their known world, e.g. a house plant that they own. Or they may see their representational image in a familiar landscape, e.g. their childhood garden. As discussed in the instructions for eliciting the building image, it is important to gently explore the significance of these autobiographical references. The main question to resolve is whether this is an indication that the person is strongly identified in some way with a particular environment (see the vignette, titled *The Rose with No Thorns*, presented later on in the chapter).

    Sometimes people are unable to visualise a plant form. This could be an inner resistance that indicates that the plant form is not going to be a helpful starting point (see the discussion and illustration of multiple starting points in Chapter 11). Or it may be that the plant form is unusual in some way. Some gentle inquiry can be used to help the client explore this lack of obvious imagery. Sometimes, as with the other framing images discussed in this book, it may be that the person is censoring imagery that does not appear to them to fit the conventional plant forms – such as the previously mentioned image of desert plants that look like stones. Another possibility is that the plant form is represented in an ungerminated state buried under the earth (for a discussion of this particular condition see the vignette titled *The Underground Bulb)*. However, it is important not to press clients too much, and if the resistance persists then I would usually suggest that we abandon the procedure for the time being.

5   Then get some sense of the initial response to their plant form by asking clients to identify their main emotional reaction to it. As a prompt it can sometimes be helpful to remind them that they are looking at a picture of themselves.

6   Suggest that they are going to explore their plant form a little more in order to get some more information about it. Then, depending on what is appropriate to the individual and the particular image, it is worth attending to the following:

Ask the person if they sense there is anything about the plant that needs attention. This might be obvious, for example: the plant could be wilting; a branch might be splitting off from the trunk; the stem is bending; or the container might be too small. Or it could be less apparent, for example: the trunk of the tree looks solid but it is in fact hollow; the root system of the plant is too shallow; or the soil is very poor. It could also be something with more positive connotations such as a flower that is blossoming.

Then, whatever the person indicates as noteworthy will need some further exploration. If at all possible, gain some indication from clients as to how long ago they think that a particular development occurred in the plant. Ask them what was happening in their life at that time that might be linked with this particular feature of the image. This information is important because it can help the person to begin to make correspondences between the internal image of growth and related outer events. It will also suggest ways in which psychological growth can be promoted. An example of this might be asking how long the client thinks that the tree has been in its winter season; if it has been like that for a long time it could indicate an arrested depressive state (see the vignette titled *A Tree Stuck in Winter*). Other examples could be: if the plant is damaged, how might this correspond with a traumatic event? If the flower is opening then what positive life events is this connected with? In order to elicit these links I would try some general questions along the following lines:

'What do you feel the. . . . (specify what this is) . . . . means?'
'Can you get any sense of how long that . . . (specify what this is). . . . . has been like that?'
'How do you think that . . . (specify what this is) . . . shows up in your current life?'

It is important to do this in a sensitive way as the corresponding events or conditions may have been traumatic. It is a good idea to let the client know that you are not going to initiate any further exploration at this point. Reassure them that you are looking at it purely to gain basic information in order to understand the plant form better and see what it needs in order to grow.

7   When the above steps have been completed, advise the person that you are now bringing this initial procedure to a close. Ask them to stand in front of the plant. It can be useful to give them a minute to visualise it clearly. Then instruct them to turn around with their back to the plant form and create a blank screen.
8   Instruct them to switch their attention back to their physical body. Let them know that you are going to bring them back into their everyday state of mind. Then use a simple basic procedure designed for this purpose.
9   Finally, at the end of the procedure, it is helpful to summarise their account of the plant form as a preparation for a discussion of their experience.

Starting to work with the plant: the diagnostic and reparative functions

After the client has produced a plant image this will then usually become the site for exploration and meaning-making and this means that the diagnostic function will come to the fore. If there are any significant problems with the state of the plant that need immediate attention then the reparative function would also come into play, for example, if the plant is wilting through lack of water.

In this section I discuss how to begin using the client's plant image as a means of facilitating self-insight and identifying the focus for therapeutic work. As stated earlier in the introduction, I have structured this section along the two main dimensions of the plant image, i.e. type of plant and growth processes. In the first part I will consider how the type of plant can provide a means for understanding the self and this will include related issues such as self-evident and cultural interpretations. This part will include some discussion of common types of plants that I have observed in clinical practice as well as the important matter of the ground or container in which the plant is growing. In the second part I will move onto how stages of growth and development can be revealed in the plant image. At the end of the section I discuss some potential reparative interventions for common problems presented by clients when working with the plant form.

Attitude towards self

This section opens with the important matter of the client's attitude towards the plant as this will impact on therapeutic work and process. I noted how often substance misusers displayed negative attitudes towards their plant images and the following vignette, titled *The Tiny Potato Plant*, is drawn from that particular client group. In this case, the negative fearful response a client held towards her own growth was particularly problematic.

> Ann was attending a rehabilitation programme to help her with the challenging combination of long-term alcohol dependency and clinical depression. Initially, she appeared shut down and uncommunicative; however, over time, her warmth and sensitivity became more apparent. At the beginning of our

work together, she visualised herself as a potato plant that had only recently begun to emerge above ground. Ann's reaction to this was one of alarm and anxiety. She explained that the plant had been safe when it was underground but now that it was above ground it could be destroyed. I understood where her fear came from – she had spoken to me previously of her childhood and how it had been dominated by an abusive violent father. I decided at this juncture to make a process management intervention and I suggested that she could imagine some kind of temporary cover over the shoot to protect its growth. Initially, she wanted to create something dark without any openings. I explained to her that if the plant were to be completely sealed off, it would die. Ann's fear of exposure was so great that she was willing to sacrifice her new growth and it took some considerable time to work through the resulting impasse. Finally, we reached a makeshift compromise: she would allow one small window in the container. As a further precaution she imagined a curtain behind the window that she could open and close. I was still concerned about the well-being of the plant but that was all that Ann would accept.

Over the next few sessions I made a point each time of getting her to picture the plant and imagine watering it despite her reluctance. Finally, she felt secure enough to leave a permanent small opening for the plant to receive light and water by itself. At no point would she reveal to me if the plant had grown and I had to bide my time until our final session when she reported to me that the plant had grown considerably and was stronger. By the end of her rehabilitation programme she had become more assertive in the community and it was clear that she had begun to break through the fear that had constrained her for the whole of her adult life.

Types of plants

In general, the kind of plant that clients report can be usefully explored as a symbolisation of dominant personality traits such as their strengths, pre-occupations, outlook, support needs and way of relating to the world. I have noted that clients usually grasp the self-evidential nature of plant imagery and easily make connections with the type of plant they visualise. Sometimes, the client may produce plant forms that are not part of the therapist's repertoire. However, an inquiry that elicits a detailed description of the unfamiliar plant form will usually identify the salient factors. Having said this, though, it is always important to bear in mind other aspects of interpretation – in particular, the culturally constructed meanings of plants. When working with clients from a different culture or country it is important to ask them if their plant form has any particular cultural associations as these may well be useful in generating further insights. In this section I give two examples of how the plant image can be used as a site of self-exploration and I consider some of the classic plant types that clients produce as self-representations.

Trees have been particularly common plant forms in my clinical work. It is important to ascertain, if possible, the particular species of tree as this will often generate further insights for the client. It is worth adding that I have noted some particular psychological issues that often seem to be present for people who represent themselves as trees. These difficulties are linked to both how they experience themselves in relation to their peers, i.e. they are often late developers, and also how they are perceived by others, i.e. as possessing an inner strength. In the following vignette, titled *A London Plane Tree*, the client viewed his particular type of tree as a helpful confirmation of his sense of self.

> I had last seen Tom, a cheerful and energetic Londoner, five years ago on a previous admission to the crisis centre. During the intervening period, he had been to a rehabilitation centre and had remained drug free while he worked as a drugs worker. He had recently relapsed on crack cocaine and he described the extreme paranoia he had experienced. At one point, he had become convinced that he was being followed by undercover police officers and had presented himself at the police station demanding to be arrested for his own protection. The desk sergeant found it difficult to persuade Tom that the police were completely uninterested in him. It was this experience that made him realise that he could not smoke crack again. Although he recounted this experience with rueful good humour, he stated that he could not afford to put himself through another relapse. I was aware that Tom had undertaken considerable therapeutic work on his previous rehabilitation programme, so I suggested to him that he might like to see a picture of his psychological growth in order to gain a wider perspective.
>
> In the session, Tom viewed himself as a big London plane tree growing on one of the main North London urban routes. The tree looked healthy and, from the state of the leaves, he guessed that it was in its summer season. Tom resonated with this image and said that it just about summed him up – he was a tough survivor, born and bred in a rough inner city environment. The tree was undamaged; in fact, it appeared to be flourishing. This image prompted him to accept that he needed to channel all this energy back into something constructive. Over the next couple of sessions, Tom and I explored his long-term goal of pursuing youth work in the community. He reported that his frame of mind was becoming more optimistic and that he was using the image of the plane tree to restore his confidence in himself.

Another example of a client making productive connections with the type of plant and her sense of self can be seen in the following vignette, titled *The Cactus in the Snow*. The client represented herself as a cactus – a plant type that invites self-evidential interpretations of a well-defended and self-reliant personality. Some of the psychological issues that appear to be associated with this plant form relate to the ways the person manages emotional processing. Generally speaking, they need little emotional input and do not thrive in environments that flood them emotionally.

> Sonia, an articulate and self-contained woman in her early thirties, was highly motivated to let go of her crack cocaine habit – an addiction which had taken away her job and given her a criminal record. However, her stay in

the rehabilitation centre had involved the unwelcome return of an old depressive state. She was very concerned that this would drag her under and that she would be tempted to use drugs again. When she visualised her psychological growth and development, she saw a tiny cactus growing in a terracotta pot that had been placed out in the snow. She made a link between the snow and her experience at secondary school. This had been a cold and lonely time for her when she had experienced rejection by the other girls. Ever since then, she had felt mistrustful of other women. It seemed to her that she had not been able to really move on in her life since that point and that all her energy had been used for her own survival. We explored the imagery further, in particular, the mismatch between the cactus and the snow. Sonia resonated with the idea that a cactus needs very little attention in order to flourish; she said that it was easy for her to live on her own and she liked her own company. However, although the cactus had clearly survived, it had not been able to grow in such an emotionally cold climate. It became clear to Sonia that she needed to find a way of releasing herself from the wounding experience of school so that she could grow and develop.

NB: The next part of Sonia's work is presented in the vignette (titled *The Cactus in the Greenhouse*), which is used to illustrate the section on the process management function.

In the rest of this chapter there will be further illustrations of the range of plant forms that clients produced. Although these examples have been chosen to illustrate particular aspects of working with the plant image, some of them include references to how the type of plant form itself generated insights for the client. These illustrations include some of the most common types that have occurred in my clinical practice.

The ground or container

The earth or ground that the plant is growing in represents the basic conditions that support the person's growth and development. Sometimes the imaginal perspective will deliver imagery that indicates most emphatically that there is a very serious problem with the client's environment. In the following vignette, titled *The Cherry Tree in the Wrong Ground*, the imagery pointed to the long-term negative consequences of an unsuitable environment and the toll it took on the person's life.

> I did a short piece of therapeutic work with Madeleine, a courageous and free-spirited woman, who had been diagnosed with terminal liver cancer. When I first encountered her, she was still holding down a part-time teaching job but she was finding it more and more difficult to manage the increasing pain levels of her illness. Madeleine wanted to find a way to draw on her inner resources to help her in this final stage of her life. She was familiar with a range of practices such as chi gong that employed mental visualisation

techniques and she was interested in using mental imagery to help her gain more insight into how to manage her anger and despair.

Initially, she produced an image of a cherry tree moving into its winter season. It had been growing in ground that was poorly suited to it and the root system had not established itself properly – in fact, parts of it had become rotten. There was a sense that the tree needed to be dug up and replanted somewhere more conducive to its growth. Madeleine said that the meaning was clear to her – she had come to live in London when she was a young woman and, at first, it had suited her perfectly. However, over the last decade she had increasingly felt that she did not belong in this big city. The culture had changed and she expressed her belief that it had become psychologically toxic for her. She said ruefully that she had missed her opportunity to leave years ago and had regretted staying put. Now she was consumed by thoughts of moving into a spiritual community away from the city where she believed she might be able to re-energise and heal herself. She thought that her cherry tree could be carefully dug up and lifted out of the ground. However, the prospect of such a radical move when she was so ill was not a realistic one: her physical condition was deteriorating rapidly. We focused, instead, on helping her visualise props being placed under the branches to give the tree some form of extra support. She interpreted this as allowing herself to let go of her fiercely independent stance and, instead, open up to receiving help from others and the services provided by the hospice and cancer support agency. Very shortly afterwards, Madeleine moved back into the hospice where she later died surrounded by her family and friends.

Another possibility is that the imagery of the ground or container will deliver information about formative conditions in the person's life (similarly to the foundations of the building discussed in Chapter 8). A good example of this can be seen in the vignette (titled *A Single Blade of Grass*) presented later in this chapter. Occasionally, the continued impact of the person's childhood growing conditions is made explicit when clients report that their plant is growing in a familiar past environment such as their parents' garden (see the vignette titled *The Rose with No Thorns*).

Plants may not be growing in the ground at all: it is quite a common occurrence in my clinical practice for clients to report that their plant form is growing in some kind of container. I have already written about this in the earlier vignette (titled *The Cactus in the Snow*). In general, it is helpful to facilitate clients' exploration of the container, in particular how it maps onto their world. In the following example titled *The Pot Bound Plant*, the person was able to use and work with the image of the container to help her make sense of a big change she needed to make. Drawing on both the rational and imaginal perspectives led to a successful outcome of a personal crisis.

Deborah had been living for several years next door to her long-term partner in a small village in a remote part of the Scottish Highlands. During this period, she had thrived in the rugged conditions that suited her practical and resourceful nature. When she first viewed her plant representation, she reported that it was a healthy plant (she was unable to identify the species) and it was growing in a small red pot – there was a sense that this container represented her relationship. She reported that the roots were beginning to feel cramped but this feeling was not strong enough to warrant any further attention at that time.

Over the following two years, Deborah began to find the remote conditions more challenging, particularly when her cottage was snowbound during the winter. In addition, her long-term relationship was showing clear signs of coming to an end. She found herself sinking into a depression. Usually energetic and motivated, she was disturbed to find herself unable to summon up any enthusiasm for her house and garden and she felt uncharacteristically emotionally vulnerable. I suggested to her that it might be time to return to her plant image to see if it could shed any light on her depressive state. To her evident surprise, she reported that the roots had cracked open the red pot and the plant was now lying on the ground. This picture began to make sense to Deborah as she linked the vulnerable state of the plant with her own feelings of insecurity. Concerned by the compromised state of the plant, I suggested an immediate reparative intervention to her: she could imagine the plant's roots being temporarily contained in something. Deborah immediately visualised a strong plastic bag tied around the roots that would keep them safe and moist whilst she worked out where the plant needed to go. This represented a turning point for her as she accepted the truth of her feelings – her life in this part of the world was over and it was now time to move. The imaginal perspective on her depression gave her the means to contain her problematic feelings while she attended to practical matters. As her emotional state began to improve, she was able to consider her options. Over the next couple of months, she used the plant image to support all the practical decisions she would need to make during this transition. The first step was to begin to visualise a new suitable container for her plant form. Deborah reported that an image of a simple, aesthetically pleasing, grey ceramic pot was coming into view. This process corresponded with the search for a property to buy in the South of England near her family. As she went through all the stages of setting up home, this was mirrored in the plant imagery as she visualised her plant being established in its new container. Within a relatively short period of time, the process was completed and Deborah had begun a new chapter in her life.

Stages and cycles of growth and development

After the initial clarification of the type of plant, attention will often turn to exploring other aspects of the image. Of particular relevance to therapeutic work would be the plant's current stage of growth. Sometimes, this aspect can be especially illuminating as illustrated in the two following vignettes, titled *The Underground*

Bulb and *A Single Blade of Grass*. In both cases, the plant image conveyed information about arrested psychological growth in a concrete and unambiguous fashion that allowed both clients, in their different ways, to make more sense of their current experience.

> Nick, an ebullient and charismatic man in his mid-thirties, had experienced a long period drug-free while working abroad. However, on his return to London he had relapsed on heroin. He felt he had the potential to develop as a musician and he was very interested in looking at a picture of his psychological growth. Initially, Nick could not conjure up any plant image at all. He appeared to be standing in a landscape and could imagine the ground under his feet but, despite repeated requests to his subconscious mind, nothing appeared. I asked him to notice where his attention was being drawn to and he replied that he kept looking down at the ground. It was then, to his surprise, that he pictured a large and unusual bulb that was buried in the earth. It had not yet begun to grow. This image had a powerful impact on Nick. He had felt for a long time that he had an undeveloped potential that he was neither exploring nor fulfilling. It seemed to him that most of his adult life had consisted of finding ways to suppress the boredom of an unfulfilling life – using heroin being the most damaging one. Unfortunately, I did not have the chance to explore this with him in further sessions, as he was due to leave the crisis centre the following day.
> A year later, Nick arrived back at the crisis centre having relapsed on heroin and crack cocaine. He was very enthusiastic about engaging again with the imagery work and he also felt very positive about his detoxification programme. We returned to the image of the bulb buried in the earth. He reported a development; a whole network of roots had begun to grow out of the base of the bulb. Nick was very clear that this had begun during a recent experience in jail. He explained to me that his six-month prison spell had been a deeply positive experience and that he had used this time to practise meditation and play music. Although this was an unusual trigger for positive growth (he had been remanded in an inner London jail, notorious for its overcrowded conditions and bullying regime) it was evident that his time in prison had been very productive.

NB: A further extract from Nick's work is presented later on in the vignette, titled *One Bulb Produces Many Shoots*.

In the following vignette, titled *A Single Blade of Grass*, the image produced by the client revealed how the harsh conditions of his childhood had delayed his development. As with the preceding illustration the image also shows how new adult experiences operated to stimulate new growth.

> Mick, a forty-year-old man with a twenty-year heroin habit and associated forensic history, was determined to address his chronic anxiety and low

self-esteem. He traced this back to a very abusive upbringing. Being a devoted father, he was determined that his children should receive a better upbringing than he had done but he was finding it difficult to develop his self-confidence.

In the first session, Mick explained to me that he wanted to use the imagery to look at his low self-esteem. I suggested that it might be more helpful if he widened that out to the bigger picture of his psychological growth and development, and he was happy to do this. In response to the first instructions of the process, he said he felt he was standing in an empty desert and that all he could see was a tiny single blade of grass that had only recently grown. This was such a powerful image that I felt an emotional response welling up inside me. He said he knew exactly what this meant – the desert was his childhood environment where he had not been able to grow so he had stayed inside himself just like this plant had stayed as a seed under the desert surface. In response to my question as to when the shoot had first emerged, he said it had happened when he came to the rehabilitation centre and, for the first time in his life, people paid attention to his feelings. I asked him what he felt when he saw this blade of grass and he replied that it gave him a great sense of hope. We discussed the plant's needs and how important it was to look after it. He said it would need regular watering and in the inner picture he imagined sprinkling it with spring water. We talked about the meaning of water and how it related to emotional release and support (he said he had not cried for many years). We concluded the session with Mick reflecting on the new experience of feeling hopeful that, finally, he might have a chance to begin to really grow as a person instead of being riddled by chronic anxiety.

NB: A further extract from Mick's work is presented later in the vignette (titled *The Vulnerable New Plant Shoot*).

The seasonal stage of the plant can also deliver helpful insights particularly in relation to the person's emotional and energetic state. Quite often, natural developmental and cyclical life processes can be experienced in the initial stage as strange and alarming, therefore it can be useful to have a way of reframing them from a more positive perspective. The plant form image can help the client differentiate between pathological conditions that need some kind of intervention and nonpathological processes that need to be accepted and understood. An example of this can be found in clients who represent themselves as trees in their winter season (a quite common theme in my clinical work). These clients usually report depressive states associated with this imagery. The work would usually focus initially on investigating this seasonal stage to gain a better understanding of the depressive symptoms. The following vignette, titled *A Tree Stuck in Winter*, is an example of working with this particular theme.

> When I first encountered Jessica, she told me she had been struggling with depression for a long time and had been prescribed Prozac for the previous two years. She wanted to find a way of moving on with her life and

stop relying on anti-depressants. Her life history had been a challenging one: she had been brought up by a mother with mental health problems who had dominated the family. Jessica had been subjected to daily cruelties that included, as a small child, being locked in dark cupboards for hours at a time. I was struck by how, despite these harsh formative experiences, her attitude to others seemed sensitive and open-hearted. Also, although she felt that her upbringing had created difficulties in creating a fulfilling life for herself, she was clearly a resilient woman.

Jessica's self-representation took the form of a tree in winter (she was not sure about its species). She was concerned by its state – the ends of the branches were dried out and the tree needed watering. On further exploration, she came to the conclusion that her tree had gone into winter when she was eighteen years old and had experienced a severe depression. Now, in her late-thirties, she had never fully emerged from that earlier depressive episode. She interpreted the dried-out state of the branches as the cumulative effects of years of stress. We discussed the likelihood that watering the tree would involve processes of emotional release. Jessica felt that this was the only way she could move forward in her life and that she was ready to do whatever was required to release her tree from winter.

Over the next few months, under medical supervision, Jessica cut down her antidepressant dosage to zero and, as predicted, experienced a very difficult time as long-suppressed emotions rose to the surface. Particularly difficult for her to tolerate and process was the rage from her childhood. There were times during this period when she felt so overwhelmed that she doubted she had the strength to endure it. Yet, she was able to draw on deep reserves of resilience, and little by little, she started to feel that she was making some progress. She acknowledged that, even though the waves of feelings were very difficult to cope with, this stormy passage was preferable to the never-ending depression.

When, after several months of processing her feelings, she returned to the image of the tree, she reported that buds had developed on the branches and were beginning to open out into new leaves. This hopeful image was a confirmation for Jessica that her work had paid-off. She decided to stop the therapy at that point – she believed she had completed a very important task and needed time to get on with her outer life. She sensed that it was time now to find more fulfilling work and she was now more confident in her abilities and own resources.

The vignettes of stages and cycles of growth presented in this section are examples of some of the possible ways in which plant forms can be helpful in making sense of clients' presenting issues. These illustrations represent just a few of the wide range of possible images and more examples can be seen in the vignettes in the rest of the chapter. Before ending this brief discussion, it is worth highlighting the power of the plant image to instill hope. This can be particularly important during life crises that often involve letting go of an old identity. I recall a client who was recovering from nasal cancer that involved significant facial reconstructive surgery. She was struggling with her self-image. She represented herself as a sunflower that was going to seed. Through reflection on this inner image she was able to accept that an old cycle of growth was at an end – she could not hold on to her previous glamorous self-identity – but if she allowed seeds to fall to the ground then she would be able to re-establish her naturally extroverted self in a new way.

The condition of the plant and common reparative interventions

The diagnostic procedure will not only show the type of plant and its stage of growth, it will also give a clear indication regarding its condition. Usually the state of the plant is clear-cut (e.g. the dried-out branch tips in the previous vignette, titled *A Tree Stuck in Winter*) and I will be discussing some of the common problematic states I regularly noted in my clinical work accompanied by some suggestions for reparative interventions. However, sometimes problems with the condition of the plant are not immediately apparent and I begin this section with an example, titled *The Manicured Evergreen Shrub*, of hidden difficulties.

> Jason, an introspective man in his mid-forties, had been very ill for several months and had lost a lot of weight. Despite visiting his doctor on several occasions he had been unable to get a diagnosis. Finally, when his weight had reduced to life-threatening levels, he had been rushed into hospital where the doctors discovered he had cancer of the colon. Since the subsequent medical treatment, he had been making good progress and was hopeful that his disease had gone into remission. However, on returning from a much needed holiday, he was called in for more blood tests that revealed his blood cell count had risen again. He was disturbed by the possibility that his recovery was compromised and wanted a means of making sense of what was happening to him and help with managing his thoughts and feelings. I suggested that a representation of his inner growth and development in the form of an image of a plant could give him a concrete starting point.
>
> Jason reported that his plant form appeared to be a highly manicured evergreen shrub bearing bright red berries. He was surprised by how healthy it seemed. However, as he explored the image in more depth, the message of the seemingly healthy plant became more ambiguous. In previous sessions with Jason, he had disclosed to me the difficulties he had experienced in his upbringing. He described his childhood as one of living in fear of his mother's unpredictable temper. He made connections between the controlled symmetrical shape of the shrub with the way he had learned to control his self-expression in order to be acceptable to others. It seemed to him that the only way that the shrub could grow was within this confining shape. Consequently, its core had become very dense. Jason felt that this intense

self-control exhibited in the plant form was linked in some way with the cancer. It seemed to him that if this shrub was left to its own devices it would grow into a taller tree form, less symmetrical in shape and with greater variation in its greenery.

In following sessions when we discussed his plant form, Jason reflected on the extent to which the imagery had confirmed what he had already long suspected – that breaking through old patterns of self-control was vital for his future health and well-being. However, he was doubtful about the prospects of being able to achieve this in the near future. Self-control lay at the heart of very early survival strategies and, for the time being, he did not feel able to combat the intense anxiety that always arose for him when he tried to change this behaviour.

Although the state or condition of the plant form is unique to the individual and, as illustrated in the previous vignette, is linked to the person's particular life history and personal experience, there are some conditions that are more general. One such condition comprises plant forms that have been compromised by lack of water. Dried-out plants were commonly reported by the substance-misusing clients. This theme is unsurprising as water, in symbolic terms, is usually linked to emotion and chronic substance misuse clearly interferes with the ability to be emotionally engaged with life. Sometimes, the inevitable therapeutic focus on emotional processing will be enough to begin the process that would be symbolised as watering the plant. However, there are times when a reparative imagery intervention might be appropriate particularly if the plant form is very dried out. In these cases I would introduce the idea of visualising the plant being watered. It is important that this process is done in stages and also that the client is prepared for the emotions that may rise to the surface. Otherwise, using the reparative intervention could become counterproductive with the client finding it difficult to manage and regulate overwhelming emotions. The type of plant form also needs to be taken into consideration. Clearly, there are some plants that thrive in dry conditions and the prime example of this is the cactus. This plant form suggests a self-contained temperament that does not require much emotional sustenance. These plants take badly to excessive watering. The basic rule is that the watering process needs to be adapted to the type and condition of the plant.

Other common reparative interventions that I have used with plant forms address difficulties with the growing environment and issues of support. In the first case, people sometimes report that where their plant form is growing is problematic in some way. This could be a container that is now too small or ground that no longer supports the continued growth of the plant. Sometimes the change process has already started and an example can be seen in the earlier vignette (titled *The Pot Bound Plant*) where the roots of the plant had broken the pot. Similarly, I have also occasionally seen plant forms that have started to uproot themselves from the earth in order to move to more suitable ground. Sometimes a more active imagery intervention is called for to either trigger the change or facilitate it.

Therefore, depending on the client's imagery, I might suggest reparative strategies such as repotting a pot bound plant or transplanting a plant form to more suitable ground. I must stress that these reparative strategies cannot be reduced to a simple formula. These interventions need to be completely adapted to clients' images and be guided by their needs. A good example of considering this type of reparative intervention can be seen in the vignette presented later on in this chapter (titled *The Rose with No Thorns*).

Another condition that can benefit from a reparative intervention is a plant that requires support. These might include: trees where branches are sinking down to the ground; plants with large flower/seed heads on tall thin stems; and climbing plants in general. Depending on the individual requirements, a whole range of suitable reparative images could be introduced such as temporary stakes and climbing frames. An example of propping up tree branches can be seen in the previous vignette (titled *The Cherry Tree in the Wrong Ground*). In all cases it is important to get clients to identify what the imagery might represent in their external world. This could range from short-term support symbolised by temporary stakes holding up plant stems or longer-term solutions symbolised by the more permanent structures needed by climbing plants.

Developing the work with the plant image: the monitoring, processing and process management functions

After the initial diagnostic procedure (that may also include reparative interventions to address immediate difficulties), the plant image can become a site for ongoing therapeutic work. Other imagery functions will now come to the fore as required. In this section I discuss the use of the monitoring and processing functions and how they might operate in the unfolding process of therapeutic work. I will also be considering how productive use could be made of the process management function in working with the framing image of the plant. At the end of the section I give a more detailed vignette of a piece of therapeutic work with the plant image.

The monitoring function

The monitoring function is particularly relevant to ongoing work with this framing image. This is not hard to understand as the plant image symbolises dynamic processes of growth and development. Using the plant image to track and monitor these psychological developments seems to be particularly helpful for clients in gaining increasing self-awareness and insight. I have noted that the plant image is particularly useful when people are going through processes of inner change. This is because one of the first indications that a change is happening is often a sense of unease. It is very easy to automatically interpret such feelings through a negative lens. However, when these feelings are investigated through monitoring the person's plant image, a more helpful perspective often emerges that suggests the feelings are natural symptoms of moving into a new stage of growth. Interestingly, I have noted on occasion that a client's sense of generalised anxiety has been linked to a blossoming process – a stage that would usually be viewed as exceptionally positive.

The monitoring function is particularly useful in determining how a developmental and seasonal stage is progressing. In the following example, titled *The Bulb with Many Shoots*, I return to Nick's work presented earlier in the vignette (titled *The Underground Bulb*). In this case, returning to monitor the image of the bulb revealed a rapid change process and a clarification of the original image. The changes in the imagery were then used to make sense of a new development in his life.

> After a gap of a few days, Nick returned to focus once again on his image of inner growth. He said that he was experiencing withdrawal aches and pains but these he could manage, where he really needed to focus was on deeper psychological issues. He reported that a change seemed to be happening to the image of the bulb – it was growing but in an unusual way. Instead of one main shoot emerging from the tip of the bulb, there were little shoots forming on the root junctures and they were about to emerge above ground. At first, neither of us could make much sense of this new development as it did not represent the usual way a bulb would grow. However, as we discussed it further, the idea arose for Nick that this form of growth was much more sustainable than one big shoot and also much more difficult for other people to eradicate. Nick was pleased with this interpretation. He believed that this represented a very important new stage in his life and the priority was for him to protect and nurture his development. Rather than thinking he had to be a star performer, he recalibrated his expectations of himself along more realistic lines. He said that the little shoots suggested that he had a range of potential skills and talents, and that he needed time for these to grow and develop. In line with this more realistic self-appraisal, he made plans to move to a supportive environment when he left the crisis centre, rather than be tempted to try and go it alone as he had in the past.

Other examples of the monitoring function in action can be seen in the following vignettes: *The Tiny Potato Plant*; *A Single Blade of Grass*; *A Tree Stuck in Winter*; *The 'Scraggly' Geranium*; and *The Rose with No Thorns*.

The processing function

The processing function appears to operate in the plant image in a similar way to the building image. This is due to the fact that earlier experiences have imprinted themselves onto the plant and shaped how it has grown and, consequently, repressed material and experiences are held in a stable form. Just picturing the plant will not necessarily activate the processing function. However, paying sustained attention to the plant image can allow a conduit for the repressed material to emerge into the person's awareness. If the person can withstand the reliving of the repressed experience, particularly in the form of disturbing emotions and memories, this allows the material to be processed and consciously integrated. The following vignette, titled *The 'Scraggly' Geranium*, is a classic example of the processing function at work.

> Janine was a creative woman in her late thirties who was in remission from breast cancer. Due to her professional arts background, she was attracted to the use of creative visualisation to help support her continued good health. When she pictured her plant form, she described it as a 'scraggly' geranium bush growing in a plastic pot. She noted that the little branches were starting to sprout new growth and she could also see the beginnings of tiny flower heads. When she reflected on the possibility that she might be beginning to blossom, she stated that this was the first time that this had happened to her. Janine made connections with this new stage and her recent struggles to break through old restrictive mental conditioning. She thought that the plastic container represented the time she had spent in a boarding school from the age of eight to seventeen. She described this as a very unhappy time for her where she was conditioned to be compliant with authority. This session ended with Janine's realisation that her geranium plant could not continue to grow if it was left in the plastic container.
>
> In the following session, Janine returned to focus on the little plastic pot. It was clear to her that her plant needed to be repotted in something more individual than a factory-produced plastic container and she imagined a much more suitable replacement in the form of a substantial terracotta pot. As she visualised easing the geranium plant out of its little pot, she found herself flooding with tears – memory upon memory rose to the surface of her time at boarding school. Most of the session was taken up with Janine experiencing waves of emotion and recounting stories of her experience in the repressive regime of the school.
>
> In our last session, Janine was calm and reflective. She had been making sense of her experience of the imagery process and had identified the main theme running through her memories – being forced to comply with the expectations of unempathic authority figures. When she took a final look at her plant form she reported that it was looking less 'scraggly' in its new terracotta pot and she realised it was a scented geranium. She concluded that she had reached a point in her life where it was now time for her to rely on her own instincts rather than fall back on an outworn negative script instilled in her by authority figures from the past.

The process management function

Process management interventions would comprise new elements that are introduced into the client's image to promote or facilitate helpful therapeutic processes.

Over a period of several years, I have refined two main process management procedures that appear to suit this particular framing image. Both of these are similar to the ones used for the building image but, in this case, are focused on the particular aspects relating to growth and development. In this section I discuss the first procedure of offering temporary structures that are designed to provide security and optimal growing conditions and I then go on to make some comments about the potential for introducing generic helpful figures.

Sometimes clients produce images of plant forms that indicate they might benefit from a process management intervention. These indications are usually self-evident such as: vulnerable young plants that need protection; or plants that, temporarily at least, require controlled growing conditions in order to flourish. In these cases I would suggest that the client can design an appropriate temporary structure to help protect the plant while it grows. Over time, I noted that, unsurprisingly, clients would often produce an image of a greenhouse, and so now I will often suggest this as the template. Usually, this procedure is straightforward but there are some instances where defensive patterns in the self can generate unhelpful versions of this suggested template. An example of such imagery can be seen in the earlier vignette (titled *The Tiny Potato Plant*) where the client's fear of exposure resulted in a protective cover that threatened the growth of the plant. Therefore, it is important to make sure that the client's imagery will suit the purpose for which it was originally intended. In addition, as with all the imagery work presented in this book, it is also important to help the client make connections between the inner image and what this might represent in their life. The two following vignettes illustrate the way that images, representing temporary protection for the plant form, can be incorporated into the client's imaginal landscape. The first example, titled *The Cactus in the Greenhouse*, is another extract taken from Sonia's work seen earlier in the vignette (titled *The Cactus in the Snow*) where she is considering how she can help herself move on from the negative impact of her experiences at school.

> I broached the possibility with Sonia of moving the cactus out of the snow and into a warmer environment. It seemed to me that this move would not pose too big a challenge as it was already growing in a container. Sonia's immediate response was that the cactus should go into its natural terrain of a desert. However, upon further reflection she came to the conclusion that a sudden and dramatic change of environment would be too much of a shock. I suggested she might consider an intermediate option such as a heated greenhouse that could help the cactus adjust in stages to a change in its environment. Sonia responded positively to this suggestion and was able to visualise placing her cactus plant inside a small greenhouse within the snowy landscape. She interpreted this as her planned move on to a second stage rehabilitation centre. Originally, she had seen this move purely as a pragmatic step that would give her more time in a supported environment to get used to living drug free. However, the picture of a greenhouse implied that there might be

an emotional dimension to this next stage. On reflection, Sonia began to consider the possibility that allowing herself to experience the warmth of a supportive community might be a key to releasing herself from earlier damaging experiences of school. Over the next few sessions, Sonia and I used the time to prepare for her move on from the rehabilitation centre. As we did so, she became more committed to the idea she could use the experience of communal living to develop her capacity for establishing and maintaining a network of relationships. By the end of our work together Sonia felt optimistic about the prospects for further psychological growth offered by the next stage of her recovery programme.

The second example, titled *The Vulnerable New Plant Shoot*, presents another extract from Mick's work and picks up from the end of the earlier vignette (titled *A Single Blade of Grass*) which described the impact of an emotionally supportive environment on his sense of self.

I saw Mick for one further session a fortnight later. In the meantime, he had been asked to leave the rehabilitation centre due to an altercation with a member of staff. He had been readmitted after a week and I was pleased to see him in a positive frame of mind. I expressed my concern that his psychological state could have been damaged by leaving the supportive environment of the rehabilitation centre. However, when Mick returned to the image of the new plant shoot, he reported that it had grown a little bit more. He explained that leaving the rehabilitation centre had been a positive experience for him because he had not relapsed on drugs during that time: he had been determined to return to the rehabilitation centre and complete his programme. On closer inspection of the plant form, he began to think that this might not be a single blade of grass but an, as yet, indeterminate plant shoot. We discussed what the plant might need and Mick felt that some form of protection, while it was in its early stages, would be helpful. I suggested he could visualise a temporary structure and he immediately imagined a tall greenhouse forming around the little plant shoot. He reported that it had no roof so that the plant could grow and be open to the rain and air. Mick interpreted the greenhouse structure to be the residential centre and, as long as he followed the programme, his new psychological development would be safe. He expressed his new feelings of optimism, 'I never thought I would ever get to this point in my life – a point where I would feel that there really was some hope for me. I am even beginning to like myself.' And, on this optimistic note, we completed the short piece of work we did together.

Linked to the temporary structures discussed above is another potentially useful process management procedure. I sometimes suggest that clients can symbolise a positive helpful part of the self in the form of the figure of a gardener. The client can then interact with this figure in terms of asking for advice on how the plant can be nurtured. Sometimes the figure can be imagined taking care of the plant through watering it and feeding it. This procedure seems to be particular useful when the plant might need significant ongoing attention, e.g. when it is in a nursery or greenhouse.

An example of a longer piece of work

In this final vignette I give a more detailed example of how the range of therapeutic functions can operate together across the stages of therapeutic work with the plant form image. The following illustration, titled *The Rose with No Thorns*, shows how the plant image can both encapsulate an ongoing psychological difficulty and reflect developmental progress over time.

> Sam was a sensitive and introverted man in his late thirties who had a long-standing alcohol problem. He was artistically gifted but he had not been able to complete his art school training due to his alcoholism. When I met him in the rehabilitation centre, he was suffering from chronic depression and anxiety. He was interested in experimenting with therapeutic imagery as he already had a well-developed visual imagination.
>
> During the first couple of sessions, Sam sketched out his background for me and it became apparent that he had not really separated from his parents, having continued to live in their home all of his adult life. His mother suffered from a similar disabling chronic anxiety state as himself. I wondered at this point whether it might be useful for him to get a picture of his inner psychological state in the form of a plant. He described this as a single rose growing in the middle of a lawn. On closer inspection, it became clear to him that it was the lawn in his parents' garden. He said he understood that this environment was not right for the rose and that it was time for it to be moved. However, he also admitted that he had known for years that he needed to move away from his parents but he had never been able to accomplish it: something held him back. I mooted with him the possibility of transplanting the rose in stages by, first of all, gently uprooting it and planting it in a pot. The idea of a stage-by-stage move was clearly interesting to Sam but he wanted to leave it where it was for a while so he could mull this over.
>
> A couple of weeks later, we returned to the rose image and Sam made a curious discovery – the rose had no thorns. He could imagine where the thorns had been on the stem but each one had been removed. This discovery was a breakthrough for Sam as he made clear links between the lack of thorns and his inability to stand up for himself. He had found it very difficult to establish himself outside his family environment because he had always been unassertive. It seemed to him that his family conditioning had created this behavioural trait and he came to the conclusion that, in order to move

on, he would need to learn the skills to protect himself. At that point I suggested a reparative intervention: he could try regrowing the thorns on his rose plant. He responded enthusiastically and creatively to this by imagining a thorn-regeneration liquid that he painted onto the stem where the thorns had once been. He had a sense that the thorns would take about a week to regrow and we left the session at that point.

When Sam came back a fortnight later, I was naturally curious to hear what had transpired for him after his insight. He reported that, much to his surprise, he had been more assertive in the community the previous week. This behavioural change had given him a bit of confidence although he felt it would take more time for him to fully trust that he could defend himself. I agreed with him that it was early days and that we should leave the rose plant for a month or so. When he checked the image he said that the plant was looking stronger with small but clearly defined thorns. In addition, he could see another group of roses some way in the distance where he felt his rose should go. He made the connection between this picture and making plans to move on to second-stage supported housing. A short while later, Sam decided that it was time to begin the transplantation of his rose and he imagined very gently digging it up and putting it into a terracotta pot. He left the pot standing on the lawn; he realised it would stay there until the time came for him to actually move into his room in the second stage supported house. We ended our work there, with Sam feeling more confident about moving out into the world.

Conclusion

This chapter has provided an introduction to using the framing image of the plant as a site for therapeutic work. This image is particularly useful as it offers both a concrete representation of an individual's dominant personality traits and also a means of capturing the dynamic processes of human development. Although I have identified some common themes and patterns in the plant forms, in the end, each imagery representation is unique to the individual. Once clients have a clear picture of their plant form, this image can operate as a means of facilitating and tracking their growth and development over time. Furthermore, this image provides a particularly helpful and positive means for clients to deepen their self-understanding – representing oneself as a plant highlights the natural cyclical processes of life and engenders hope. In addition, it can offer a corrective to the pathologising tendencies evident in contemporary Western culture's attachment to models of linear progress. I will be returning to more discussion of the plant image in the next chapter when I examine how it can be integrated with the other two framing images into a powerful multi-aspected vehicle for ongoing therapeutic work.

References

Assagioli, R. (1965). *Psychosynthesis*, New York: Hobbs, Dorman & Co.
Hall, E., Hall, C., Stradling, P. and Young, D. (2006). *Guided Imagery: Creative interventions in counselling and psychotherapy*, London: Sage.
Jolles, I. (1971). *A Catalog for the Qualitative Interpretation of the House-Tree-Person: H-T-P*, Los Angeles: Western Psychology Services.
Kövecses, Z. (2002). *Metaphor: A practical introduction*, Oxford: Oxford University Press.
Lakoff, G. and Johnson, M. (2003). *Metaphors We Live By*, 2nd edn, Chicago: University of Chicago Press.
Leuner, H. (1984). *Guided Affective Imagery in Short-term Psychotherapy: The basic course*, New York: Thieme-Stratton Corp.

Chapter 11

Integrating a more inclusive approach to mental imagery into ongoing therapeutic work

As stated in the introduction, the main aim of the more inclusive approach to theory and practice presented in this book is to promote a deeper integration of mental imagery into talking therapies. Instead of using mental imagery either just as a specific procedure within counselling and psychotherapy or in the form of a primarily image-based therapeutic approach, it is viewed as an integral part of the whole therapeutic enterprise. In other words, mental images are viewed as a language that, combined with verbal communication, can facilitate significant long-term therapeutic shifts. This chapter discusses how this type of integration can be achieved and uses the three framing images presented in the previous chapters to illustrate this practice.

I begin with some general observations about the therapist's approach before going on to examine some of the different aspects of incorporating imagery into ongoing clinical work (other important matters such as safe practice and the therapeutic relationship will be addressed in the following chapter on practice issues). For the sake of imposing some structure on this chapter, it is arranged around the beginning, middle and end of therapeutic work. Before beginning this discussion, it is important to note that the guidance and comments in this chapter are provisional – they represent distillations of my own personal and clinical experience combined with some commonalities observed in other therapists' practices with these framing images.

Integrating the use of mental imagery into the therapist's approach

As has already been emphasised, the work presented here is not designed to be another new therapeutic approach comprising a set of systemised imagery procedures. Instead, the focus is placed on mental images as significant sites for ongoing productive dialogue between the rational and imaginal perspectives. Using imagery in this way does not replace other processes and procedures in therapeutic practice, instead it needs to be more fully integrated into the whole therapeutic endeavour. And, inevitably, its effectiveness depends on other factors such as the wider context of a good therapeutic relationship. Therefore it is hoped that therapists will draw on this work in a way that resonates with their own approach and that they will adapt it to their own practice.

However, although therapists will have different ways of integrating the use of mental imagery into their practice, I think it is possible to identify the generic components of a more inclusive therapeutic stance towards its use. The first relates to the position the therapist maintains in relation to the rational and imaginal perspectives. In more inclusive work with mental imagery, the two perspectives are judged to be equally important and this has significant implications for therapeutic practice. Holding this position means that the therapist will actively work on behalf of the dialogic process between the two perspectives; favouring neither at the expense of the other. It will involve advocating for the neglected perspective, examples being: supporting the imaginal viewpoint by not colluding with clients who want to impose drastic changes on their imagery; and supporting the rational viewpoint by challenging clients who want to use imagery for escapist ends. In order to maintain a balance, it is important to keep the client's focus on the communicative process going on between the two perspectives. One of the simplest and most direct means of doing this is to help clients make links continuously between inner imagery and their lived experience, and vice versa.

Another important component of a helpful therapeutic stance is a deep appreciation of the creative unfolding processes exhibited in working with mental imagery. In particular, care needs to be taken to ensure that the directive functions are not used to impose a rational or ego-based agenda on the client's therapeutic or developmental process. It is important to respect the ongoing interactive process between directive procedures and receptive processes. Sometimes, the surprisingly rapid shifts and changes that can be observed when using mental imagery have encouraged therapists to actively force processes. An example of this type of directive work can be seen in one of Desoille's (1966) illustrations of using his classic theme of ascending a mountain. In this particular case, his patient stopped and said that she did not want to go any further. Desoille pushed her to overcome her resistance by getting her to imagine that her daughter could accompany her up the rest of the mountain. Although Desoille argues that the end result was therapeutically beneficial for the client – she could visualise herself pushing through old defeatist patterns – my experience has been that attempts to force processes are often counterproductive. I would agree with Leuner's (1984) observation that defences, in particular, are resistant to this kind of operation. He gives an example of how an inexperienced therapist tried to help his patient break through inner defences that were visualised as an enclosing wire fence. When the therapist suggested that the patient could imagine a pair of wire cutters, the wire fence immediately turned into a high wall.

The particular characteristics of framing images in therapeutic work

Having said that this work is not a new therapeutic approach, it is important to acknowledge that there are some differences in the way that mental imagery is used in this more inclusive approach with framing images. In the field of counselling and psychotherapy, there are two main ways in which mental imagery is integrated into therapeutic work. The first type comprises one-off or short-term episodes of working with a particular mental image, examples would be: a client's dream image; a spontaneous client metaphor; specific guided visualisation exercises; or an image elicited through other types of established procedures such as Gendlin's (1981) 'focusing' method. In these cases, the imagery usually represents a particular presenting issue or an as yet unclear feeling or sensation or an unconscious process or dynamic. Although reference may be made back to this imagery in the process of therapy, the image is not explicitly viewed as a site for further ongoing work. When imagery is being used in this way, it is a technique that is resorted to for particular therapeutic purposes but it is not the main method for therapeutic work and, although useful, often remains somewhat peripheral. The second category comprises the use of mental imagery as the main method of therapeutic work. This would include the clinical innovators such as Leuner and Desoille who, it would appear, usually spent most of each therapy session with their clients directly working with their visualised inner landscapes. It also includes the contemporary imagery-rescripting approaches developed within the CBT school (Smucker and Dancu, 1999) where clients are helped to change their memories of traumatic experiences by purposefully shaping new autobiographical imagery.

The use of framing images in ongoing counselling and psychotherapy does not fit neatly into either grouping and, instead, displays a mixture of characteristics from both types of work. The framing image provides a significant focus or referent for therapeutic work that is ongoing. The use of mental imagery is formalised along similar lines to the European waking dream tradition through introducing a specific starting point for the client's visualisation process that is understood to represent a particular dimension of the person's self. However, apart from the initial diagnostic procedure, the work on the image is not systemised – it is viewed as a unique unfolding process over time that the therapist supports but does not direct. The interventions of the therapist are mainly restricted to explicitly prompting clients to return to the image at appropriate points and to use this as a means of monitoring and working with their therapeutic processes and development. Another difference to image-based therapeutic approaches is that, instead of the imagery always being at the forefront of therapeutic work, it is interwoven through the therapeutic process. Sometimes the framing image becomes the focus for a whole session, sometimes it lies in the background while therapeutic processes are being mediated through other means such as verbal reflection, intersubjective processes and enactments. Every now and then, some brief work with the framing image triggers a process of change that then requires a great deal of integration which is done through talking therapy. The main point is that the framing images remain as consistent threads running through the therapy – they are sites for therapeutic work, sometimes to the forefront and sometimes in the background. Furthermore, it is this emphasis on continuity that differentiates this inclusive practice from the more usual short-term use of mental imagery in counselling and psychotherapy. Sometimes clients will touch briefly on their plant form, building or path imagery just to monitor their progress or state: sometimes they will engage deeply with the framing image that represents a dimension of their experience that is undergoing change. The work with mental imagery is interdependent with the work that is being done through talking in therapy. Ideally, this more inclusive practice seeks to draw equally on both communicative modes depending on therapeutic need moment by moment.

Beginning the work with imagery

The decision to offer the possibility of using mental imagery will usually be determined by the client's material. I am alert to clients' statements that might indicate issues in one of the dimensions of life represented by the three framing images such as: 'I feel insecure (wobbly, weak, anxious)' may suggest that the building image would be a useful starting point; 'I don't seem to have any energy' could point to the plant form; and 'I feel stuck' would suggest the path image. Sometimes the client may express a spontaneous linguistic metaphor that is clearly generated by one of the conceptual metaphors represented by the three framing images (I have already given examples of these in the relevant chapters). In addition, I may suggest mental imagery work if the client has expressed an interest in working creatively or is a visual artist. In such cases I might offer all three possible framing images and ask which one resonates with the person at the moment.

Of course, it is not always possible to select the most appropriate framing image based on the client's presenting issues. I have observed over the course of my clinical practice that if my suggestion of a particular framing image is not suitable, sometimes a more appropriate one will appear in its place. My work with Jessica is an example of this process (see the vignette titled *A Tree Stuck in Winter* presented in Chapter 10). In the assessment session, Jessica reported that she just could not make any progress in her life – she felt completely blocked with regard to developing any meaningful work and she also felt depressed. Because she was explicit about her depression being a function of her inability to make any progress, I suggested that she might want to look at the path image. When I took her through the procedure of representing her journey through life, she reported that she was imagining a tree stuck in its winter season. After some more discussion and exploration, it appeared that this image of herself as a plant form was showing her that her depression was causing her inability to make progress rather than the other way round. In other words it was the dimension of growth and development that was more significant than the dimension of living a purposeful life. In this case, it appeared that the imaginal perspective had used the opportunity of the visualisation procedure to substitute a more relevant framing image than the one that I had initially suggested.

Introducing the use of imagery to the client

I tend to discuss the possibility of using imagery with the client quite early on as I will expect it to play a significant role in facilitating the therapeutic process.

But, introducing it in the early stages of therapeutic work is not an absolute requirement; it will depend on the particular therapist's practice and therapeutic needs of the client.

After I have established a good enough working alliance and I have ascertained that there are no obvious contra-indications to its use (see the detailed discussion in Chapter 12), I will usually introduce the possibility of using mental imagery. I generally frame it as a creative experiment that can be tried out by the client. Of course, this introduction depends on the client's sophistication with regard to drawing on the imagination in this way. Some people may well have tried simple guided visualisation processes before. Notwithstanding the level of sophistication, there are three main points I would usually want to cover in the introduction before starting the particular diagnostic procedure as follows:

- **The rationale for this method**. Sometimes a very simple explanation will suffice along the lines of: 'The subconscious mind communicates in images not words so if we think in pictures we can get another useful perspective on our current situation.' Sometimes clients require more information and explanation. I am happy to discuss this further but other therapists may have different inclinations.
- **The procedure**, i.e. a relaxation process followed by a series of instructions. It is important to reassure clients with no experience of this method that this is not like stage hypnosis and that they will be conscious of what they are doing. I have found that clients often have negative fantasies about the nature of hypnotism mainly informed by its presentation in the media as a means of manipulating people for the entertainment of an audience.
- **The client's autonomy**. Finally, I emphasise the most important operating rule for the use of mental imagery, i.e. that the client is in control of the process and the procedure can be stopped at any point for whatever reason. This rule is so important that I will restate it during the initial work with imagery. My intention is to reassure clients that they can make their own judgment as to whether they feel working with imagery is helpful for them or not.

Then after completing the introduction I would take the client through the initial diagnostic procedure that begins the work.

Working to correct an imbalanced view of the imagination

In my experience, many clients have difficulties accepting their mental imagery as a trustworthy source of information. It is common to hear clients dismissing the validity of their mental images in statements such as, 'I'm just making this up.' I consider that one of the therapist's tasks, certainly in the early stages of working with mental imagery, is to offer a corrective to this de-privileging of the imagination. Otherwise it can lead to a lack of appreciation on the client's part of the importance of details and changes in the framing image. I regard it as part of my role to help consolidate clients' skills in using mental images as a reliable source of information about their inner processes. This is not to say that mental imagery should be accepted uncritically – the conscious mind can and does interfere with the process; producing images that are not true representations of the person's inner world and I will be discussing this particular issue in some detail in the following chapter.

Sometimes the opposite attitude presents itself where clients overvalue the imagination. This position can lead to people believing that if something arises within their imagination it is automatically true. Some developmental theorists view this as a type of 'magical thinking' and link it to an early developmental arrest. Other theorists, informed by a transpersonal perspective, take a different view: Wilber (1999), for example, has coined the term 'pre-trans fallacy' for this condition and argues that it arises through mistaking preverbal imagery for transpersonal symbols. Examples of this imbalance would be clients who read everything they encounter in the world symbolically without subjecting their interpretations to scrutiny by the rational perspective. In these cases I would encourage clients to develop a more discriminating attitude towards the products of their imagination.

What I have noticed is that over time, if clients become more used to working with the framing images, this imbalance begins to right itself. The people who begin by dismissing their imagination start to employ mental images more easily and are able to make productive use of them. Leuner notices a similar trajectory and observes how his patients became more creative in their approach to imagery over the course of therapy. The clients who, more unusually, over-privilege their imagination seem to become more able to evaluate their mental images realistically and work with them in a more balanced way.

Developing the work

The aim is always to interweave imagery with talking therapy as seamlessly as possible, the one supporting the other. However, it is impossible to predict the way this process will unfold as the work has a rhythm that is unique to each client. There are times when the image comes to the fore, for example when the first diagnostic procedure is done or when there are changes happening within that particular dimension of the person's life. Sometimes several sessions might elapse with no reference to the image; that dimension of the self is either stable or dormant or is being eclipsed by other pressing issues. Sometimes the imagery work will take up most or all of the session: sometimes it is just a few minutes to monitor the image. Sometimes the image goes through a burst of activity and change: sometimes it remains exactly the same for quite long periods. These framing images depict the self and reflect its processes of inner change and development as well as revealing the way in which it is being impacted by outer experience.

Yet, despite the unique nature of these processes, it is possible to make some general observations. This section discusses two significant aspects of work with the framing images: first, how the therapist encourages the client to make ongoing use of the imagery; and second, the importance of processing changes that happen to the image. It will then go on to discuss the interrelationship between the three framing images in practice illustrated by a detailed vignette.

Returning to the image

As discussed earlier, the monitoring function of mental imagery is particularly helpful in ongoing therapeutic work as it allows clients and therapists to track therapeutic processes and changes. In the early stages of therapeutic work with the framing images, it is more likely to be the therapist who prompts a return to monitor it. I will tend to suggest such a return when the client reports a new behaviour or insight; on the grounds that it might be helpful to see if this change is represented in the pertinent framing image. This return to the image can often lead to fruitful exploration and can also consolidate the client's grasp of the way that imagery can provide a helpful interactive mirror. I recall one client who, after a very long period where she felt defeated and hopeless, had had a powerful verbal fight with her partner in which she was finally able to express her feelings more truthfully. I noted a subtle change in the way that she was holding herself: she appeared more energised. I suggested that she return to check her building image. To her surprise she reported some changes to her house – a red carpet leading to the front door had appeared and the lights inside had been switched on. She believed that this was a confirmation of the positive impact of the argument and it allowed her to accept the possibility that she might be emerging from a long period of passivity and despondency.

I may also suggest a return to the image if a client reports problematic emotional states or behaviours accompanied by an expressed fear that everything is getting worse. The diagnostic and monitoring functions of imagery are particularly useful here because they can help clients identify if their feelings are symptoms of an actual deterioration or damage to the self. If there is no change to the image or, in fact, a change that looks positive, this can help to allay their fears. A common experience in clinical work is that clients experience change as threatening and returning to the image can be a way to help them understand what is happening.

There are other more general circumstances that would also prompt me to recommend a return to the image. I would suggest this if the client has gone for a considerable period of time without making any reference to the framing image. As a general principle, it is important to consolidate the use of imagery as a means of supporting and enhancing therapeutic processes. If this is the case, I would just suggest a check-up to see what state the picture is in. It may be that this procedure reveals no change in the image indicating that this aspect of the person's life is stable and does not require any attention. On the other hand it might show that a change has occurred and would benefit from some further reflection. It is worth noting at this point that, occasionally, when I have prompted clients to monitor their framing image, they have reported difficulties in seeing it clearly. Clients have described this phenomenon in various ways such as: the image is obscured by a fog or mist; the image is indistinct; or there is veil or barrier between the person and the image. Initially, I was puzzled by this phenomenon and I used to encourage clients to push through what appeared to be a form of mental resistance. However, trying to force the clear viewing of the image is generally unproductive often resulting in confusion for the client. Through experience, I began to understand that unclear representations are often linked to active change processes; at these times, the dimension of life represented by the particular framing image is in a fluid state of transition. When the transitional state stabilises, the mental image becomes fully accessible again. Now, when clients encounter this phenomenon I usually explain that it suggests that changes are taking place and it would be better to return at a later point.

The purpose of revisiting the image is both to monitor developments in the client's process and also to initiate further work on the image if appropriate. As the work develops, imagery is much more interwoven into the fabric of the therapy sessions and clients tend to take more ownership of the framing images. It is common, then, for them to report changes in the imagery that they have noticed between sessions and this would usually prompt a return to the image in the session to explore it in more depth.

The importance of processing changes that happen to the mental image

Active engagement with imagery that represents fundamental dimensions of the self can trigger a range of processes. This phenomenon is particularly likely to happen when changes happen to the images themselves. These changes can either come about spontaneously or they may have been initiated by some directive work on the imagery such as a reparative or process management intervention. Sometimes, the triggering of these processes happens immediately within the therapy session itself. However, whether the process begins immediately or a little later on, it is quite likely that it will continue over a period of time. I noted early on in my practice that clients would often be taken by surprise by the power of these processes and would sometimes find it difficult to contain them. Consequently, I consider that it is important to prepare clients for the possibility that working directly with the imagery can result in a period of feeling destabilised. All of the reactions and responses triggered by changes in the imagery that would include insights, arising related memories, emotions, physical sensations and cognitions need to be processed so that they can be fully integrated into conscious awareness.

A lot of this work will need to be done through the medium of verbal reflections and explorations in the following therapy sessions. A good example of this process in action can be seen in the vignette (titled *The 'Scraggly' Geranium*) presented previously in Chapter 10. In this example, the reparative action of repotting the plant triggered a powerful reliving of the client's experience at boarding school (symbolised as the small plastic pot). The painful memories rising to the surface needed a considerable amount of talking through in order for the client to make sense of the earlier life experience and find ways of integrating it more positively into an expanded sense of self. Although, it is important to note that I am not suggesting that change processes operate in a unidirectional way, i.e. that change only originates at the level of the image. The rational and imaginal perspectives are interdependent. In other words they are two different views of the one phenomenon or dimension of existence. Therefore significant experiences or changes happening in the person's external life will show up as changes to the imagery representations of the self. A good example of this can be seen in the vignette (titled *An Unexpected T Junction*) presented earlier in Chapter 9. Here, the impact of being fired from his job is reflected in significant immediate changes to George's path image.

I have found that the following general questions can be helpful prompts for clients in order to make the correspondence clearer between changes to the imagery and external events and/or psychological states. The use of the term 'sense' rather than 'think' in the following questions is deliberate. This word is used to steer the client away from trying to employ analytic reasoning skills.

- In the first case, if the client returns to monitor a framing image and reports that it has changed, ask the following:

    'When do you sense that the change happened?'
    'What do you sense is the change related to?'
    'How do you sense this change is showing up in your external life, behaviour or psychological state?'

- In the second case, if the change happens in the work with the image within the therapy session, the following questions can help the client manage the ensuing processes.

    'What do you sense you need to do or not do over the next few days/weeks in order to support this process of change?'
    'What do you sense you may experience over the next few days as a result of this change?'

How the three framing images work together

Each individual framing image discloses a particular dimension of human experience: these images are partial views of the totality of the person. Relying on just one can sometimes result in an over emphasis on a particular aspect of the person's life. Therefore, it is common in my ongoing work to introduce the possibility of using one or two of the other framing images, when appropriate, in order to balance the work. After establishing the use of more than one framing image, the client then has two or possibly three potential sites for therapeutic work. A set of framing images can deliver a broader view of the client's experience than just one by itself. An example of this can be seen in George's work presented earlier in vignettes (titled *The Light in the Hallway*; *A Fire Is Lit* and *An Unexpected T Junction*).

After he had seen how the picture of his path represented the impact of losing his job, I suggested that he return and check his building image. George reported that he visualised a hole in the roof. He gained the impression that it had been hit by a wrecking ball, which represented the shock of suddenly being fired from his job. Although initially somewhat skeptical as to the veracity of his imagery, after some further reflection he accepted that he had sustained some psychological damage: he was feeling hopeless about his future. The building imagery indicated that this blow to his confidence needed to be addressed before he could move on.

Using more than one framing image inevitably adds another level of complexity to the ongoing work with mental imagery. However, in general, this complexity seems to be manageable because the framing images tend to come to the fore dependent on therapeutic need. Sometimes, for example, one particular framing image such as the building will be the focus of a period of intensive work and there is no reference to other images for a while. Then, at the end of this particular piece of work, the client may remark spontaneously that it seems as if the plant form might also be changing. Then the focus will shift to that dimension of the self. The way that the framing images interrelate in therapeutic work displays the same creative and unpredictable characteristics of this type of imagery work in general. At the end of this section I give an example of how this can unfold in practice over a lengthy piece of therapeutic work. However, it is important to bear in mind that increasing complexity also has the potential to generate unhelpful confusion. One way of guarding against this possibility is to maintain the distinctions between the framing images through visualising them as separate landscapes. Even though these images are different conceptual metaphors for dimensions of the self, it can become confusing if, for example, the building is pictured in the same landscape as the path. Conflating the two landscapes is likely to introduce an artificial tension between psychological structure and the journey through life.

In the following vignette, titled *Three Framing Images*, I give a highly compressed example of using the building, path and plant images together in long-term psychotherapy. When I first met Amelia, she was in her late twenties and was experiencing considerable difficulties in living. I have presented two extracts earlier from her work with the building image in two vignettes (titled *The Damaged Roof* and *The Sad Little Girl in the Basement*). There I also briefly described the negative formative conditions of her childhood that was dominated by an extremely controlling father, and noted the later impact of this conditioning in the form of debilitating mental health issues. It is important to acknowledge that the imagery work presented below does not represent the totality of the therapeutic work. Other helpful and equally significant therapeutic processes were facilitated by the containment offered by a boundaried therapeutic relationship. However, the consistent use of the three framing images appeared to give Amelia a reliable means of understanding, tracking and managing her subjective world over time. The development of the three images reflect the solid progress that she made during these few years of intensive work.

In our early meetings, it was evident that Amelia was very sensitive and intelligent but had little capacity for regulating her emotions. She lived in a state of overwhelming emotional turbulence and she felt a sense of despair about ever being able to establish herself as an adult in the world. Her feelings of vulnerability were exacerbated by chronic poor health in the form of debilitating bouts of M.E. (Myalgic Encephalomyelitis).

The first framing image that we used was the building; Amelia's main complaint being that she felt fundamentally unstable and insecure. She initially visualised it as an old fortified stone mansion – the walls were solid but there was a big hole in the roof and no one had lived there for a long time. The first stages of the work involved helping her overcome her fear and negative attitude towards her building and begin to accept responsibility for it. When she started to explore the interior, most of the work focused on the basement which contained a significant amount of repressed material. This work included overcoming an initial revulsion to nonhuman images, in particular, a giant spider, and beginning to accept and befriend a neglected part of the self in the form of a young girl (described previously in more detail in the vignettes in Chapter 8 referenced above). Quite early on in the work, she also looked at the other two framing images. She visualised her plant image as a vulnerable sapling that needed protection. Meanwhile her path image showed how she was struggling on a difficult journey up the side of a forbidding and daunting mountain (described briefly in Chapter 9).

Through the therapeutic work she undertook over the seven years, Amelia made consistent productive use of all three framing images; using them to monitor her progress and as sites for active therapeutic work. This work was embedded in relational work where I endeavoured to provide her with a reliable empathic reparative relationship. A large proportion of the time spent in the sessions was devoted to witnessing and validating Amelia's lived experience. However, the threads of mental imagery work were woven through all the work we did together. Sometimes a whole session would be devoted to one particular image; on other occasions there would be little more than a passing reference. Each framing image would come to the fore depending on the dimension of life where Amelia was currently experiencing difficulties. Over time she became more able to tolerate and contain her emotions and little by little she began to establish herself in the world through doing voluntary work.

By the end of seven years all three framing images had disclosed significant developments and improvements. Most of her work had focused on the challenges presented by her building. Bit by bit she had explored the extensive cellars with their disturbing contents; uncovering hidden damage to the walls as well as neglected crumbling outbuildings. All of these building features seemed to relate to parts of the self that had formed up during her childhood. It was a big challenge for her adult self to work through the integration processes required to make changes. As she learned to tolerate the re-experiencing of primitive emotions and early memories, the building began to display subtle changes and it appeared warmer and more inhabitable. In terms of her current outer life experience, she accepted that her emotional self had become more manageable and this was reflected in her increasing ease in establishing good relationships with people. In later stages of the work, Amelia became ready to address the damaged roof, which she linked to the mental damage inflicted by her upbringing. It appeared to her that this part of the roof covered a large empty hall and she sensed that this space represented her unlived potential.

At the same time, her journey image had displayed parallels as over the seven years she had slowly made her way up the side of the mountain, encountering many difficult challenges. During the course of her journey, there had been long periods when she needed to rest up in temporary shelters in order to recoup her strength and energy. Finally, when she arrived at the summit, she reported that the landscape was opening out into a flat plain with a tree-lined path. This new vista resonated with her inner sense that she had finally found a real direction in terms of her work in the world.

Meanwhile the little sapling also grew substantially over these few years into a large tree. This particular framing image appeared as the main site where Amelia's debilitating health condition was symbolised. At various stages, the tree disclosed signs of poor health; one example being fungal infections that seemed to be connected to difficulties in getting clear diagnoses for her physical conditions. The image of the tree also disclosed the extent to which Amelia resisted being in her body. She often stated vehemently that she had not wanted to be born and this resistance was represented in problems with the tree's roots: they did not go down deep enough into the ground to provide a secure enough anchor. Although there was a significant focus throughout the therapy on helping her to change this basic negative attitude towards her life, this default position would often re-emerge in times of stress. At these times some of the roots would retract back into the trunk, thereby threatening the stability of the tree. However, it is hoped that over time this unstable default position will exert less power as Amelia experiences ongoing evidence that she is secure in the world and that people recognise her contributions and gifts.

It is interesting to note that Amelia's framing image of the path took the form of climbing up a mountain and that this is a common motif used in some of the established image-based therapies. The self-evidential nature of this type of journey imagery requires minimal interpretation – the climb up the mountain captured Amelia's struggle to establish herself as an independent and self-reliant adult. Other clinicians who work with this particular motif over time are in agreement that ascending the mountain is linked to positive developments for the client. But the way they interpret these changes is predicated on what they consider this particular theme to represent. Leuner, for example, sees climbing the mountain quite specifically as symbolising mastery over the world. Consequently, he interprets the changes in the panoramas reported by clients as they ascend as reflections of their increasing power and authority.

Concluding the work

If imagery, in the form of these framing images, has been an integral part of the therapeutic work, then it is important to bring it to a proper conclusion. Two important tasks in the ending phase of therapy consist of consolidating the therapeutic work and preparing clients for leaving therapy. These tasks are usually carried out through reviewing the course of the therapy and the developments that have occurred for the clients. It is also common practice to discuss with clients how they will maintain the gains made in the therapy and find alternative ways of supporting themselves in the absence of the regular therapy sessions. Both of these tasks need to incorporate some consideration of the role of mental imagery.

In terms of consolidation, it is important to have a final look at each framing image that has been part of the therapeutic work. These tasks can be incorporated into the general review that will usually take place during the final sessions. I will usually recommend to the client that, as part of the ending process, we revisit the image for a final check-up. This procedure can then lead into some facilitated reflection on how the framing images have developed over the course of the therapy. This final check-up is not the time to initiate any new work. However, it can be used, if appropriate, for gaining some insight into potential future developments regarding the image and the dimension of life that this represents. I will usually ask the client what they sense might be the next area of focus in their imagery. Sometimes, this future focus will be obvious, for example, when the landscape of the journey has changed significantly (for an example, see the final stage of Mehmet's journey in the vignette, titled *Traversing the Dark Woods*, presented in Chapter 9). Sometimes, the next stage is not immediately apparent when, for example, the building and plant form images appear stable and in good-enough functioning states. Depending on their response to the question about the next area of focus in the image, I may facilitate some exploration by inquiring how this particular focus could be linked with the next stage of their life. It can also be useful to get some idea of the timing of this next phase, although realistically, this is more difficult. What I am aiming to elicit from clients is their sense, however sketchy, of what may lie ahead. I think it is particularly important to do this when the clients' imagery indicates that they have broken through an old defence. It is a good idea to remind people that this kind of change often involves a process of cycling back through old patterns of behaviour and thinking; otherwise, in the absence of regular therapy, these reactions may be easily misinterpreted as evidence that change has not occurred. A good example of this can be seen in Jessica's work (presented in the vignette titled *A Tree Stuck in Winter* in Chapter 10). Jessica's self-representation as a plant form was a tree that had been stuck in its winter season for fifteen years. At the end of the therapeutic work, her tree image was displaying clear signs of moving into spring. I spent time with Jessica helping her get a sense of how this might unfold for her and her main impression was that her life was about to become more exciting and full of possibilities. I was concerned when she expressed her conviction that she would no longer have to deal with any negativity; I believed that it was important to encourage a more realistic attitude. Consequently, I allocated some time in our final session for discussing the idea of change as a process rather than an event. The challenge as I see it, in such cases, is to temper the client's natural optimistic responses to positive imagery by offering a more grounded perspective on new developments in life and the inevitable accompanying challenges.

Finally, in terms of suggesting ways that clients might support themselves in the absence of regular therapy, I would encourage clients to continue to draw on the framing images as resources for inner guidance. Ideally, this could take the form of a committed regular creative reflective practice that combines ongoing work using the framing images with reflective journal writing as described in the next section.

Creative reflective practices using mental imagery

There is no clear consensus regarding the suitability for mental imagery as a therapeutic method undertaken by an individual working without the support of a therapist. As mentioned earlier, Jung (1991) held the view that his method of active imagination was not suited for therapeutic work with a therapist; recommending, instead, that his patients should use it for the purposes of individuation work after the ending of the therapy. On the other hand, there are many clinicians such as Leuner who, although drawing on Jung's method, believe that the facilitation of the therapist is required for the full therapeutic potential of mental imagery to be realised.

My view is that, as mental imagery provides a means of communication between the rational and imaginal perspectives, its use should not be confined to the therapeutic encounter. My hope would be that, having been introduced to the use of the framing images as an effective way of working with the presenting issues, clients would then continue to make use of them after the ending of the therapy. I would introduce the idea of following a creative reflective practice using imagery emphasising the following points:

- The importance of a regular committed practice.
- The usefulness of keeping a record of the imagery. Without the presence of the therapist to witness and track the imagery, it may be harder to remember details and changes over time. Furthermore, the process of drawing or writing a description of the image allows more detail and insights to arise. These reflections can form part of a wider project such as an ongoing therapeutic journal if wished.
- The creative nature of such an enterprise. Each individual's practice will be unique.

It is important to acknowledge that there are many ways of using mental imagery that could be fruitfully incorporated into a creative reflective practice. The counselling and psychotherapy literature provides a wide range of possibilities to explore. There are also plenty of examples of visualisation techniques in the popular literature on self-development; but it is important to exercise some discrimination as the quality of these publications is variable. I often suggest people might like to start by looking at a couple of the established classics in the field such as Krystal (1993) and Glouberman (2010). In addition, it is worth noting that creative reflective practices can be used for other purposes as well as self-development – see Thomas (2014) for an example of using mental imagery to enhance researcher reflexivity.

How the framing images develop over long-term work

Before leaving the discussion of integrating more inclusive mental imagery into ongoing psychotherapeutic work, I think it is worth commenting on some patterns I have noted in the development of the framing images over the long term. At this stage I am not sure if they are indicative of general trends or are just representative of my practice with a number of clients and the reports of colleagues who have also used these framing images in their clinical work.

The general trajectory of the framing images is towards more responsiveness. In the very early stages of working with these images, they often appear static. As clients start to use the framing images as sites for interactive work, the images begin to respond and change. In longer-term therapeutic work, and also in creative reflective practice, it often seems as if the images are coming to life. This development is not surprising as it mirrors the increasing consciousness and responsiveness that is occurring within the person. Another general development is the way that the framing image can become less differentiated and start to incorporate or reflect dimensions represented by the other framing images. An example of this phenomenon would be buildings that start to incorporate more organic plant-like aspects. An illustration can be seen in Amelia's work that was used as an example earlier of using the three images together. The cold interior stone walls of her fortified manor house began to show signs of taking on the softer warmer texture of the bark from her tree form image. I have also noted the reverse when plant forms begin to disclose structural aspects. I recall one long-term client who represented herself as a rosebush that over time grew into a substantial tree – a hollow living space appeared within the main trunk that offered a safe room for her to occupy when she felt under threat. Another example would be the way that the framing images of the building and plant begin to demonstrate the agency that is usually more obviously symbolised in the path imagery. I recall my own experience of creative reflective practice when I realised that my representational tree form had begun to uproot itself. Over a period of a couple of months it moved in a determined but rather unstable manner towards a new piece of ground. This imagery was paralleled in my outer life experience of accepting, after a period of increasingly urgent inner prompts, that it was time to move to another part of the country. In my clinical practice I have also noted a couple of examples of buildings changing temporarily into vehicles that allowed them to move to another location where they resumed their building form. Such developments over time should not be so surprising as they reflect the complexity and multifaceted nature of development and growth. The framing images themselves, as I have noted, are useful but artificial constructs: they over-differentiate dimensions of the experience of the self that are, in reality, interdependent.

Each framing image also discloses its own characteristic changes. I have observed that the building image tends to display increasing complexity and size over time. In some cases, the building images have gone through significant changes in form, sometimes opening out into collections of different structures. All of these have been accompanied by significant personal expansion in terms of expressing the self in the world. In one example, the client had been working with her building image for a couple of years when she reported that an ancient and mysterious stone pillar had appeared on the ground floor. Although she was unable to make any sense of it, she had a feeling that it needed to be taken out and placed next to her building. Once that had been accomplished, over a period of time, the pillar opened out into a building site where a new structure arose. This process was paralleled by the initiation and completion of a major artistic project that established her reputation in her particular field. Looking back on this experience, my client and I agreed that it seemed as if her building image had gone through a process of giving birth.

The plant form image also appears to develop in the direction of increasing size, complexity and maturity. Sometimes different processes of growth and dying away may show up simultaneously. The rose tree with the hollow trunk briefly mentioned above started to produce flowers at the same time as rose hips. This phenomenon was linked to the way a new work project was starting at the same time as other projects were being brought to fruition. I have also observed several examples of plant forms that reproduced and created more growing plants and this development appears to be connected with the seeding and germination of creative projects in the world.

Finally, the path image can start to display wider types of landscapes. People may report that they are moving purposively across oceans in boats and through the air in planes. More complexity can be represented in the way that the path imagery incorporates multidimensional aspects. In other words, the landscape may appear less 'concrete'. These developments can be associated with new perspectives on life goals. People sometimes report that their sense of space and time has become more fluid. Transpersonal material and past life meta-narratives can emerge depending on the client's and therapist's belief systems.

Of course, these tendencies described above are only anecdotal. For the time being I regard the observations presented above as tantalising hints of the potential of these framing images to operate not only as sites for therapeutic work but also as an ongoing means for representing and promoting highly complex developmental processes.

Conclusion

This chapter has offered some thoughts on how to incorporate a more inclusive approach to mental imagery into ongoing therapeutic practice. It is not possible to give any prescriptive rules: the effective integration of mental imagery into therapy depends on the skills, inclinations and sensitivity of the practitioner. However, it has been possible to say something about the way that using mental images that represent fundamental dimensions of human experience can be interwoven through talking therapy. There is an emphasis in this more inclusive approach on regarding mental images, not simply as a therapeutic technique, but instead offering an ongoing site for therapeutic work. The framing images discussed here can continue to serve the client as a means of self-development after the end of therapy. In the following chapter I go on to examine some of the more concrete and specific practice issues that can arise in a more inclusive therapeutic practice with mental imagery.

References

Desoille, R. (1966). *The Directed Daydream*, New York: Psychosynthesis Research Foundation.

Gendlin, E. T. (1981). *Focusing*, 2nd edn, New York: Bantam.

Glouberman, D. (2010). *Life Choices, Life Changes: Develop your personal vision with imagework*, 3rd edn, Shanklin, Isle of Wight: Skyros Books.

Jung, C.G. (1991). 'The Archetypes and the Collective Unconscious', in *The Collected Works of C. G. Jung*, vol 9, part 1, 2nd edn, trans. R.F.C. Hull, London: Routledge.

Krystal, P. (1993). *Cutting the Ties that Bind: Growing up and moving on*, Boston: Weiser Books.

Leuner, H. (1984). *Guided Affective Imagery in Short-term Psychotherapy: The basic course*, New York: Thieme-Stratton Corp.

Smucker, M. R. and Dancu, C. (1999). *Cognitive-behavioral Treatment for Adult Survivors of Childhood Trauma: Imagery rescripting and reprocessing*. Northvale, NJ: Jason.

Thomas, V. (2014) 'Drawing on Creative Reflective Practices in Counselling Research: An example of using mental imagery to enhance researcher reflexivity', *British Journal of Counselling and Guidance*, 42, 1: 43–51.

Wilber, K. (1999). *The Collected works of Ken Wilber*, vol 3, Boston: Shambhala.

Chapter 12

Practice issues

It is important to acknowledge that there are important practice issues related to using mental imagery in counselling and psychotherapy. In this chapter I consider some of the more significant ones in relation to developing a more inclusive practice with mental imagery. I begin by reviewing some of the more general matters such safe practice, which includes: contra-indications to its use; working with induced relaxation states; and managing clients' problematic reactions to imagery. This overview will be followed by a discussion of issues that are particularly relevant for a more inclusive practice such as strategies for increasing the client's capacity for making productive use of their mental images. Finally, I make some comments regarding the way that utilising mental imagery in counselling and psychotherapy affects the therapeutic relationship and how this work, in its turn, is also shaped by the intersubjective context.

Safe practice

It has long been acknowledged that mental imagery is a potentially powerful therapeutic method that needs to be treated with caution. Practitioners who already use techniques such as guided visualisation with their clients will be familiar with some of the guidance presented in this section. The obvious dangers are predicated on the way that mental images can bypass conscious defences and access repressed experience. Other issues concerning safe practice are linked to the increased vulnerability of clients who will be working in induced relaxed states with their eyes closed. In this section I discuss ways in which the therapists can ensure that their practice is safe.

Contra-indications for this work

Before engaging in therapeutic work with mental imagery, an assessment needs to be made to determine if this type of work is appropriate for the client. As a general rule I would want the client to make that assessment. As described in the previous chapter, I usually frame my introduction to the use of mental imagery as an experiment and this allows clients to make a choice based on their direct experience.

However, not all clients may benefit from this type of experiential introduction to the work. In general there are two main contra-indications where it is potentially unsafe to offer the possibility of working with the more inclusive approach to mental imagery presented in this book. They are:

1. The client has a history of serious mental health problems, particularly if this has included episodes of delusional ideation. Difficulties in distinguishing between creations of the mind and external reality would indicate that working with mental imagery could become counter-therapeutic.
2. The client is suffering from post-traumatic stress disorder (PTSD) – either medically diagnosed, self-reported or indicated by the initial assessment. Although there are methods for using mental imagery to rescript traumatic memories, these are specialist contemporary CBT applications. The processing function of mental imagery allows a conduit for repressed material to come into conscious awareness. Consequently, using mental imagery with clients with PTSD can trigger flashbacks to the original traumatic experience. Without proper management and containment these experiences are potentially unsafe and counter productive.

In my experience, there are other conditions that, although not necessarily contra-indicated, do not tend to respond very well to the use of mental imagery. I have noticed that people who have a tendency towards being overly intellectual or controlling can find imagery a bit threatening. Clients who are concrete thinkers often find the process of symbolisation difficult to grasp and make use of. Quite often these clients will not be attracted to the possibility of using imagery in the first place.

In the end, the decision regarding the suitability of offering mental imagery rests on the therapist's assessment of each individual client. I think that as long as the two main contra-indications are observed, it is generally safe enough to offer it so that clients can make their own mind up regarding its usefulness. I always emphasise that mental imagery does not suit everyone. Some clients will decide, based on the therapist's explanation of the method, not to proceed, while others will be willing to try it out. If their initial experience is not particularly helpful then it can just be viewed as an experiment: nothing has been lost.

Guidance for working with clients in induced relaxation states

This guidance is particularly important during the early stages of working with clients using mental imagery particularly with regard to the initial diagnostic procedure. Later on, in ongoing work, the procedure for inducing relaxation states is more informal and oftentimes dispensed with altogether as the client becomes more skilled in visualisation. The main thing to bear in mind is that the therapist is required to actively manage the procedure when clients are in an induced relaxed state and deeply focused on their inner experiences. I include the following directions for therapists who are less experienced with using mental imagery:

- **Stay in verbal contact with the client.** The client cannot see you therefore you need to convey your presence through your voice. Obviously there are times when it is important to remain silent, e.g. when the client needs to be fully immersed in an unfolding inner process. However, as a rule-of-thumb it is best not to let more than a couple of minutes pass without speaking even if it is only to say a word or two. If you stay silent for too long, one of two things may happen; either clients may lose their way in the process or they might become unnerved by your verbal absence.
- **Do not let the client remain silent for more than a couple of minutes.** Again, for similar reasons listed above, the silence might indicate that the person is either drifting away or going into problematic psychological territory. It is your job to track the client and the best way to do this is by eliciting a running commentary.
- **Pay close attention to any physiological signs that could indicate emotional or psychological distress during the process**, e.g. change in breathing pattern or skin pallor. If these occur ask clients how they are feeling. Sometimes people become emotionally uncomfortable but are not able to volunteer that information unless asked.
- **Do not press the client for information they appear reluctant to give.** Memories or associated thoughts may rise up during the process that the client is not ready to divulge. There are different opinions regarding the necessity of understanding how clients are making links with their imagery. Some clinicians believe that working purely with the image itself is sufficient. Others, myself included, do not think this is advisable – I need to have some rough idea about the nature of the associated material so that I can make an assessment of whether it is wise to proceed. Therefore, in such cases, I may ask clients if they feel able to tell me in a very general way what the image is linked to. If this is not forthcoming or if their response indicates traumatic material, then I would usually suggest to the client that we bring the imagery to a close. After bringing them out of the relaxed state we would then have an opportunity to discuss their experience.

Managing difficulties that may arise

No matter how safe the practice, there are occasions when difficulties arise, particularly during the initial stage of working with mental imagery. In this section I discuss some of the more common problems that may occur and I offer some thoughts about strategies that can be used to manage them effectively.

It is important to bear in mind that clients have differing responses to induced relaxation processes. Some people are particularly susceptible and may slip into a deeper altered state of consciousness. It is very important that the therapist remains alert to signs that this may be happening. It is the therapist's job to help clients stay conscious of what they are doing and maintain their focus whilst in a conscious relaxed state. Deep altered states of consciousness are not, of themselves, necessarily problematic: these states can facilitate powerful, transformational processes. However, I believe that such episodes need careful management. Signs that people are moving deeper into an altered state of consciousness would include the following: the breathing pattern changes; they become motionless; and they either stop speaking or find it difficult to respond coherently. If any of these signs occur then I would ask the client what is happening and I would persist until I got a clear answer. When they respond verbally to me this is an indication that they are regaining more conscious awareness. I would usually then continue to speak giving gentle but firm instructions designed to bring them out of the relaxation state. Then I would discuss their experience with them in order to assess whether it is appropriate to continue the imagery work or not.

There are other possible responses to the induced relaxation state that may be problematic. Sometimes clients report troubling sensations that may include altered perceptions of their body, e.g. their hands start to feel very large or their body feels like it sinking through the chair. These are quite normal signs that the person is going into a deep state of relaxation and I would usually verbally reassure the person along these lines. If they continue to express unease about the sensations then I would help them readjust their state by using verbal instructions to bring them back more in touch with their conscious awareness (the instructions the therapist uses will depend on the type of relaxation script that they usually employ). If they elect to stay where they are then it is important to monitor their state because these symptoms indicate they are hovering on the edge of an altered state of consciousness.

Another possibility is that clients experience a strong emotional response that is triggered by the imagery. This is a common experience for people due to the processing function of mental images allowing access to repressed experiences. When clients are used to using imagery in their therapeutic work, this is not usually problematic. However, if this occurs in the first couple of times when clients are being inducted into this way of working, it can cause difficulties. Common reactions would include: clients feel overwhelmed and fear that they are losing control over their emotions; or they might feel disturbed by the power of the method. In such cases I would usually manage the session in order to help clients contain their emotional responses. This intervention would usually involve bringing the imagery work to a close and gently but firmly bringing clients back into everyday awareness where I would work with them to make sense of what has occurred. I would use this opportunity to normalise their reactions and explain further how images access repressed experience and emotions. It is also important to reassure people that if they choose to continue to work with imagery, they will be able to do this in a way that works for them.

Strategies for helping clients make more effective use of mental imagery

As mentioned in previous chapters, most clients will present culturally conditioned attitudes towards the imagination and little experience of consciously and purposively using mental images. It takes time and experience for people to understand how mental imagery operates. One of my aims is to help consolidate clients' knowledge and understanding of the communicative process operating between the rational and imaginal perspectives that is mediated through imagery. Sometimes it can take a long period of patiently reinforcing the links between inner and outer experience symbolised in the imagery before the person grasps its possibilities and begins to use it more autonomously. In this section I consider some strategies that can be employed with specific common blocks experienced by clients.

Resistance to the image

Over time, I have noted that one of the biggest stumbling blocks in inducting clients into working with mental imagery is their distrust of the truthfulness of their images. I have discussed the historical reasons for this and also the implications for practice at some length in previous chapters. One of the complicating factors is that there is some truth to this common objection – the mind can use the imagination to create illusions. One of the main strategies that I employ with clients is to explain the differences between types of imagination, in particular, that the images produced by the imaginal perspective have a different quality to the ones produced by the rational perspective. Sheikh gives a particularly clear succinct description of the former type of imagery:

> It is fixed and cannot be altered at will by the patient. Even if the patient should succeed in temporarily altering an image, it will not fail to return to its original form as soon as he loses conscious control or relaxes. The image can be manipulated and mutated only under concentrated attention and only in accordance with the laws under which these images function. Furthermore, when a series of changes are made, they have a corresponding impact on the psyche.
>
> (1978: 203)

In the early introductory stages of mental imagery work, an additional strategy is often required to help clients get past this initial resistance. Over time I have found that the best way to do this is to acknowledge with clients the possibility that they might be producing 'false' pictures. I will sometimes say explicitly that it is fine to think they are just making up the pictures and to go ahead in this way; they will be able to judge how 'real' they are afterwards. This strategy can often bypass the resistance. The imagery that the client produces can then be assessed as to its validity. Superficial images are usually fugitive and often appear to be two dimensional with little associated affect. Images generated by the imaginal perspective remain consistent, as Sheikh notes above, and are accompanied by physiological and emotional responses. There is a sense that the client is experiencing the image rather than merely seeing it projected onto a screen.

Other forms of resistance can arise when clients see a mental image that is quite different to the one that they expected; a not uncommon experience as Sheikh notes, 'It needs to be highlighted that the experience that emerges in the eidetics often is at variance with the patient's conscious views of it' (1978: 218). This mismatch between the imaginal and rational perspectives can often be implicated in the client's presenting issue and would therefore indicate a potentially fruitful area of exploration and reflection. As a point of interest, I have noticed a tendency for clients to be resistant to framing images that convey intimations of significant maturity and stature. In my experience, it has been quite common for clients to react with surprise when their imagery representations are large buildings or mature tree forms. Their responses are usually along the lines of a perceived mismatch between the picture and their sense of self. The converse is rare in my experience, i.e. people appear to find it easier to accept representations of the self in the form of modest-sized structures and smaller plant forms. However, the majority of my clients have been British and this tendency might be reflective of cultural conditioning.

Finally, it is worth noting that people might use another objection to their mental images that is informed by a view that the imagination just reproduces whatever the person has previously seen or experienced. Similar objections are made to dream imagery. This mechanistic view can be traced right back to Hobbes's (1588–1679) assertion in his philosophical treatise, *Leviathon* (Hobbes, 1996) that imagination is just a record of decaying sense impressions. I would try to counter this position by encouraging the client to question why, out of the vast number of images previously seen, this particular one has been selected. I would then explore with them the possibility that this particular image has something meaningful to communicate regarding their current situation. Of course, the client's attachment to a mechanistic view to the exclusion of other perspectives might be too powerful to dislodge at this time.

Difficulties in making connections between the image and outer experience

I have already addressed the importance of helping clients make sense of their imagery from three perspectives i.e. personal, cultural and universal (see the detailed discussion in Chapter 7). Clients have varying degrees of success with linking the mental images to their own lived experience. But, in general, most will require the therapist to prompt and facilitate this meaning-making process until it becomes a more established part of their reflective processes. In order to do this, I will rely on a process of inquiry that adapts the set of basic questions given for the diagnostic procedures for the framing images.

However, there are other ways of supporting this linking process. Desoille (1966) suggests another type of interpretative strategy that relies on the embodied nature of mental imagery. He gets his patients to return to the feeling evoked by the image and make connections with where they have the same feelings in their everyday life. I have used this with some success when clients are not able to make sense of their image using the basic questions and verbal instructions described earlier. A very similar strategy to Desoille's makes use of metaphoric linguistic expressions. Even though people might find it difficult to link an actual image to an area of experience, they will be used to thinking in metaphorical terms. An example of such a strategy would be helping a client whose path image takes the form of a steep hill. A simple question framed metaphorically – 'Where are you experiencing life as an uphill struggle at the moment?' – should be sufficient for the person to begin to make links between inner and outer experience.

Mental imagery and the therapeutic relationship

Using mental imagery in counselling and psychotherapy focuses on the client's subjective experience and this therapeutic work takes place within the intersubjective context of the therapeutic relationship. In the writings of 20th-century clinical innovators on the use of mental imagery in psychotherapy, not much attention is paid to intersubjectivity. It was generally believed that this method lessened the potential for unconscious relational dynamics to be enacted within the therapeutic relationship – instead, these dynamics would be projected into the imagery. For some practitioners, this perspective was informed by a critical view of psychoanalytic practice, as can be detected in Watkins summing-up of the position taken by the oneirotherapists, 'The transference is often seen as an unnecessary dependence on the therapist that prolongs therapy and promotes a more passive, irresponsible attitude to one's unconscious contents' (1984: 54). Nowadays, developments in intersubjective theory along with the disclosures of neuroscience have led to a more sophisticated understanding of the co-constructed nature of therapy. It is beyond the remit of this book to examine the relationship between the subjective and intersubjective dimensions of the therapeutic process – this is a complex theoretical area. However, it is important to consider how working with mental imagery both impacts on the therapeutic relationship and is also itself, in turn, influenced by unconscious relational dynamics. In this section I discuss some of the implications of this interdependence in more concrete terms for clinical practice.

Any time that the therapist initiates a procedure or technique in the therapeutic work, it has the potential to impact on the therapeutic relationship. Much has been written in the literature about how such usage can place the therapist in the role of the expert thereby exacerbating the already-existing power imbalance inherent in the therapeutic dyad. The use of mental imagery brings with it particular difficulties that are generated by its requirement for conscious relaxed states and also its potential for triggering powerful emotional processes. I have noted that clients can sometimes attribute the power of the imagery process to the therapist. In other words the therapist becomes the screen for the client's projection of 'magical healer'. This projection can be very seductive. It needs to be gently and firmly refused. In such cases I will spend some time discussing with the client the taking back of this projection. It is important that clients re-situate the power within themselves. I have also observed that this projection can arise with clients from non-Western cultures that retain indigenous healing practices employing altered states of consciousness.

Another problem that may occur when clients become more familiar with this practice is that mental imagery can become a way of escaping from difficulties arising within the therapeutic relationship. Closing their eyes and going into an induced relaxed state can operate as an escape hatch that allows clients a means of avoiding the conscious working through of relational dynamics. This subtle misuse can sometimes take a little while to detect. I pay attention to my embodied counter-transferential responses to alert me that something in the therapeutic relationship is off-key. I also note the different quality of feeling evoked by mental imagery work when it is harnessed to nontherapeutic ends; there is usually less vitality and less engagement with the process and the images appear two dimensional. There are times when the relational requirements take precedence over engaging with mental imagery. Part of the therapist's skill in integrating mental imagery into their work involves being able to identify when a focus on the client's subjective world is counter productive.

As mentioned above, proponents of imagery-based therapeutic approaches assert that transference and counter-transference play a relatively minor role when mental imagery is the main vehicle for therapeutic processes. On one hand I would agree with the idea that mental imagery – particularly the framing images that represent fundamental dimensions of the self – appears to offer a container for the working through of some early unconscious material that might otherwise be acted out within the therapeutic relationship. However, in my experience, the situation is not so clear-cut and unconscious relational dynamics will impact on the use of mental imagery in a variety of ways. I believe that it is important not to underestimate the way in which the client's unconscious relational patterns will actually shape the encounter with the work. One way that this might operate is through the client's over-compliance. This response might arise from a transference onto the therapist of an earlier authority figure. Or it might arise from a more general deference to the therapist as expert. I have had experiences where, to my surprise, clients have revealed to me later on in the therapy that they had only engaged with the imagery to humour me. Rennie's (1994) ground breaking research studies into the client's experience helped me understand the extent to which clients will defer to the therapist and conceal their own, often quite different, opinions. Another possible cause of over-compliance is when the client has had abusive formative experiences that have resulted in an inability to hold a boundary. This is particularly problematic as it is possible for the therapist to inadvertently step through a breach in the client's defences and in so doing reenact the original relational dynamic. The building image is the most likely site where this could happen.

Conclusion

In this chapter I have outlined some of the main practice issues that can arise when using mental imagery in therapeutic practice – the most significant ones are concerned with safe practice. The power of a method that bypasses conscious defences is, of course, also the source of its greatest danger. Many of the difficulties and challenges that arise in practice are concerned with the processing function of imagery as clients can easily be overwhelmed by the triggering of repressed memories. Most of the guidance given in this chapter is designed for the early stages of working with more inclusive imagery. My experience has been that as clients become more familiar with accessing and working with mental images they become more skilled and confident in this practice. However, it is always important to bear in mind the intersubjective context of this work and that clients' relational patterns also shape how they engage with the imagery work itself.

Finally, I would argue that the most basic issue, colouring all aspects of this practice, is the client's culturally conditioned attitude towards imagination: many clients with a Western heritage will find it difficult to accept the validity of their mental images. Consequently, there is an educative dimension to this work. This chapter has included some strategies designed to increase clients' understanding of the way that mental imagery operates as well as increasing their skills in its use. One of the implicit aims of a more inclusive practice with mental imagery is to help clients reclaim a neglected inner resource – memorably encapsulated in the title of Fromm's (1951) classic text *The Forgotten Language*.

References

Desoille, R. (1966). *The Directed Daydream*, New York: Psychosynthesis Research Foundation.
Fromm, E. (1951). *The Forgotten Language: An introduction to the meaning of dreams, fairy tales and myths*, New York: Rinehart.
Hobbes, T. (1996). *Leviathon*, ed. R. Tuck, Revised student edn, Cambridge: Cambridge University Press.
Rennie, D.L. (1994). 'Clients' Deference in Psychotherapy: A qualitative analysis', *Journal of Counselling Psychology*, 41: 427–437.
Sheikh, A.A. (1978). 'Eidetic Psychotherapy' in J.L. Singer and K.S. Pope (eds) *The Power of Human Imagination: New methods in psychotherapy*, 197–222, New York: Plenum Press.
Watkins, M. (1984). *Waking Dreams*, 3rd revised edn, Dallas, TX: Spring Publications Inc.

Chapter 13

Conclusion

This book has been an attempt to answer the main question posed in the introduction, i.e. how can we develop a more inclusive framework for the practice of mental imagery in counselling and psychotherapy, one that allows integrative therapists a means of drawing upon the wide range of valuable insights, theories and methods produced by different schools and clinical innovators? The answer I have proposed in this book is simple; identifying commonalities in its practice is a starting point for constructing a model that transcends the limitations of school-based theories.

However, a transtheoretical model of mental imagery lays the ground for an even more radical project, i.e. revising the role of mental imagery within talking therapies. The therapeutic use of mental images has usually taken two forms: either it is used as a technique or procedure within counselling and psychotherapy; or it is an image-based approach where imagery is the main vehicle of therapeutic process. The more inclusive approach presented in this book argues for a deeper integration, one where the use of mental imagery is an integral part of the process, inextricably interwoven into the fabric of the therapy. Clients' mental images can be used to represent fundamental dimensions of the person's self and, in so doing, these images then become sites for ongoing therapeutic work.

The faculty of imagining was effectively removed as a healing modality in the West and marginalised as a 'primitive' mode of thinking. Psychotherapy's rediscovery of the therapeutic power of mental images was one of the first steps in the reclamation of imagination as a valid means of knowledge about the self. This journey is not complete: another step is required. The task of integrating a premodern imaginal consciousness with a modern rational worldview involves the contributions of many disciplines and takes many different cultural forms. Cognitive linguistics, in particular, has developed our understanding of the way that imagination and metaphor are deeply implicated in cognitive processes. Therefore, clients' mental images should be regarded as a fundamental part of therapeutic work. Once mental imagery is properly theorised from a transtheoretical perspective and integrated more deeply within talking therapies, then the disciplines of counselling and psychotherapy will have made some more progress towards healing an old split that has shaped Western culture. In the context of a therapeutic practice, mental images provide the means for each individual client to honour both the rational and imaginal perspectives and re-establish a productive and creative inner dialogue between them; a dialogue that in the end, despite all of the instructions, procedures and guidance delivered in this book, is unique, ever-changing and at its heart, a mystery irreducible to conceptual analysis – a mystery to be embraced and fully lived.

Index

Abandoned Victorian House, The, vignette 96–7
absence of image: building image 90; path image 117–18; plant image 138–9
Achterberg, J. 13–14, 46
Ahsen, A. 34, 53; *see also* image/somatic/meaning (ISM) model
aims of book 3
analytical psychology 25–7
anger, metaphoric conceptualisations of 48–9
animal magnetism 17
anxiety and building image 94, 106
archetypal psychology 27
Aristotle 14
Arriving at a Crossroads vignette 124–5, 127
art therapy 4
Asay, T. 30
Asclepian tradition 14
Assagioli, R. 28, 57, 133
attic of building in image 106
attitude toward building 92–3
audience for book 3
autobiographical memory and reparative function 56

back of building in image 98–9
Bamber, M. 57, 68
Barnard, P. 44
basement of building in image 106
Beck, A. 35
bedrooms of building in image 106–7
behaviourism 19
Blake, William 43
Bruner, J. 4
building image: changes to over time 174; conscious relaxation state and 77; diagnostic and reparative functions, using 92–101; framing function, using 88–91; guidelines for working with 87–8; longer-term work with 109–10; monitoring and processing functions, using 101–8; overview 85–7, 110; process management function, using 108–10
Bulb with Many Shoots, The, vignette 152
Butler, G. 60

Cactus in the Greenhouse, The, vignette 143, 154–5
Cactus in the Snow, The, vignette 142–3, 144, 154
Cartesian dualism 2, 15–19
casebook, illustrations drawn from 7–8; *see also specific vignettes*
Caslant, E. 32
CBT *see* cognitive behavioural therapy
challenge, facing, and path image 125–6
changes to image, processing 166–7, 173–4
Charcot, Jean-Martin 19, 24
Cherry Tree in the Wrong Ground, The, vignette 143–4, 151
Chestnut, W. J. 59, 68
childhood home, image of 90
Clarkson, P. 69
clients: attitude of 79–80; in induced relaxation states, working with 177–9; introducing use of imagery to 162–3; over-compliance of 183–4; way of being of 102; *see also* substance misusers, clinical experience with
clinical innovators 31–5
CMT (compassionate mind training) 37

co-constructed nature of therapy 30
cognitive behavioural therapy (CBT):
    empirical view of imagination and 43–4;
    reparative function of imagery in 55–6;
    rescripting techniques of 20, 63–4;
    schema therapy 57; structured imagery
    interventions 35–9
cognitive linguistics theory 48–50
cognitive processing, types of 4
The Royal College of Physicians,
    founding of 15
compassionate mind training (CMT) 37
conceptual metaphors: convention in
    representation of 8; framing images
    as 82–3; LIFE IS A JOURNEY 111–12;
    overview 49–51; PEOPLE ARE BUILDINGS
    85–6; PEOPLE ARE PLANTS 134
conceptual metaphor theory 86, 134
condition of building in image: door
    or doorway 100–1; foundations
    99–100; front and back 98–9;
    highly-compromised 94–5; roof
    damage 97; uninhabited 95–7
condition of plant in image 149–51
consciousness, deep altered
    state of 178–9
conscious relaxation state 76–8
consolidation of therapeutic work 171
container in plant image 143–5
contra-indications for therapeutic work
    with mental imagery 176–7
counter-transference 183
covert modelling 36
creative reflective practices 172–3
cultural level of interpretation 81
cultural perspectives on imagery 80
Cummingham, A. 18

Damaged Roof, The, vignette 97,
    106, 168
Dancu, C. 38
decision making and path image 124–5
delusional ideation 177
Descartes, René 15–16
desensitisation technique for phobia 36
Desoille, R.: directed daydream method
    of 32–3; importation of known figures
    and 130; on interpretative strategy 182;
    mountain ascent theme of 62, 160;
    on triggering images 58; on view of
    imaginal 78
development, process of, and plant image
    135, 145–9

diagnostic function of mental imagery:
    building image 92–101; overview
    59–61, 67; path image 116–26; plant
    image 135, 140–9
dialogic imagery techniques 54
directed daydream method 32–3
directive/active imagery 54, 67
door or doorway of building in image
    100–1
Dossey, L. 18
dreams 4–5, 28–9
drifting or floating theme and path image
    121–4

Edwards, D.J.A. 35
effective use of mental imagery 180–2
effort, making, and path image 125–6
eidetic psychotherapy 34, 45–7
embodied experience of imagery 48–9,
    50, 83
emotional responses triggered by
    imagery 179
empirical view of imagination 42–5
Erickson, M. 48
escapism: misuse of mental imagery for
    183; path image and 121, 131–2; use of
    imagery and 79–80

Ferrucci, P. 28
figures: helper, in building image
    108; helper, in plant image 155–6;
    spontaneous appearance of, in inner
    landscape 130–1
Fire Is Lit, A, vignette 105, 107, 120, 167
five relationship framework 69
forest, motif of 57
foundations of building in image
    99–100, 103
framing function of mental imagery:
    building image 88–91; overview 58–9,
    67; path image 114–16; plant image
    137–40
framing images: beginning work with
    162–4; characteristics of, in therapeutic
    work 160–2; as conceptual metaphors
    82–3; concluding work with 171–3;
    developing work with 164–71;
    development of, over long-term work
    173–4; as working together 167–71;
    see also building image; path image;
    plant image
Frank, L. 31
Frétigny, R. 33, 58

Freud, Sigmund 1, 20, 24–5, 31, 85
Fromm, E. 184
front of building in image 98–9
functional equivalence theory 44, 51
functions *see* therapeutic functions of mental imagery

GAI (guided affective imagery) 33
Galen 14
Gallese, V. 49
Gatekeeper's Cottage, The, vignette 108–9
Gendlin, E. T. 28, 39, 161
gestalt therapy 28–9
Gibbs, R. W. 49
Glouberman, D. 173
Greece, shamanic practices in 14
Grey, N. 64
ground: contact with, and path image 114, 122; in plant image 143–5
growth, process of, and plant image 135, 145–9
guide, appearance of, in inner landscape 131
guided affective imagery (GAI) 33
guided imagery scripts 58–9, 61–2, 68

Hackmann, A. 4, 39, 83
Hall, E.: building image of 85; climbing mountain theme and 111; on guided imagery scripts 58–9; on interpretation 60; 'magical' interventions and 132; processing function and 64; on reparative function 56; on tree image 133
Happich, C. 31, 76
Harpur, P. 15
Hartley, David 17
Hastrup, J. L. 13
head/mind and roof damage in building image 97
healing tool, imagination as: impact of Cartesian dualism on 15–19; premodern use of 13–15; psychology and 18–21
health of plant form 136
Hegel, G.W.F 43
helper figures: in building image 108; in plant image 155–6
highly-structurally compromised building in image 94–5
Hillman, J. 4, 20, 27, 45, 78
Hobbes, T. 16, 42–3, 181
Hollis, J. 27
Holmes, E. A. 60

hope, power of plant image to instill 148–9
house image *see* building image
House-Tree-Person exercise 133
humanistic school 27–9, 57, 58–9
human potential movement 21
Hume, David 43
hypnotherapy 4, 19, 48

ICS (interacting cognitive subsystems) model 44
ideo-motor action 18
image/somatic/meaning (ISM) model 45–7, 50, 63, 71
imaginal perspective 4, 75, 76–7, 160, 185–6
imagination: correcting imbalanced view of 163–4; empirical view of 42–5; historical perspective on therapeutic use of 13–21; mechanistic view of 181; phenomenological view of 3, 45; *see also* healing tool, imagination as
immune system, imagery of 17–18
imploding psychodynamic themes technique 25
Imposing Façade, An, vignette 98–9
inclusive practice: development of model of 66–9; functions of mental imagery and 64; issues related to use of mental imagery 176–84; overview 6–7, 185–6; *see also* integration of mental imagery; interactive communicative model
inclusive theory: historical perspective on therapeutic use of imagination 13–21; imagery work presented and 7–8; overview 5–6; *see also* integration of empirical and phenomenological views; therapeutic approaches
Incomplete House, The, vignette 94–5
individuals, contributions of 31–5
integration of empirical and phenomenological views: commonalities of therapeutic practice 53–64; in explanations of therapeutic efficacy 45–51
integration of mental imagery: beginning work 162–4; concluding work 171–3; developing work 164–71; framing images, as working together 167–71; overview 159–60, 175; processing changes to image 166–7; returning to image 165–6
interacting cognitive subsystems (ICS) model 44

interactive communicative model: advantages and limitations of 69–71; balance principle of 75–6; client attitude 79–80; clinical work 82–3; conscious relaxation state 76–8; framing images 83–4; interpretation, matters of 80–2; overview 69, 70; therapist attitude 78–9; *see also* building image; path image; plant image
interactive imagery techniques 54
interior of building in image 104–8
interpretation, matters of 80–2
intersubjective theory 182
introducing use of imagery to client 162–3, 180–1
ISM (image/somatic/meaning) model 45–7, 50, 63, 71

James, William 18, 19
Janet, Pierre-Marie-Félix 20, 24
Johnson, M. 2, 48–9, 50
journey, metaphor of 111; *see also* path image
Jung, Carl: on active imagination method 172; analytical psychology and 25–7; archetypes and 43; building image of 85; mental imagery and 28; mental images and 1

Kant, I. 43
Kopp, S. B. 48
Kosslyn, S. M. 44, 51
Kövecses, Z. 48, 134
Krystal, P. 173

Lakoff, G. 2, 48–9, 50
Lambert, M. 30
landscape image *see* path image
Lawley, J. 49–50
Leuner, H.: bedroom in building image and 107; building image of 85; defences, dealing with 160; on diagnostic function 59; forest motif of 57; on framing function 58; guided affective imagery and 33; meadow motif of 111; monitoring function and 62; mountain ascent image and 170–1; rose image and 133; on state of relaxation 77; on view of imaginal 78
life experience and building image 86–7
Light in the Hallway, The, vignette 96, 102, 104–5, 107, 120, 167

linguistic metaphors and mental imagery 47–50
living room of building in image 107
Locke, J. 42–3
London Plane Tree, A, vignette 142
longer-term work: with building image 109–10; development of framing images over 173–4
lost theme and path image 117–18
Luthe, W. 31–2

'magical' interventions 131–2
Malamud, D. 61–2, 68
Manicured Evergreen Shrub, The, vignette 149–50
Mathews-Simonton, S. 17–18
McMahon, C. E. 13, 15
mechanistic view of imagination 181
meditative zone 76
mental imagery: in creative reflective practice 172–3; effective use of 180–2; historical and cultural contexts of 1–3; nature of 42–5; patchwork development of theory and practice of 1, 39–40; therapeutic efficacy of 42, 50–1, 180–2; therapeutic relationship and 182–4; *see also* integration of mental imagery; therapeutic functions of mental imagery
Mesmer, Franz 17, 19
metaphorical imagery 38–9; *see also* building image; path image; plant image
mirror neurons 49
monitoring function of mental imagery: building image 101–8; overview 61–2, 67; path image 116–27, 117; plant image 151–2
multi-functionality of mental images 67–9; plant image 156–7
Myers, F.W.H. 19, 20, 45
mythopoetic 20, 45, 75

narrative therapy 30
Naruse, G. 34, 57
New Conservatory, A, vignette 109–10

O'Brien, J. 49
One Big Space vignette 105–6
One Bulb Produces Many Shoots vignette 146
oneirotherapy 33, 80
Orbiting the Planet vignette 121, 122–3

outer life: inner landscape and 116; making connections between image and 181–2
over-compliance 183–4

Paracelsus 15
parallelism 17
path image: changes to over time 174; decision making and 124–5; diagnostic, reparative and monitoring functions, using 116–26; drifting or floating theme 121–4; framing function, using 114–16; guidelines for working with 114; importation of known figures and 130–1; lost theme 117–18; 'magical' interventions and 131–2; making effort and 125–6; monitoring and process management functions, using 126–7; overview 111–13, 132; processing function, in ongoing work 128–32; struggling theme 118–20; as symbolisation of dynamic process 116–17, 126; trapped, stuck or blocked theme 120–1
Perls, Fritz 21, 28–9
personality structure: building image and 86; plant image and 135, 136, 140–3
personal level of interpretation 81
phenomenological view of imagination 3, 45
phobia, desensitisation technique for 36
plant image: attitude towards self 140–1; changes to over time 174; diagnostic function, using 140–9; framing function, using 137–40; ground or container in 143–5; guidelines for working with 135–6; monitoring function, using 151–2; multifunction work with 156–7; overview 133–5, 136–7, 157; processing function, using 152–3; process management function, using 153–6; reparative function, using 149–51; types of plants 141–3
postmodern perspective on nature of self 30
post-traumatic stress disorder (PTSD) 37–8, 177
Pot Bound Plant, The, vignette 144–5, 150
practice issues: increasing effectiveness of use of mental imagery 180–2; overview 176, 184; safety 176–9; therapeutic relationship 182–4
preparation for termination 171–2

pre-trans fallacy 164
Price-Williams, D. 25–6, 75
processing function of mental imagery: building image 101–8; overview 62–4, 67; path image 128–32; plant image 152–3
process management function of mental imagery: building image 108–10; overview 56–7, 67; path image 127; plant image 153–6
psychoanalysis 24–5
psycho-imagination therapy 34, 63
psychology: analytical 25–7; archetypal 27; emergence of 18–19; mental imagery and 19–21
psychotherapeutics 20
psychotherapy 20
PTSD (post-traumatic stress disorder) 37–8, 177
Pulling a Heavy Truck vignette 119–20
purposeful life, leading *see* path image

Rachman, S. 36
rational perspective 4, 75, 76–7, 160, 185–6
receptive/passive imagery 54, 67
relational turn in counselling and psychotherapy 2, 29–30
relaxation states, working with clients in 177–9
Released from the Jelly vignette 119, 126–7
Renaissance, healing practitioners during 15
Rennie, D. L. 183
Repaired Building Needs Work on its Foundations, A, vignette 103–4, 109
reparative function of mental imagery: building image 92–101; overview 55–6, 66–7; path image 116–26, 120, 122, 123, 125–6; plant image 149–51
Repositioned Door, The, vignette 101, 102–3
repressed traumatic experience, accessing 62–4, 102, 152–3, 176
rescripting 37–8, 63–4
resistance to image 180–1
Resisting the Building vignette 92–3, 119, 126
responsiveness, trajectory of framing images towards 173
returning to image 165–6
Romantic poets, view of imagination of 43

roof damage on building in image 97
Roof with a Hole, The, vignette 126
rose image 133
Rose with No Thorns, The, vignette 138, 144, 151, 152, 156–7
Rowe, D. 112–13

Sad Little Girl in the Basement, The, vignette 97, 106, 168
safe practice: for clients in induced relaxation states 177–9; contra-indications 176–7; managing difficulties that arise 178–9; path image 114, 125
Schelling, F.W.J. von 43
schema therapy 57, 68
Schmid, H. 111–12
Schultz, J. H. 31–2
scope of book 4–5
'Scraggly' Geranium, The, vignette 152, 153, 166
seasonal stage of plant image 147–8
Seeing With the Mind's Eye (Samuels and Samuels) 21
self: attitude towards 140–1; boundary between private and public 100; building as representation of 85–6; change in conception of 30; mental images as representations of aspects of 82; mismatch between public and private 98; neglect of, and building image 96
self-help and self-development literature 5
shamanic cultures 13–14
Sheikh, A. A. 1, 46, 180–1
Shorr, J. E.: on diagnostic function 59–60; monitoring function and 61; multi-functionality of mental images of 68; on projective devices 58; psycho-imagination therapy and 34, 63; on reparative function 55; reverse time imagery and 62; on role of imagination in therapy 1; on view of imaginal 79
Silverman, L. H. 25, 60–1
Simonton, O. C. 17–18
Singer, J. L. 47, 53, 64
Single Blade of Grass, A, vignette 144, 146–7, 152, 155
Sinking into a Swamp vignette 113, 114
size and type of building in image 93–4
Smucker, M. R. 38
social media, excessive use of 100
spider, as symbol 106

Stopa, L. 39
structural issues with building in image 94–5, 103
structured fantasy 58
struggling theme and path image 118–20
Stumbling Along in the Desert vignette 112
substance misusers, clinical experience with: building image and 86, 94, 95–6, 97, 108; framing images and 83; overview 8; path image 112, 120, 124; plant image 134, 140–3, 145–7, 150, 154–7; resistance to rational perspective 79–80
Suler, J. 63
support for plant in image 151
symbolic modeling 50
symptom relief and reparative function 56

Tajima, S. 34, 57
Teasdale, J. 44
temporary structures: in building image 108–9; in plant image 154–5
terms and conventions 8
therapeutic approaches: analytical psychology 25–7; cognitive behavioural 35–9; humanistic school 27–9; psychoanalysis 24–5; reflections on 39–40; *see also* integration of mental imagery
therapeutic functions of mental imagery: commonalities in clinical practice 53–5; diagnostic 59–61; framing 58–9; monitoring 61–2; multi-functionality and 67–9; processing 62–4; process management 56–7; relationships among 66–7; reparative 55–6; *see also* building image; path image; plant image
therapeutic relationship 182–4
therapeutic use of imagination, historical perspective on 13–21
therapist facilitated inquiry 76
therapists: attitude of 78–9; importance of expertise of 94–5
The Royal College of Physicians, founding of 15
Thomas, V. 173
Three Framing Images vignette 97, 126, 168–70
Tiny Potato Plant, The, vignette 140–1, 152, 154
Tompkins, P. 49–50

Tower Block with a Side Door, The, vignette 100–1, 105, 109
transference 183
transpersonal imagery 5
transtheoretical perspectives in practice of mental imagery 45–7, 185–6; *see also* interactive communicative model
trapped, stuck or blocked theme and path image 120–1
Traversing the Dark Woods vignette 118, 127, 128–30, 171
tree image 133, 141–2
Tree Stuck in Winter, A, vignette 139, 147–8, 149, 152, 162
Tsubo mental imagery method 34, 57
Tuke, Samuel 17
two-chair procedure 29

unconscious: Freud and 24–5; humanistic school and 28; hypnotic states and 19–20; Jung and 25–7

Underground Bulb, The, vignette 139, 145–6, 152
Unexpected T Junction, An, vignette 120–1, 167
Ungerer, F. 111–12
uninhabited building in image 95–7
universal level of interpretation 81

Virel, A. 33, 58
Vulnerable New Plant Shoot, The, vignette 147, 155

waking dream tradition, European 58, 161
Watkins, M. 31, 45, 78, 81–2, 182
Watson, J. B. 19, 20
Western view of nature of mental imagery 42–5
Wickman, S. 50
Wilber, K. 164